THE EXECUTIVE'S
HANDBOOK
OF TRADE AND BUSINESS
ASSOCIATIONS

THE EXECUTIVE'S HANDBOOK OF TRADE AND BUSINESS ASSOCIATIONS

How They Work—and How to Make Them Work Effectively for You

Charles S. Mack

Foreword by
R. William Taylor, CAE

President,
American Society of Association Executives

Q

QUORUM BOOKS

NEW YORK · WESTPORT, CONNECTICUT · LONDON

Library of Congress Cataloging-in-Publication Data

Mack, Charles S.
    The executive's handbook of trade and business associations : how
they work, and how to make them work effectively for you / Charles
S. Mack ; foreword by R. William Taylor.
        p.   cm.
    Includes bibliographical references and index.
    ISBN: 0-89930-531-8 (lib. bdg. : alk. paper)
    1. Trade and professional associations—United States.   I. Title.
HD2425.M28   1991
338'.006'073—dc20   90-8957

British Library Cataloguing in Publication Data is available.

Library of Congress Catalog Card Number: 90-8957
ISBN: 0-89930-531-8

First published in 1991

Quorum Books, 88 Post Road West, Westport, CT 06881
An imprint of Greenwood Publishing Group, Inc.

Printed in the United States of America

The paper used in this book complies with the
Permanent Paper Standard issued by the National
Information Standards Organization (Z39.48-1984).

10 9 8 7 6 5 4 3 2 1

To ''Alcharl''

Contents

PART V: MEETING THE NEEDS OF THE '90s—AND BEYOND

Foreword

Trade and business associations are, without a doubt, an unknown quantity to much of the general public and even to those close to associations. To give an idea of the vast size of the non-profit sector, which includes nearly all trade associations, let me refer to the findings of a 1988 study by Hodgkinson and Weitzman titled *Dimensions of the Independent Sector:*

- Non-profits employ 7.7 million workers—more civilians than the federal and fifty state governments combined.
- The combined annual budgets of the American non-profit sector exceed the budgets of all but seven nations in the world.

Although trade and business associations form just one segment of the enormous non-profit community, their impact on society is far-reaching and important. In tackling the challenge of explaining the role and nature of these business organizations, Charles Mack has succeeded in preparing a discussion that is enlightened and informative.

As Mack points out, trade and business associations offer broad benefits that otherwise would have to be provided (presumably at a higher cost) by government. These associations:

- educate their members on technical and scientific matters, business practices, innovation and technology transfers, legal issues, and environmental concerns. For many industries, there is no more knowledgeable source for continuing education.

- inform the public about the efficiency, quality standards, and safety of products and services, thereby bolstering public confidence in the marketplace.

- perform a vital function in setting professional, performance, and safety standards, ethical canons, and other guidelines, all of which reduce risk to the consumer.

- act in partnership with government to provide technical information. In this partnership, the federal government relies heavily on trade and business associations to disseminate and explain new regulations and guidelines, and to provide feedback to lawmakers about the impact of proposed legislation on the affected industries and consumers.

- conduct research and statistical analysis that is unavailable from other sources.

- provide the structure and resources to call forth extraordinary amounts of volunteer labor. Associations mobilize and train volunteers, often helping to develop a public focus on the strength of the American spirit.

In all these examples, the responsible collective interest of association members—in advancing technology, improving productivity, developing professionalism, and enhancing legislative positions—has a tremendous impact on our nation's quality of life.

I am confident that you will find this book well worth careful study and use.

R. William Taylor, CAE
President, American Society of Association Executives

Preface

Trade and business associations exist to improve the business climate for their members. They also have a sweeping and pervasive impact on public policy formation, the economy, and society at large. Despite their importance to the operations of individual businesses, however, few companies analyze the value of these organizations or take the steps necessary to maximize their influence within their associations.

This book is intended as a guide for corporate and association executives to help them evaluate the effectiveness of their associations as instruments for the advancement of each member's corporate or individual objectives, as well as the collective needs of the industry, profession, or business community that the association represents. The book is also designed to provide a comprehensive survey of the association field for executives, students, journalists, government officials, and others who want to understand how these important interest groups have developed and how they operate.

Four decades have passed since publication of the last work on the use of associations. Business organizations have undergone dramatic changes during the intervening years, particularly the rapid growth of government relations as their chief priority. Early books devoted almost no attention to chambers of commerce, to international or state trade associations, or to business-oriented professional societies. In particular, the concept of cost-effective evaluation of individual associations from the standpoint of the participating members is a very recent one. My intention has been to fill these gaps and to bring the analysis of business associations up to the present.

This book grows out of material in my earlier book, *Lobbying and*

Government Relations: A Guide for Executives (1989), and subsequent articles that dealt with the analysis and utilization of business associations. Those publications stimulated considerable interest and led to a decision to provide a book-length treatment of the subject.

The business associations discussed in this book cover a broad spectrum of groups: multi-industry umbrella organizations, trade associations, certain professional societies, and chambers of commerce. The scope of these institutions is vast—international, national, state, regional, and local.

A word about terminology is in order. Virtually all trade associations, chambers of commerce, and other umbrella organizations are comprised either of companies and enterprises or of other business associations. In this book, therefore, organizations with company memberships (except chambers of commerce) are described as either trade or umbrella associations, whether or not they choose to use those terms to describe themselves. Similarly, professional associations or societies are almost always individual membership organizations; those expressions are used synonymously here unless there is a reason to differentiate.

I wish to express my gratitude to the individuals and organizations that generously provided assistance and material without which this book could not have been written. These particularly include many helpful staff members of the American Society of Association Executives (ASAE) and the U.S. Chamber of Commerce. ASAE's resources, surveys, and publications are an invaluable lode of data and information that I freely mined.

My deep appreciation must also be expressed to executives of the associations who provided documents and other information essential for the profiles that appear in several chapters. They include: Nancy Nord, formerly with the American Corporate Counsel Association; John L. Pickitt of the Computer and Business Equipment Manufacturers Association; Lewis D. Andrews, Jr., of the Glass Packaging Institute; Norman Vale and Richard M. Corner of the International Advertising Association, and Mary W. Covington, formerly with IAA; James Barrett of the Michigan Chamber of Commerce; James T. Rogers of the New York State Food Merchants Association and NYSFMA's general counsel, Richard G. Hickey; Richard Breault, Lawrence B. Kraus, Donald J. Kroes, and Bill Mitchell of the U. S. Chamber of Commerce; and James V. Olsen of the Utah Retail Grocers Association, as well as members of their staffs and other individuals, too numerous to name individually, who shared with me their knowledge and perspectives on these and other associations.

Especial thanks are owed to R. William Taylor, president of ASAE, for the foreword he graciously contributed; and, for their helpful comments on the manuscript, to Dr. Richard A. Edwards, former senior vice president of the Metropolitan Life Insurance Company and Kappel Professor of Business-Government Relations at the University of Minnesota, to Hugh McCahey, manager of the U.S. Chamber's Association Department, and to Raymond L. Hoewing, president of the Public Affairs Council. Of course, the author alone is responsible for any errors the book may contain.

My wife, Alice Barrett Mack, was, as always, a loving source of encouragement, support, and constructive criticism.

Underlying this book is the author's strong belief that associations are essential to meeting the growing needs of business enterprises of all kinds and sizes, for government relations, economic services, and information. If this book proves a useful guide to associations for strengthening those services and to their members for effectively utilizing them, it will have achieved its purpose.

Charles S. Mack

Part I

THE COSMOS OF ASSOCIATIONS

1

Interest Groups and Business Organizations

Americans of all ages, all conditions, and all dispositions constantly form associations. They have not only commercial and manufacturing companies, in which all take part, but associations of a thousand other kinds, religious, moral, serious, futile, general or restricted, enormous or diminutive. Wherever at the head of some new undertaking you see the government in France, or a man of rank in England, in the United States you will be sure to find an association.

Alexis de Tocqueville, 1835

The human animal is a sociable beast. Natural competitiveness is matched by an instinct for cooperation with peers in even the most primitive social groups. The drive to compete and achieve within a larger framework—social, political, economic—is what has enabled the species to build civilizations.

These dual drives emerge with equal clarity at the tribal level at one extreme and in the most complex economic organizations at the other. Modern economic man strives for gain both in absolute terms and relative to his rivals, while at the same time willingly cooperating with them to advance common interests.

Nothing illustrates this principle more clearly than the business associations that are found in every capitalist national economy that has experienced the industrial revolution. Individuals and enterprises that compete with each other in the marketplace come together within a structure of collective self-help and cooperation that provides mutual benefits.

At a meeting of the board of directors of a trade association, a relatively new member once confided to the author that "this takes some getting used to." He was asked what he meant: "We sit down together at these meetings in the friendliest atmosphere and discuss ways to improve the industry. Then we leave here to go out and cut each other's throats. We come back for the next meeting and it's all sweetness and light again."

No statement better typifies the character of business associations—organizations of enterprises and individuals that often compete with each other but, at the same time, seek to advance and protect the interests of the particular trade, industry, profession, or geographic area that the association represents.

There is probably not a single field of business economic activity that is not represented by at least one association.

Business organizations serve a variety of functions for their members. They collect and disseminate industry economic data, provide information and training, offer cost-saving economic services of different kinds, set technical and professional standards, and serve as the public voice of their memberships with the public, the press, and governments. Trade and other business associations are important to each of their members; for many, they may actually represent their single most valuable economic relationship.

THE ASSOCIATIONS' OWNERS AND CLIENTELE

The purpose of associations is to better the lot of their owners—the membership. Associations exist to meet the common needs of their members at large, but they also must serve the interests of their individual members, which is not at all the same thing. The members of each association share many qualities and desires with each other—else why belong to the association? That commonality should not disguise the fact, however, that none of the shared interests is identical with each other. Each member, whether individual or corporate, has its own special, perhaps even unique, needs that it looks to the association to satisfy—that it *pays* the association to satisfy.

In that sense, the member is not only the association's proprietor but also its client. Associations are thus businesses owned by their customers. They are enterprises that exist to serve not only the membership's collective interests but a number of their individual requirements as well. Often, in fact, these individual needs have a higher priority for the member than the collective ones.

For example, a member of a professional society may suddenly find herself in need of new employment. If the society's job referral service helps the individual gain a new position, she is likely to value the organization quite highly, even if it is utterly failing in its overall organizational goals.

To use another example, if a trade association or chamber of commerce fails to achieve one of its low-priority objectives that nonetheless happens to be of great importance to the profitability of one of its member companies, that firm is unlikely to hold the group in high esteem, even though the association is otherwise blazingly successful.

The governing board of each association appraises the organization's effectiveness and value to the membership at large. Individual members of the association—its clientele—should make a somewhat different evaluation using these criteria:

1. How well the association serves those of their needs shared by others in this interest group.
2. How well the special needs and priorities of the individual "client" are being met.

A major purpose of this book is to help the "clients" of business associations utilize their organizations to satisfy both sets of interests. This brings us to the subject of what associations are all about.

INTERESTS AND INTEREST GROUPS

Business associations belong to a major class of organizations known as interest groups.

Americans are joiners. Alexis de Tocqueville's observation is even truer today than it was 155 years ago. We create organizations and clubs for every conceivable interest shared by even the smallest groups of people. Organizations of bald-headed men, aardvark aficionados, barbed wire collectors, prostitutes, flying chiropractors, and descendants of the illegitimate offspring of British monarchs all actually exist. A four-volume encyclopedia,[1] updated annually, is required to list these and the thousands of other groups that teem throughout American society. The number of associations in the United States grows by about a thousand every year.

People join such groups to give expression to their particular interests and values. Individuals and institutions in every society have multiple interests: family, economic, social, political, religious, cultural, artistic, ad infinitum. Interest groups are organizations created to advance and protect a particular interest.

For example, bowling enthusiasts share an interest in their sport. They want to be able to engage freely in this activity and to have bowling alleys available and accessible. For that reason, they may wish to promote the sport through publicity, advertising, recruitment, and skills training to increase its popularity. They also want the sport to have a tangible, coherent identity with established rules, alleys of specified dimensions and physical construction, balls within an established range of weight and composition, and so forth.

The class of people who are bowling enthusiasts may be termed an interest group, but a narrower use of the term would denote a formal organization of some kind created for the purpose of advancing the interests of bowlers. This interest group of bowlers would seek to protect their interest against those whose actions might threaten or blur its identity. For instance, some action (economic, legal, or political) might be taken against a rival group that sought to use the word "bowling" to describe a sport involving fifteen pins instead of the traditional ten. They might seek the enactment of laws to codify bowling standards and perhaps initiate litigation to protect the integrity of bowling as they define it.

We see here a number of activities characteristic of many interest groups: defining and safeguarding the identified interest, promotion and training to upgrade it, setting standards, and legal or political action to protect it.

Important distinctions among bowlers might lead them to create organizations that represent more narrowly defined bowling interests. Owners of bowling alleys have different interests from their customers. Amateur bowlers may have goals separate from those of professionals. The bowlers of Akron may create a local association of individuals to promote the sport in that city, separate from those in other cities and states and distinct from local bowling teams, leagues, or associations of leagues.

Interest groups fractionate in this way when individuals develop subinterests and wish to distinguish themselves from others who share the larger interest. Presbyterians, to take another example, share a common interest in their faith, but there may nonetheless be good social, political, economic, or other reasons why Presbyterian clergy might choose to develop their own interest group distinct from that of the laity.

As individuals, each of us shares multiple interests that in a sense compete for our time, attention, and involvement. Our Akron bowler may also be a Presbyterian, a daughter, wife, and mother, a consumer, an accountant, an environmentalist, a feminist, a Democrat, and a devotee of science fiction, Dixieland jazz, and the paintings of Jackson Pollock—all simultaneously. Each of these is an interest that may or may not be represented by an organized interest group, in which the individual may or may not choose to be involved and active.

No other society in the world appears to have as many varied interest groups as does the United States. Indeed, its rich abundance of interest groups is a distinguishing characteristic of American society.

There are few interests that seem not to have organized into groups.

Indeed, it is hard to conceive of a class of individuals in America unrepresented by some group. Even individuals at the bottom of society, the poor and the homeless, are an interest represented by various and varied philanthropic and advocacy organizations of one kind or another. This example demonstrates that the organization representing an interest need not be a membership group, although most are.

NON-BUSINESS INTEREST GROUPS

Interest groups may be comprised not only of individuals but also of institutions and other interest groups. This book deals with sets of economic interest groups that represent business enterprises and certain business-related professions.

In addition, there is a vast array of non-business interests that are highly active, vocal, and effective. It is worthwhile to look briefly at a few of them.

Labor

It is ironic that both labor unions and business organizations, contentious throughout their entire history, trace their lineage to a common ancestor, the earliest medieval guilds (see Chapter 2). In the United States, labor unions arose in the nineteenth century to win rights for workers from employers, who saw labor as a resource to be used like any other asset—for maximum output at minimum cost.

Because employers and employer organizations viewed the rise of organized labor as a major threat, it is not surprising that labor history is rife with contention, strife, and violence. Legal recognition of the right to strike was hard won. Although strike violence (by both employers and workers) is far less prevalent now than it was in the last century and the first third of this one, it is not uncommon to this day (for example, during the 1989 coal miners' strike and the 1990 Greyhound bus strike).

The extreme difficulties that organized labor generally experienced in winning concessions on wages and working conditions from employers led some individual labor unions into direct political and lobbying activities very early. Trade and craft unions joined in 1886 to create the American Federation of Labor (AFL) to give labor a united voice.

The rise of the socialist movement, here and around the world, is inextricably entwined with the history of the labor movement. If socialism never caught on in America, its offshoot, modern liberalism, did. Liberalism as we know it in the twentieth century (quite different in many ways from liberalism of the classic tradition) has been characterized by its support of governmental intervention to achieve labor goals.

The alliance of liberals and labor was cemented in 1933 with the com-

ing of the administration of Franklin D. Roosevelt. This was the beginning of labor's political zenith. Although the New Deal fulfilled many of
labor's most cherished goals, none was more significant than the passage
in 1935 of the Wagner Act, which provided labor unions with the right
to organize workers free from employer coercion or interference. Strongly
supportive of Democratic administrations, Congresses, and candidates
in the decades that followed, labor was arguably the dominant economic
interest group in America from the 1930s through the 1960s.

Another major development in labor organization occurred in 1935. A
group of unions seceded from the AFL to form the Congress of Industrial Organizations (CIO), a group whose member unions were organized
largely along industry lines in contrast with the AFL, which was comprised of craft unions. Reunion came twenty years later, and the newly
merged organization adopted the CIO's political activism. The AFL-CIO's
Committee on Political Education (COPE) was the first political action
committee and has been a major force in American politics, particularly
in support of liberal Democrats and policies.

But eventually there was a price to be paid for labor's success in winning higher wages and better working conditions through legislation and
collective bargaining. High labor costs led many American manufacturers to transfer operations first into the southern states (historically the
region least friendly to organized labor and its objectives) and then to
other countries where labor costs were far lower. Labor's position was
further weakened by consumers' ready acceptance of lower-cost, often
higher-quality imports, as well as by a changing labor force and declining
union membership.

By the 1980s, the unions' position had weakened to the point where
their agenda was marked by successive major legislative losses (for instance, the failure to win expansion of minimum wage legislation for the
first time in decades) and by negotiations with employers that were characterized by labor "give-backs" rather than management concessions.
The success of the Reagan administration in breaking a striking public
employees union, the air traffic controllers organization, epitomized the
weak political state to which labor had fallen.

Labor unions and their national organization, the AFL-CIO, may never
completely regain the political and economic strength that they had a
generation ago. Nonetheless, an economic and political interest group of
such size and strength undoubtedly will remain a major force in America
in the foreseeable decades.

Medicine

Along with the law, medicine remains the premier profession in America. There are about five hundred national medical organizations and

probably thousands more at the state and local levels. As professional organizations, in contrast with trade associations, these groups are comprised of individuals rather than firms. Medical associations provide their members with a variety of economic and educational services, often including certification programs to regulate the professional quality of practitioners in medical specialties.

The high esteem in which the public has historically held the medical profession, together with the political activity of many individual physicians, has enabled organized medicine to exercise a high degree of legislative influence. The national umbrella organization, the American Medical Association (AMA), has long been one of the nation's most influential lobbying forces. Its most significant victory came during the Truman administration when political liberals sought to enact a program of national health insurance. After a protracted struggle, the AMA succeeded in defeating the proposal, despite strong support for it from the White House, organized labor, and other liberal interest groups then at the peak of their power.

The AMA was a pioneer in the establishment of political action committees (organizations that collect voluntary contributions from large numbers of individuals, donate the aggregate funds to political parties or candidates, or affect campaigns and elections in other ways).

Although social and economic changes (including some within the medical profession) have reduced the AMA's membership and influence, it continues to be a significant legislative force.

The Law

Lawyers belong to a variety of professional organizations, typically called bar associations, that are found at the national, state, and local levels. There are also associations serving various legal specialties, ranging from the American College of Probate Counsel to the Trademark Society. Not all attorneys are associated with private law firms, and there are also associations representing attorneys by place of employment, such as those with corporations or who work for colleges and universities.

All these groups, including their umbrella organization, the American Bar Association (ABA), provide the range of educational and economic services typical of professional associations. The very nature of their profession has always led lawyers to be deeply involved in politics and government. Law has historically been the predominant profession among legislators at all levels of government, although this is less true today than it once was.

It is not surprising, therefore, that the ABA has long played a highly influential role in governmental processes. Its prestige has flowed from a concentration on broad public policy concerns and issues, not merely those that benefit the legal profession. The ABA's Antitrust and Trade Regulation Section, for example, is undoubtedly the primary interest group affecting federal antitrust policy, and senior Justice Department antitrust officials have often come from the section's leadership. Professional ratings by another ABA group have long played a major part in the selection of federal judges, although its reputation was somewhat tarnished by the charge of allowing ideological factors as well as professional assessment to affect the evaluation of Robert Bork's failed nomination to the Supreme Court.[2]

Recent ABA positions on various social issues have drawn criticisms from Bush administration officials who have denigrated the organization as "just another lobbying group".

This is not to say that professional associations of attorneys abstain from involvement in legislative issues affecting their economic welfare. The trial lawyers' association, whose members' fees are frequently a percentage of court judgments for their clients, has been exceptionally successful in lobbying against such federal and state legislative proposals as product liability reforms and no-fault insurance that are intended to place limits on the sums that can be won in litigation.

Veterans

Assuring health and economic benefits for those who served in the nation's armed forces is the major purpose of such individual-membership organizations as the American Legion, the Veterans of Foreign Wars, and other less well-known but often influential veterans groups.

Veterans' organizations are perhaps the epitome of the informal but highly effective lobbying alliances known as "iron triangles." Iron triangles are a form of coalition politics in which particular interest groups ally with both friendly legislators and the government officials responsible for administering programs beneficial to the interest group's members. In this case, veterans' organizations and their active members give strong political backing to helpful legislators who vigorously support continued and expanded government programs for veterans. The lawmakers also provide political and legislative support to executive branch officials who administer these programs and often assist in their career advancement. Lobbyists and officials of the veterans' associations provide the liaison and coordination that keep this iron triangle functioning.

A recent illustration of the continued influence of veterans' organizations was their success in upgrading the Veterans Administration to cabinet status as the Department of Veterans Affairs. The legislation creating this department had the endorsement of President Reagan and was passed by Congress overwhelmingly despite arguments from critics that it was an added public expense that would do little to enhance benefits for veterans.

Senior Citizens

Some interest groups are united by demographic characteristics. Blacks, Hispanics, women, and Americans of Italian or Korean ancestry are examples of demographic interests represented by various organizational champions. Another demographic interest group has, in just a few years, become one of the most significant in the United States: the aging.

The older segment of the population has grown not only in size but also in political influence. This is partly because of the governmental programs and legislative issues affecting these people, but also because, as a group, they have the time and the inclination to take an active and vocal interest in legislative affairs. The oft-repeated pledges of Republican presidents and Democratic congresses to exempt Social Security from any federal budgetary cuts are as much a tribute to the political power of the aging as to social concern for the elderly. No governmental program for any other social group, whether children or the homeless, has been granted such a blanket exemption by either political party.

A number of organizations represent the interests of the aging, but the largest by far is the American Association for Retired Persons (AARP), which is a group that is twice the size of the AFL-CIO and that represents one-fifth of all voters. With a membership of 30 million over the age of fifty, the AARP is the second largest institution in America; only the Roman Catholic Church is larger.

With an annual budget of $235 million and a staff of 1200[3], the AARP dwarfs other economic interest groups in its political influence. Only 5 percent of all associations have more than 100 employees; AARP has more than that number (120) on its legislative staff alone.

AARP is by no means the only organization seeking to represent senior citizens, however. A rival group, the National Committee to Preserve Social Security and Medicare, was instrumental in stimulating an enormous outcry from older Americans in 1989, urging the repeal of the Medicare catastrophic coverage surtax that had been enacted with strong AARP support only the year before.

The committee may represent a new form of advocacy group. Although it is a membership organization, the committee has a close relationship with a direct marketing firm in California. The committee is funded not only by dues but also by the sale of its mailing lists. Its 1989 budget of $48 million is remarkable for an organization founded only seven years earlier.[4]

However these senior citizens advocacy groups may sort themselves out, the interest they champion will become an increasingly important political force. With the "baby boom" generation now in middle age, the ranks of the aging can only swell. As an interest group, its influence is likely to continue its ascent until well into the twenty-first century.

Cause Groups

The members of cause groups share an interest in the advancement of a single issue or a particular ideology. Cause groups are a relatively new phenomenon in American political life in that they function as advocacy organizations, unlike their nineteenth- and early twentieth-century counterparts, which usually constituted themselves as small political parties. One of the oldest of these organizations is the Americans for Democratic Action, a highly influential umbrella group for liberal political interests during the quarter-century of liberal dominance following World War II.

Cause groups began to mushroom during the 1960s, initially concerned with consumer issues and the environment.

The consumer movement, which actually dates back to the early years of this century, became an important influence during the Kennedy administration. The Consumer Federation of America was created as an organization of local, state, and national consumer and labor groups. It was instrumental in the passage of much legislation at all levels.

A variety of environmental organizations also began during this period and have been similarly effective in the enactment of clean air, water, and other environmental laws.

The establishment of so-called "public interest" groups is another relatively recent development. A number of these groups, some with formal memberships, others without, are the creation of the populist activist and advocate, Ralph Nader. Ideologically, they tend to have a strong anti-establishment orientation in their political and economic issue positions.

Numerous other cause groups have also sprung up in recent decades. Some, like Common Cause, are devoted to governmental and political reforms. Others are devoted to the advancement of ideological points of view, such as the various conservative organizations that helped to elect Ronald Reagan and actively supported his policies. Still others are single-issue groups including, for example, those on both sides of the abortion issue.

Several thousand cause groups of widely differing views operate at the national level, and a large (if unknown) number exist in states and localities.[5]

BUSINESS ORGANIZATIONS

These descriptions merely sample the rich variety and breadth of interest groups active in America. However, no other sector of major interest groups comes close in number to those representing business. There are more than 10,000 business associations in the United States. Their budgets total more than $20 billion.

American business associations are a varied complex of organizations. All are interest groups, but no two have identical interests. All have memberships, but the needs of their constituencies range widely; even within an association, membership needs and interests are at best similar, never identical. Business associations are widely diversified by size, type of membership, range of specialty, and geographic scope. A classification of these associations is important to understanding their similarities and differences.

Types of Business Associations

Associations representing American business enterprises are of several different types, ranging from broad-based "umbrella" organizations, to trade associations representing highly specific industries, to many of the professional societies comprised of individual practitioners in particular fields. These groups are found at all levels: international, national, regional, state, and local.

Business associations differ among each other according to the range and composition of their memberships, and therefore of their interests. They can be classified as follows:

Broad national umbrella organizations representing business enterprises without regard to industry. For example, the U. S. Chamber of Commerce and the Business Roundtable.

Statewide umbrella organizations with a similarly broad base. Examples include the Pennsylvania State Chamber of Commerce and the Business Council of New York.

Local umbrella groups, generally called chambers of commerce (or boards of trade or business councils), which represent businesses of all kinds within specific geographic areas.

Restricted national umbrella organizations comprised of businesses in broad aggregates of industries, such as the National Association of Manufacturers (NAM) and the National Retail Federation (NRF). Such groups differ from the broad umbrella organizations in that they exclude certain classes of businesses. Thus, retailers cannot join the NAM nor manufacturers the NRF.

Restricted umbrella groups are also prevalent at the state level—for instance, the California Retail Council and the New Jersey Manufacturers Association—but are rare locally. Local chambers of commerce usually fill this niche.

Trade associations representing specific industries, lines of business, or other interests both broadly and narrowly defined. Within the food industry, for example, there are broadly based organizations like the Grocery Manufacturers of America and the National Food Processors Association. There are also a number of manufacturer trade groups representing very specific product lines, such as peanut butter, bakery products, frozen foods, soft drinks, cereals, and so on. Even these relatively narrow product line groupings may be further segmented; different kinds of baked goods, for example, are represented by different trade associations. The members of a trade association are almost invariably competitors in the marketplace.

In general, the manufacturers and distributors of the same products tend to have separate organizations, sometimes called *"vertical associations."* However, *"horizontal associations,"* representing both the manufacturing and distribution sectors, are also found in some industries.

The strongest trade associations generally operate at the national and international levels. Local and state trade associations tend to be smaller but are widespread and often quite powerful; multi-state or regional groups exist in some industries.

Professional societies representing individual practitioners in distinct professions or occupations. Like trade associations, professional societies may be international, national, state, or local in scope. They almost always accept only individual memberships, in contrast to umbrella and trade associations that are comprised mainly of companies (or, in some instances, of other associations; see *Federations,* below.) Examples of professional organizations include the American Institute of Architects and the World Future Society.

Many of these societies are composed of professionals in business, such as the American Society of Corporate Secretaries or the Association of Information Systems Professionals.

However, not all individual membership groups are business organizations, by any means. A great many represent scientific, medical, or other non-business specialties. In a sense, labor unions fall in this latter category although their members are usually employed in specific trades, occupations, or industries rather than in the professions. Conversely, a few professional organizations, particularly those in education, really act more like labor unions (for example, the American Association of University Professors and the National Education Association).

One important professional group is the American Society of Association Executives (ASAE), whose members are the staffs of trade, business, professional, and other associations. Although its members are association management employees rather than the associations themselves, ASAE is in many ways the "association of associations."

Federations are associations of other associations; some may also have direct company or individual memberships as well. Federations may be national organizations with state and local members; their members may also be other national (or international) organizations. To add to the confusion, some groups whose members are solely companies or individuals, rather than other associations, choose to call themselves federations—strictly speaking, a misnomer.

There are also a variety of specialized organizations with business memberships. Although they are not analyzed in any detail in this book, for the record they include such groups as the following:

Employers' organizations, a form of trade association that specialize in labor matters, usually including group collective bargaining with an industry union on behalf of all their members. These groups are on the wane as individual companies undertake direct labor negotiations.

Export associations (sometimes called "Webb-Pomerene associations," after a federal law that authorized many of them). These operate under a limited antitrust exemption for the purpose of promoting sales abroad.

Commodity and stock exchanges, such as the New York and American Stock Exchanges and the Chicago Board of Trade. These are membership organizations, highly regulated by government, that provide centers for the trade of standardized commodities, whether bushels of corn or corporate stocks.

Better Business Bureaus, local organizations that, together with their national federation, the Council of Better Business Bureaus, focus on improving business-consumer relations, such as investigating unethical or fraudulent business practices, policing advertising, and providing consumer guidance.

Business research or policy organizations, such as the Conference Board or the Committee for Economic Development.

This classification of business associations represents general patterns but barely sketches the lush complexity of organizational and membership arrangements. A number of associations straddle classifications. Some have both corporate and organizational members, for example; others have both as well as individual members. Almost every conceivable structure can be found somewhere.

Characteristics of Business Associations

The different classes of business associations have characteristics that can be compared for a better understanding of these interest groups, so an initial word about sources of statistical data describing them is in order. ASAE surveys its members every few years regarding a variety of operating characteristics and policies. The most recent of these surveys, conducted in 1987, provided a statistical portrait of 2,005 business, trade, and professional associations,[6] a group that represents about 20 percent of all such organizations.

The U.S. Chamber of Commerce makes similar surveys of state and local chambers of commerce, most recently in 1988 for the former[7] and 1989 for the latter.[8]

Trade and Professional Associations. ASAE's data are reported by type of membership. In this book, organizations with company memberships are considered to be trade or umbrella associations. The terms "individual membership organizations" and "professional associations" are used synonymously. Trade associations comprise about 60 percent of total associations (exclusive of chambers of commerce), and professional societies the remaining 40 percent.

One-fifth of American trade associations are national in scope. Another fifth have some international members, although most of their members are probably U. S. companies. About two-fifths are state associations, and one-fifth are local groups.

The average number of corporate members among business associations is over a thousand but the size of the largest associations inflates this number. A better measure is the median membership: 315.[9] The median for state and local associations is about 75 percent of that for international and national groups. Among professional associations, the average number of members is almost 17,000. The median is 3,125.

Half of the national and international associations have annual revenues *over* $1 million. More than half of the state and local associations have annual revenues *under* $500,000.

The median number of full-time association staff employees is six. National and international organizations have almost twice as many employees as their state and local counterparts.

Chambers of Commerce. In the United States, there are thousands of local chambers of commerce (sometimes also called business councils, commerce and industry associations, or similar names). These organizations are found in the smallest communities and the largest metropolitan areas, but more than half are in towns with under 75,000 in population. State chambers of commerce exist in almost every state, sometimes known by the above alternative names.

Local chambers in the smaller population centers typically have annual budgets under $300,000. Those with incomes over $1 million a year are mainly in communities with populations of 250,000 and up. Like the local organizations, state chamber budgets tend to be related to population. Annual incomes range from less than $300,000 to nearly $5 million. The median for chambers in the most populous states is $2.6 million and in the smallest states, about $400,000.

Dues constitute about three-fourths of total state chamber revenues. Among the larger state chambers, which have a variety of alternative revenue sources, only about 40 percent of incomes derives from membership dues. Membership income provides only about 40 to 50 percent of local chamber income on the average. The rest derives from publications, insurance programs, and special projects, including tax-financed activities. Government funds typically provide perhaps 25 percent of total revenues to support chamber programs in industrial and economic development, tourism, conventions, and general advertising and promotion.

Staff size in local and state chambers is comparable to numbers of employees in local and state trade associations. Again, there are wide variations by size of organization. The smallest state and local chambers may have only a handful of employees; the largest have between twenty-five and fifty.

The focus of this book is the vast array of American business organizations that have a pervasive impact on the nation's economic well-being. No other complex of private organizations, not even the huge corporations and labor unions, has so great a collective capacity to influence public policy at every level of government, nor to affect so profoundly the conduct of business in enterprises both great and small.

NOTES

1. *Encyclopedia of Associations,* 4 vols. (Detroit: Gale Research, annually). (Thanks to Ed Lucaire for drawing these examples to the author's attention.)

2. See, for example, Patrick B. McGuigan and Dawn M. Weyrich, *Ninth Justice: The Fight for Bork* (Washington: Free Congress Research and Education Foundation, 1990).

3. John Tierney, "Old Money, New Power," *New York Times Magazine,* October 23, 1988, p. 52. See also: Dan Balz, "Never Underestimate the Power of an Angry Senior Citizen," *Washington Post National Weekly Edition,* September 25–October 1, 1989, p. 7. See also: "AARP's Catastrophe," *Wall Street Journal,* October 2, 1989, p. A14.

4. Martin Tolchin, "How the New Medicare Law Fell on Hard Times in a Hurry," *New York Times,* October 9, 1989, p. A-1.

5. Detailed characteristics of some of these organizations will be found in a directory of 250 cause groups: Foundation for Public Affairs, *Public Interest Profiles* (Washington: Congressional Quarterly Press, 1989).

6. American Society of Association Executives (ASAE), *Policies and Procedures in Association Management* (Washington: ASAE, 1987).

7. U. S. Chamber of Commerce (Office of Chamber of Commerce Relations), *1988 Survey of State Organizations* (Washington: 1988).

8. U.S. Chamber of Commerce, *1989 Survey of Local Chambers of Commerce* (Washington: 1989.)

9. Half those reporting fall above the median, half below.

2

The Development of
Business Associations

People of the same trade seldom meet together even for merriment
and diversion but the conversation ends in a conspiracy against the
public, or in some contrivance to raise prices.

Adam Smith, 1776

Wherever and whenever they have arisen, business associations have
sought to enhance the environment in which their members operate in
whatever ways they can. The significance of the history of these groups
is that this purpose has universally included attempts to strengthen business conditions, modulate competitive forces, and influence governmental policies. Although there has been much interaction between business
groups and government throughout history, antitrust laws restraining anti-
competitive actions date back only about a century. An understanding
of the evolution of trade and business associations is important to an
understanding of how they operate today.

Modern business associations are largely creatures of industrialized
societies. Their evolution has followed similar general patterns everywhere. Small local trade associations are the earliest developments in
individual industries, followed somewhat later by regional and then national associations. As a business community develops in a particular
locality, a chamber of commerce will be formed. National and state umbrella business groups arise after a number of single-industry associations are flourishing, when it becomes apparent that they have common
problems that they cannot address alone. International associations develop still later.

Such has been the pattern in Europe, North America, and Japan. Although business and trade associations as we know them today are largely the creatures of industrialization, they nonetheless have a lineage that can be traced back to antiquity.

THE MEDIEVAL GUILDS

Merchants and artisans with a common trade have banded together throughout history in civilizations across the world, if only by setting up businesses in the same street or part of town. Records of ancient civilizations in China, Japan, India, Egypt, Phoenicia, and Rome contain references to trade groups of different kinds. The *collegia* of artisans in Rome are known to have created apprentice training programs and to have set wages and prices.

Historians have found references in sixth-century Italian cities to societies of bakers and soap makers and, in the twelfth century, to organizations of clothiers, furriers, wool merchants, bankers, physicians, druggists, tanners, armorers, innkeepers, and so forth.

Such societies eventually evolved into the guilds of the middle ages, which are the forerunners of contemporary economic organizations.

The rise of the medieval guilds occurred as towns throughout Europe became self-governing and started to grow into cities. Because guild leaders were often the same individuals who sat on the town councils, the guilds rose in both economic and political power simultaneously. The guilds contributed to the growth of their towns and the town fathers abetted the power of the guilds. Often, guilds and government became virtually indistinguishable.

Initially, the guilds were comprised of artisans and craftsmen who both made and sold their products. Later, guilds of merchants and bankers arose. The merchant guilds grew by their ability to determine whose goods were sold, where, and at what price. They came to dominate not only the craft guilds but all economic life in their communities.

Although the guilds were organized by town and city, many of the larger ones formed important alliances. The most powerful was the Hanseatic League, a confederacy of German cities, guilds, and trading posts that further allied itself with guilds elsewhere in northern Europe and eventually controlled trade and commerce from London and Rouen to Novgorod. The Hanseatic League was a major political and civilizing force. It made laws, fought pirates, cleared and charted waterways, controlled prices and the quality of goods, "and in general substituted order for chaos in northern European trade."[1]

The Hanseatic League and its members were also "frankly institutions in restraint of trade. They usually persuaded their towns to keep out, by a high protective tariff or elsewise, goods competitive with their own" or, "if allowed to enter the town, [to be] sold at prices fixed by the affected guild."[2] Craftsmen were required to work for the guild or, if independent, only with its consent.

The activities of the guilds ranged from wholesale cooperative purchasing, loss insurance, price control, and the regulation of product quality to police protection, patronage of the arts, and the organization of food supply, sewage disposal, and other public works. Thus, the guilds were major factors in the growth of their towns, intricately intertwined in their economic and political evolution into independent cities. They were also instrumental in reducing the power of kings, local lords, and the church, thereby altering the course of European history.

But great power always corrupts. Ultimately, the guilds became as despotic as the institutions they helped to replace, evolving "into an oppressive oligarchy of merchants and financiers."[3] For a time, the craft guilds acted as a check on the merchant guilds but eventually they also became nepotistic, oligarchic, protectionist, and exclusionary.

The power of the guilds declined with the emergence of capitalism, the rise of the nation state, and ultimately the industrial revolution. The decline was long and slow, however. The Hanseatic League expired in 1669, but guilds in some European countries endured into the early years of the nineteenth century. Nor were guilds confined to Europe. Local guilds also dominated Japanese commerce, lasting until the early 1870s when they were abolished and local trade associations rose in their place.[4]

The dominant economic institution of their day, the guilds' historical impact has shaped modern economic institutions. The craft guilds were the distant progenitors of modern trade and craft labor unions. The merchant guilds evolved into today's corporations, trade associations, and cooperatives.

The significance of the guilds to the rise of trade associations lies in two realms of activity. First, the guilds sought to protect and advance the economic interests of their members in every way possible, including the regulation and restraint of competition—just as trade associations have in every country, including the United States before the enactment of the antitrust laws and, briefly, during the Depression of the 1930s.

Secondly, like the guilds, trade associations have always been the interface between their members and the government. Of course, only in Japan have associations had the political power of the guilds even remotely, but the impulse appears universal.

There are also important differences between the guilds and the business associations of today. Guilds restricted their memberships, generally making the entry process a long and expensive one; trade and business associations admit anyone who meets their membership criteria. Indeed, in some European countries, membership in trade associations and chambers of commerce is mandated by law. Restricted membership was only one of the many means by which the guilds were able to enforce decrees and decisions. Trade associations, by contrast, have no enforcement power except where government chooses to grant it.

DEVELOPMENT IN THE UNITED STATES

The earliest recorded American trade association was established in 1724 by house carpenters in Philadelphia. In 1761, the Boston Society for Encouraging Trade and Commerce was formed; the next year, in New England, the Association of Spermaceti Chandlers was set up to regulate the prices of wax candles. The oldest business group still in existence is the New York Chamber of Commerce, organized in 1768. The second oldest is the New York Stock Exchange, established in 1792. Marine underwriters founded a trade association in 1820. A scattering of other business associations took shape during the decades prior to the Civil War, of which what is today the American Iron and Steel Institute (1855) is the most significant.

Some national trade associations began as local organizations. The Hampden County Cotton Spinners Association (1854) became a New England regional organization and then eventually (1890) the National Cotton Manufacturers Association. Still later (1956), it again became a regional group, the Northern Textile Association.

The Post-Civil War Period

The history of business associations in the United States is, in many ways, the history of antitrust development. During the quarter-century between the end of the Civil War and the passage of the first antitrust laws, trade associations were widely established in a number of industries. These groups "were more in the nature of offensive than of defensive organizations. They seem to have been formed for the purpose of enabling their members more effectively to take advantage of favorable business conditions, rather than as a means of safeguarding the trade against wasteful, demoralizing, and ruinous practices, or of striving for constructive achievement through cooperative action."[5]

Put less euphemistically, these early U. S. trade associations sought, though often in vain, to fix prices, restrict output, and allocate markets. Pools formed by purported competitors to allocate production and customers and fix prices were a favorite technique. Few worked very well, however, since there was nothing to prevent other competitors from aggressively breaking the pool agreements to their own advantage.

Indeed, the

records of these old trade associations are replete with the agonies of evolution; they would all agree to something that might work a few weeks, then some would forget and do differently, a wail would go up, the agreement fly to pieces, the association would gasp and die or go to sleep for a number of months until the storm of wrath had passed. Then the members with suspicion and hope would foregather once more and do it all over again.[6]

Laissez-faire and Antitrust

Thus was mercantilism challenged by laissez-faire economics. Unbridled capitalism developed swiftly and spread widely through the country during this period. The unsuccessful production and pricing pools were succeeded by trusts and other monopolistic combinations of such economic power that competitors were driven to the wall by practices that often included discriminatory forced rebates from suppliers, predatory pricing to capture customers, assorted financial manipulations, and plain bribery.

A series of major recessions (or "panics") during this period put an end to public support for laissez-faire economics. The pools, trusts, and monopolies were cast as the villainous causes of the nation's problems by the press and public. The resulting outcry led to the passage in 1887 of the Interstate Commerce Act which, for the first time, put a major industry, the railroads, under the regulatory jurisdiction of a federal agency. Railroads themselves supported the move in order to end cutthroat competition. Public uproar over the actions of John D. Rockefeller's Standard Oil trust and similar combinations resulted in the passage of the Sherman Antitrust Act in 1890, which outlawed any monopoly or combination in restraint of interstate commerce—a law that completely changed the face of trade associations in America.

It did not happen immediately, however. Federal courts repeatedly overturned rate-making and other decisions of the Interstate Commerce Commission. They also undermined the Sherman Act for the remainder of the century. For instance, the Supreme Court ruled in 1895 that the sugar trust's control of 98 percent of the nation's sugar refining business did not involve interstate commerce and therefore did not violate the Sherman Act! Not until the "trust-buster," Theodore Roosevelt, became president in 1901 did serious antitrust enforcement begin.[7]

The Umbrellas Unfurl

As trade associations expanded (to about a hundred national organizations in 1900), it became apparent that there was a need for an organization to represent those broad interests of American industry that were beyond the scope of any individual trade association. Thus was born the first of the two major umbrella associations, the National Association of Manufacturers (NAM). The NAM was established in 1895 to promote foreign trade, rehabilitate the merchant marine, advocate higher tariffs, support a trans-Isthmian canal, and foster the manufacturing industry.

The NAM represented only industrial companies, however. In 1912, President Taft urged the business community to form a "central organization" that would advise Congress on national economic problems and issues. The Chamber of Commerce of the United States was created at a conference in Washington that year.

These two organizations have coexisted uneasily ever since, often acting in cooperation but also often in rivalry. (See chapter 10.)

From Roosevelt to Roosevelt

Theodore Roosevelt undertook strenuous antitrust enforcement against a number of industries, and Congress expanded the jurisdiction of the Interstate Commerce Commission (ICC) to include other transportation industries in addition to the railroads, later adding telephone and telegraph companies as well. Roosevelt's antitrust policies did not oppose business consolidations if they met a legitimate need, preferring to regulate them against abusive practices rather than break them up. The courts eventually came to a parallel conclusion, ruling in a case affecting the Standard Oil Trust that only monopolistic acts that affected interstate commerce unreasonably were Sherman Act violations.

In 1914, Congress passed the Clayton Antitrust Act, which banned discriminatory pricing and certain other business practices and arrangements. The same year, it also enacted the Federal Trade Commission Act, outlawing "unfair or deceptive acts or practices" and "unfair methods of competition." The law also set up the Federal Trade Commission (FTC), a regulatory agency with police powers, to enforce the antitrust laws more or less jointly with the Justice Department.

During this period, trade associations underwent a sea change and "began to assume the dignity of definite business institutions. . . . Election to office became an honor to be published, rather than a secret to be hidden."[8] A growing number of associations began holding regular conventions, opening offices, and hiring permanent staff.

Pooling and similar restraints, never particularly effective, began to disappear, and trade associations started to develop more constructive— and legal—approaches to strengthening the industries they represented. Associations initiated the development of such member services as standardization and quality inspection, research and statistical compilations to facilitate improved business practices, credit and debt collection services, commercial arbitration, and even consumer product information.

World War I contributed greatly to the growth of the trade association movement. In its need to reorient production, consumption, and the overall economy to a war footing, the Wilson administration found it easier, in many cases, to deal with entire industries than with individual companies. As a result, existing associations were strengthened and many new ones established. By 1920, there were a total of about 1,000 national business groups.

They accomplished much. The Webb-Pomerene Act, passed in 1918, gave certain kinds of associations a limited antitrust exemption for the purpose of promoting and selling their members' products in foreign markets.

But pricing and market stabilization were never far from association priorities. A book by Arthur J. Eddy[9] produced the theory of "cooperative competition" and led to creation of a large number of trade groups known as "open-price associations." Eddy's theory held that "an exchange of price information among competing businessmen . . . would stimulate competition and give individual businessmen a sound base upon which to make independent decisions."[10] Such independent decision making would, it was argued, enable competitors to approach the nirvana of economists, the state of perfect competition, while staying clear of antitrust prosecution.

The open-price associations collected and published data on such matters as "quotations, prices, orders, shipments, purchases, production, manufacturing and selling costs, and stocks on hand."[11] The associations collected this information from their members on a mandatory reporting basis and published the results for the same audience. Open-price associations did not have quite the legal sanctity that their proponents desired, however. A series of court decisions in the mid-1920s steadily weakened "cooperative competition" and the open-price associations without ever actually banning information exchanges.

In 1929, the stock market collapsed, precipitating the Great Depression that revolutionized American economic life. By the early 1930s, as the economy reeled from the worst effects of the Depression, corporate executives and business associations began denouncing the antitrust laws as obstacles to recovery and agitating for new mechanisms to stabilize and strengthen prices, production, and employment.

The Short Flight of the Blue Eagle

The intensity of the Depression led many business people to develop a variety of proposals to bring about economic recovery. Most of these involved antitrust relaxation, if not its actual repeal, in order to facilitate industrial cooperation.

The most significant of these proposals was made in 1931 by Gerard Swope of the General Electric Company. Swope proposed that all companies with over fifty employees be required to join the trade associations for their industries and that these associations be given the power to regulate and manage production and prices to mesh with consumption demands.

Today, almost sixty years later, it is difficult to imagine the desperation of the economic circumstances that would prompt a major corporate executive to offer such a proposal.

Small wonder that during this period, even without authorizing legislation, trade groups set about to control prices and production, both secretly and through trade practice conferences conducted by the Federal Trade Commission. Economic conditions, manifest in the depression, made it seem that business-at-any-price was more desirable than stagnation and rigid adherence to antitrust principles.[12]

This sense of desperation was widespread among the country's business and political leadership. Public outrage over high unemployment and other severe symptoms of the nation's economic illness led many to express open fear that capitalism was about to self-destruct and even that the social and political fabric of America was on the verge of unraveling. In consequence, measures were advocated (and enacted) that would have been absolutely inconceivable only a few years before. The nation's brief fling with central planning grew out of one such measure, the National Industrial Recovery Act (NIRA), enacted in June 1933.

The law established the National Recovery Administration (NRA), whose famous emblem, the blue eagle, came to symbolize America's efforts to pull the nation into economic recovery. In a sense, the NRA was a cross between Arthur Eddy's "cooperative competition" and the Swope Plan. During the brief life of this offspring, American trade associations had more power than at any other time in the nation's history.

The NIRA authorized trade associations, among other groups, to develop "codes of fair competition" for individual industries. The industry codes were to be used to promote recovery through a relaxation of the antitrust laws but not (in the language of the statute) "to promote monopolies or to eliminate or oppress small enterprises." Trade associations were empowered to use their codes to ban unfair business practices and to engage in open-price reporting, among other activities. Price-fixing was not allowed, but in emergency situations the codes could be used to set minimum prices.

The NRA was established with strong support from President Franklin D. Roosevelt and Congress. The third branch of government had yet to be heard from, however. In 1935, barely two years after the NRA was established, the NIRA that had set it up was declared unconstitutional by the U. S. Supreme Court.

If the NRA was only a brief experiment in American economic history, it nonetheless had lasting impacts on the trade association movement. To take advantage of the new law's provisions, many new associations quickly emerged during this period, and older ones undertook to revise their organizational structures and expand their memberships in order to comply with the law's requirements that they truly represent their industries.

The lasting effects of the NRA on trade associations appear in the words of one association's own history: "Uneasy with its regulatory role, the officers decided that the Association must hire its first employee, a 'non-competitor.' The board approved the hiring of an assistant secretary "to do the work," and established the association's first permanent office in New York." [13] This particular association was already twenty years old by the time it was moved to take these steps. Permanent secretariats for trade associations were not new in 1933, but neither were they yet commonplace. After 1935, however, the idea that associations required the continuity of full-time headquarters and staff support became the rule and no longer the exception.

For a few more years some associations sought to continue regulating their industries. Court decisions soon made it clear that self-restraint of trade by business outside the scope of antitrust policy would be permitted only if exemptions were explicitly granted by Congress; For example, stockbrokers, who are legally regulated by their industry association, the National Association of Securities Dealers.

After the crash landing of the blue eagle's brief flight, some of the associations set up during 1933–1935 went out of business. Many remained, however, transforming their activities into programs that provided on-going benefits to their industries within the confines of antitrust law.

With the passage in 1936 of another important antitrust law, the Robinson-Patman Act, which strengthened the ban on price discrimination and certain kinds of trade allowances, it was apparent that the era of pools, trusts, cartels, open-pricing, and industry codes was finally over. The primacy of antitrust policy was fully established. Except where Congress decreed otherwise, the economic regulation of industries was henceforth the province not of trade associations but of government and particularly of the regulatory agencies that mushroomed from the Depression into the 1970s.

Far from curtailing the importance of associations, this produced another change in their roles. Eventually, they underwent a metamorphosis from economic regulators to political advocates, and the era of their greatest growth and strength would commence. That cycle would not begin in earnest, however, until after World War II and the Korean War.

The Mid-century Wars

World War II made far greater demands on American business than World War I had. The mobilization of the nation's manufacturing and transportation industries ended the Depression as abruptly as it had begun. Trade associations played an important liaison and coordinating role in economic mobilization, in rationing, and in the price and production controls that the wartime economy required. Much of this recurred, though on a greatly reduced scale, during the Korean War of the early 1950s, but not during the Vietnam War except, perhaps, during the price controls of the Nixon administration.

The economy soared during this period. America was now the pre-eminent world power—economically, militarily, and politically. The repeal of price controls at the end of World War II resulted in rampant inflation as pent-up demand suddenly spilled over and unleashed a major consumer economy. The producer was no longer king. The consumer was, and the companies and industries that flourished were those that adopted the strategies of consumer marketing as the new way of the world.

Trade and business associations, of which there were nearly 2,000 by 1945, became "clearinghouses of business information." Government relations was still only one of these functions, yet to become the associations' primary purpose.

ASSOCIATIONS ABROAD

The functions and activities of trade and business associations in different countries vary with the economic, social, legal, and political climates. There are, however, important and instructive similarities. As nations enter the age of industrialization, associations have sprung up almost universally to represent, first, the economic and political interests of members of single industries, and shortly thereafter, those of the national business community. Associations everywhere have sought to provide beneficial services to their members, to temper the forces of competition wherever allowed to do so, and to serve as the liaison between their members and governments.

It may further a better understanding of American business and trade groups to review briefly the development of their counterparts in certain other countries.

Japan

Local trade and manufacturers' associations arose in Japan after the dissolution of the guilds in the early 1870s. Initially, these groups (in which membership was compulsory) comprised local cartels—combinations akin to pools and trusts, designed to restrict competition and fix prices. These local associations regulated employment, purchasing, production, sales, inspection, and pricing. Originally regional voluntary umbrella groups representing all enterprises in a community, chambers of commerce in Japan gradually came to speak only for small and medium-sized businesses and became more regional than local in their orientation.

National trade associations were founded sporadically in various industries from the 1880s into the early decades of this century. Their period of greatest growth took place in the late 1920s and 1930s, when Japanese public policy actively promoted the development of domestic cartels. Domestic cartel agreements were not outlawed until 1947.

There are today four major national business associations in Japan:

- The Chamber of Commerce and Industry, an umbrella group representing local/regional chambers in 475 cities.
- The Federation of Economic Organizations, a major organization of trade associations grouped by industry. Probably the most powerful business asociation in Japan, it has been called ''the headquarters of Japan Inc.''
- The Federation of Employers' Associations, comprised of about a hundred local and industry-level employer groups, dealing with labor matters.
- The Committee for Economic Development, an economic research and public policy organization, not unlike the U. S. group of the same name.[14]

As a group, the trade and business associations of Japan are probably the most influential of any in the industrial world. Not only have they been major instruments of economic development, but they are also prime channels by which government has communicated with individual industries and enterprises. They are key factors in shaping Japanese policy domestically and especially internationally.

Great Britain

By contrast, British trade and business associations are among the weakest among the industrialized countries. Trade associations developed in Britain in the eighteenth and nineteenth centuries, often on a local, narrowly specialized basis. Local chambers of commerce also date back to the late eighteenth century and federated into a national organization in 1860.

This was a period in which the laissez-faire philosophy of commerce ruled supreme, and economic behaviors were largely both unregulated and unprotected. Often small and fragmented, trade associations sought to moderate market competition with no way to enforce restraint agreements and very mixed success. Restraint agreements were not necessarily illegal—just not legally enforceable. Just as victims of boycotts and other collusive acts had no legal redress, neither did associations against members who violated price maintenance or production pooling arrangements. "As many associations found to their cost, a price-fixing agreement or an output levy had the same legal status as a gambling debt; it might be an obligation of honour, but no English court would enforce it."[15]

Early twentieth century associations engaged in restrictions of prices and production where they could, sometimes in the gentlemanly fashion of continuing to pay redistributed output levies even to companies that had closed down "as a painless way of putting competitors out of business, much to be preferred to aggressive competition."[16] On the other hand, associations continued to lack power to cope with industry members who sought to maximize profits through cut-throat competition rather than through negotiations to divide market share and control production and prices.

British businesses were much more successful in combating the rise of organized labor. Local employer groups arose during the nineteenth century and lobbied with considerable success to hamper the rise of labor unions. Business groups established the National Confederation of Employers' Organizations in 1919.

Although British trade associations were actively lobbying Parliament as early as the 1840s, legislative activity did not become prominent until World War I. The first major umbrella organization, the Federation (more recently, the Confederation) of British Industries, was formed during the war, in 1916.

Several factors have contributed to the lack of effectiveness in influencing public policy by British business associations. For one thing, regional sectionalism and intra-industry rivalries have hampered the development of consensus on issues. For another, the number of large firms in a relatively small country with a strong central government and permanent bureaucracy has facilitated direct communications between those companies and policy-makers. Moreover, association staffs are neither paid well nor held in particularly high esteem; with a few exceptions, it has therefore been difficult to attract high-quality personnel to association work.

At different periods during this century, British governments have engaged in major programs of industrial reconstruction—sometimes nationalizing companies, currently re-privatizing them. The internal weaknesses of the business associations have generally resulted in their being left out of negotiations with the affected industries. Even when the British government has sought to cooperate with business through its associations, the penchant for secrecy and a laissez-faire distrust of government have often prevented these groups from getting their members to provide the requested information. Government programs to help specific industries, often begun through trade associations, have ended up by-passing them and dealing directly with individual companies.

CHAMBERS OF COMMERCE AROUND THE GLOBE

Chambers of commerce have important points of both similarity and difference with trade associations. Chambers broadly represent the interests of business in a given geographic area rather than those of a particular industry. They function to foster the interests of the local business community. In many cases, they encourage economic development, often expanding into programs that may range from promoting transportation and other public works projects to improving local school systems and supporting the arts.

Origins

The first local chamber of commerce appears to have been established in Marseilles, France, in 1650, by order of the town council. Other French cities created chambers around the turn of the eighteenth century for the purpose of keeping local merchants informed about commercial matters: "these chambers were created by the government for particular aims of its administration, but freely organized by the people concerned."[17] This became the pattern of organization in many European countries and those elsewhere in the world that had been European colonies.

The first chamber in the New World was established in Boston in 1761. The first in Britain was in Glasgow in 1773, and then in London and Liverpool. The chamber movement swept across Europe, though not without problems. Chambers of commerce were abolished during the French Revolution but later resurrected by Napoleon, who also introduced them into Italy and other countries. Totalitarian regimes in this century temporarily abolished them in Italy and Germany.

Organizational Forms and Models

There have been two main models of chamber organization. Throughout much of Europe, chambers have been established under government authorization or even edict, often financed by public funds or earmarked taxes. In these countries, membership has been mandatory for particular kinds of businesses, and there has been official representation on their governing bodies.

The second model, more familiar to Americans, is also the organizational form in northern Europe, Britain, and the countries of British heritage. These are voluntary membership organizations, funded by member dues or contributions, and without mandatory governmental representation. Chambers in these countries tend to engage in broader programs than just business development. They are also freer to engage in lobbying and government relations activities. At the national level, government relations is the predominant function in chambers in Great Britain and other northern European countries, as it is in the United States among both national and state chambers.

Local chambers in Britain, like the British trade associations, are scantily financed and staffed, with memberships comprised largely of small local merchants. As a group, they have been more notable for export promotion programs than for effective government relations. Local chambers in France, by contrast, receive public funds and rely much less on member dues. Despite this dependence on government funding, they are far more vigorous than their British counterparts, particularly as small business advocates with governmental authorities.

In a number of countries, chambers have come to represent not merely business interests but also those of agriculture and the economy as a whole, as in Italy. In other countries, notably those whose chambers operate under government authority, the chamber of commerce may be paralleled by counterparts for labor and consumers.

WHY ASSOCIATIONS ARISE

Business associations develop when the collective needs of their members outweigh competitive conditions. Trade associations in particular arose during the last century typically to try to control over-production, stabilize market conditions, and restrain high costs, especially those of labor. In some countries, remedies included the formation of cartels (for example, Japan) or less formal agreements to limit production, allocate customers, and set prices (as in Britain and the United States). Confrontations with emerging labor unions and other efforts to restrain rising labor costs were a common denominator everywhere. Associations often provided a means to pool managerial resources—for instance, obtaining foreign technology or industrywide purchasing and export promotion. As associations became institutionalized, related functions arose, such as programs to compile economic and industry statistics and develop industry standards. Other services, ranging from credit collection to publications, also developed.

Associations of all kinds in all countries found it essential to develop means to affect governmental policies in such areas as taxes, tariffs, import and export controls, labor conditions and costs, price controls, and the like. Moreover, in countries as varied as France, Japan, and the United States, the need to develop a continuity of contacts with government bureaucracies contributed to the rise of permanent association staffs.

In the United States, this has been necessary so that continuing professional expertise would be available on an industry-wide basis for negotiations with the developing complex of specialized regulatory agencies: "The growth of an active federal government with regulatory powers has been the primary factor pushing Americans toward associative functions and cooperative values."[18] The rise of an association representing one industry has often led to the formation of associations for its competing industries, lest the first gain a dominant negotiating position with regulators and lawmakers. The strong relationships among regulatory officials, affected interest groups, and friendly legislators has produced the phenomenon known in the United States as "iron triangles".

Among the major industrialized countries, business associations are strongest in the United States and especially Japan. In Japan, the political advocacy role of associations has been an important force in shaping governmental economic policy, in part because the views of Japanese associations have been actively solicited by policymakers, but also because the associations' ability to reach wide consensus has enabled them to respond with great effectiveness. Association membership by individual companies is therefore essential to their prosperity. It is safe to say that Japanese companies are undoubtedly far less prone to engage in "free-riding" on their trade and business associations than are their American counterparts.

U. S. business associations are also important influences on governmental decision making, but rarely more so than other major interest groups, all of which compete vigorously as shapers but not makers of public policy. In the United States, there is no suggestion of parity between interest groups and government. Interest groups propose, influence, challenge, litigate, and engage in a growing variety of lobbying techniques to shape governmental decision making, but in the end, it is *governmental* decision making. The lines of demarcation between government and American private interest groups are quite clear. Caesar is rendered his own.

The record of associations in Europe is more diverse. British trade associations, in the main, are small, parochial, under-financed, and under-staffed. They have not been notably effective therefore, either economically or politically. In Germany and France, effectiveness has been mixed, greater in some industries, less in others. In many cases, they have played an influential role on specialized regulatory issues, both with the ministries and the respective parliaments.

Umbrella organizations are often the most effective business associations in their countries. On the one hand, the Confederation of British Industries, probably the most respected business group in its country, has a reputation for being more progressive than its members sometimes wish, an unusual quality among umbrella associations that are more often accused of making policy at the lowest common denominator of their members' views. The *Conseil National du Patronat Francais,* on the other hand, may speak more authoritatively for French firms because it leads them where they wish to go. (As discussed in chapter 13, these different approaches to leadership have considerable significance.) National organizations of small business are active in both Britain and France, as in the United States, because of the apparently universal suspicion that the umbrella associations are the captives of large companies.[19]

European Perspectives

It is significant that "associations are more accepted, more respected, and generally larger in the United States" than in Europe, a pair of European association executives noted in a presentation to their U. S. counterparts: "Americans tend to join societies more readily than Europeans and this general pattern of behavior benefits American associations." They added several other important distinctions:

- Membership on association boards of directors is generally seen as an honor in the United States. European business people often see it as a chore.
- Board chairmen of European associations tend to have more power than their American counterparts, in large part because of the weakness of association staffs.
- Staff executives of U. S. business groups are often professional association managers. European staff managers are typically products of the industry that the association represents, with little training in association management.
- U. S. business associations are prone to expand both services and membership bases. European groups tend to concentrate on providing a narrow range of services to current members.
- Like other Americans, business associations are quite willing to take public policy disputes to court: "The European attitude [is] to keep the law out of things if possible."
- Closely related are differences in approaches to government relations which, in the United States, is increasingly considered the top-priority function of associations. "In Europe, government is something one wants to encounter only infrequently and if necessary," said the European association executives. They continued:

> The more centralised systems of government in the European nations are moreover somewhat less intrusive than the incredibly diverse United States structure. In the United Kingdom, for example, there is the local county or city and then central

government. The town, county, state, and federal structure in the United States makes it appear hugely over-governed. Only in the past few years is a stronger top tier of European government emerging, in particular in the form of the European Economic Community, and many European associations are now developing stronger government relations and looking to American experience in dealing with this new challenge.[20]

SOME LESSONS OF ASSOCIATION HISTORY

In whatever time and country, business associations exist to improve the lot of their members and industries. The aims seem well-nigh universal. Their ability to accomplish those goals, however, depends on the political and economic climate.

Business associations have sought throughout history to accomplish their purposes by controlling and regulating the marketplace. Competitive conditions have sometimes restricted the ability of associations to act in these areas, but governmental policies have been the greater restraint.

The drive to control their environment is as natural for business organizations as it is for any other human endeavor. Because the impulse to restrain competition is as strong as it is illegal in this country, association members in the United States must constantly be wary of individual or collective actions that could bring them into conflict with the law. The fact that American business groups have been ineffective in direct regulation of markets, both before and after the passage of antitrust laws, has not prevented imperiled companies and industries from making the effort.

In recent years, for example, milk dealers serving New York City and its suburbs, suffering from high labor and other costs, repeatedly undertook to structure local markets and maintain prices, despite equally repeated antitrust prosecutions by the state's attorney general. The trade association representing the dairies staved off reform legislation for many years, but ultimately was overwhelmed by consumer pressures that altered state law to allow lower-cost New Jersey suppliers to sell milk in New York. Prices then fell, and many New York dairies went under. The industry succumbed in the end to economic inefficiencies among its members. Associations and their members must be constantly wary of such situations, especially in a period of rising competitive forces, domestically and globally.

There are, however, other actions that associations can legitimately undertake to improve the climate of commerce for their members. These lie in both the economic and the political realms. For one, associations owe it to their members to identify chronic and long-term economic problems and to provide leadership before they lead to the no-win situations that befell the New York dairies (see chapter 13 for further discussion of this subject.) They also have an obligation to try to affect public opinion and to shape public policies and decisions. Efforts to enlist public opinion and the aid of governmental policymakers might have made it easier for the dairies to confront their union and restrain labor costs, instead of conspiring with it for temporary gains that led eventually to the demise of both companies and jobs.

The policies of government are the most critical single influence on the business environment in every country. For that reason, government relations and public affairs programs are an almost universal constant of associations, even if the effectiveness of those programs is mixed. As the plight of the dairies illustrates, direct association efforts to influence market conditions fail when confronted with hostile political and legal conditions.

Association effectiveness in public affairs varies in the United States from industry to industry, as it does around the world from country to country. In an era when the policies of governments will decisively affect the international competitiveness of their native companies, however, the ability of business associations to influence those policies will be vital in determining the shape of the global economy of the twenty-first century.

This will certainly be true in Europe, as new business associations form and old ones are strengthened to improve their ability to influence the policies of the European Economic Community.

It is at least as true in America. "No significant industry can afford under current conditions in the United States not to be represented by effective associational representatives," one student of trade associations has written.[21] The converse is also unmistakable: No business association can afford to be ineffective in government relations if it is to play a significant role in determining its industry's health and future.

While many association activities and undertakings are discussed in the chapters that follow, the premise of this book is that the government relations function is paramount—a point of view that American business and trade associations have increasingly come to share.

NOTES

1. Will Durant, *The Story of Civilization* IV *The Age of Faith* (New York: Simon and Schuster, 1950), 618.

2. Durant, *Age of Faith,* 634–37.

3. Ibid.

4. Fujita Teiichiró, "Local Trade Associations in Prewar Japan," in Hiroaki Yamazaki and Matao Miyamoto, eds. *Trade Associations in Business History: Proceedings of the Fuji Conference* (Tokyo: University of Tokyo Press, 1988), 87–113.

5. National Industrial Conference Board, *Trade Associations: Their Economic Significance and Legal Status* (New York: 1925), 10.

6. Emmett Hay Naylor, "History of Trade Association Activities" in U. S. Department of Commerce, *Trade Association Activities* (Washington: Government Printing Office, 1923), 303–304.

7. For a lively account of this period, see Samuel Eliot Morison, *The Oxford History of the American People*. (New York: Oxford University Press, 1965), 761–64, 817–23.

8. Conference Board, *Trade Associations,* 12.

9. Arthur J. Eddy, *The New Competition*. (Chicago: A. C. McClurg, 1912).

10. George P. Lamb and Sumner S. Kittelle, *Trade Association Law and Practice* (Boston: Little, Brown, 1956), 8.

11. Conference Board, *Trade Associations,* 18.

12. Lamb and Kittelle, *Trade Association Law,* 10.

13. Chemical Specialties Manufacturers Association, *75 Years of CSMA History* (Washington: 1988), 8.

14. Matao Miyamoto, "Business Associations in Prewar Japan" in *Trade Associations in Business History*, 3.

15. John A. Turner, "Servants of Two Masters: British Trade Associations in the First Half of the Twentieth Century" in *Trade Associations in Business History*, 177.

16. Ibid., 175.

17. Romolo Astraldi, *The Organization of the Chambers of Commerce in the World* (Florence, Italy: L. Macri, 1950), 29.

18. Louis Galambos, "The American Trade Association Movement Revisited" in *Trade Associations in Business History,* 138.

19. For a comparison of British and French associations, see Jack Hayward, "Employer Associations and the State in France and Britain" in Steven J. Warnecke and Ezra N. Suleiman, eds., *Industrial Policies in Western Europe* (New York: Praeger, 1975.)

20. Peter D. Houghton and Christian Kunz, "Contrasts Between European and American Associations" in *ASAE Fourth Annual Management Conference Proceedings* (Washington: American Society of Association Executives, 1986), 38–46.

21. Galambos, "American Trade Association Movement," 130.

Part II

OPTIMIZING THE USE OF ASSOCIATIONS

3

Evaluating and Utilizing Business Associations

The entire range of association activities . . . will, upon reflection, be found to relate to the achievement of one or both of two ends: the enhancement of efficiency in producing and marketing processes, and the circumvention of certain barriers which obstruct the fluid adjustment of economic relationships.

National Industrial Conference Board, 1925

A point frequently illustrated in this book is that business associations have many similarities as well as vast differences. The most significant underlying characteristic of all such groups in America—whether trade associations, professional societies, or chambers of commerce—is their voluntary nature. Potential members are free to join or not join. Members may take advantage of all available programs and services or use none. They may go to conventions and other meetings or not, as they choose. They may read the association's publications or ignore them. They are at liberty to be as active as they wish or to be totally uninvolved.

Those who choose to be active contribute a staggering amount of time. It has been estimated that trade and professional associations are the beneficiaries of 137 million volunteer hours per year[1]—the full-time equivalent of over 68,000 people.

VOLUNTARISM AND MARKETING

The completely voluntary nature of these organizations pervades everything they do and how they do it. Motivation and persuasion are a constant theme: How much stimulation and excitement can we build into this year's convention program to build attendance? How can we improve the readability of the newsletter? What can be done to boost interest in our educational workshops? How can we sell more insurance? How can we get the membership more involved in our programs? Above all, how can we increase membership?

The former president of the AFL, Samuel Gompers, was asked once what labor wanted. "More!" was his response. Every association executive knows exactly what Gompers meant. Each of them wants 100 percent of the industry or profession to join the association and 100 percent of the members totally involved in every association activity. Each wants his or her association to be maximally effective, influential, and respected in everything it does.

These are not fantasies; they are the objectives toward which every association executive constantly strives. The effectiveness of associations and of the people who staff them is measured, consciously or not, by growth in numbers and in qualitative achievement. Asked the same question that was put to Gompers, association executives and leaders are apt to reply, "Bigger! Better!"

Successful association executives must therefore be consummate marketers, learning what their members want, providing it, and always seeking new ways to be interesting, different, and appealing. This does not imply by any means that associations are all entertainment and hype, although those elements are often present. As in all successful marketing, however, the product must also provide quality and value, lest the "customer" be disappointed and not buy again. In a very real sense, customers are exactly what association members are. If the association does not satisfy its clientele, current members will not renew and potential ones will not join.

This alternative is unpleasant, both for the association itself and for the staff. There is a fairly high turnover rate among association executives, sometimes because of slippage in an important association program or objective, but also sometimes because the association's members have begun to find the group's staff leadership tiresome and want new faces and new styles to provide member satisfaction. If the organization's professional and elected leadership cannot resolve the problems, the association may find itself in difficulties: decreasing membership, declining revenues, and soaring dissension. Ultimately, a rival association may be formed, and both groups will find themselves diverted from the achievement of sound goals by the distractions of competitive pressures.

The satisfaction of members' needs, real and perceived, is therefore a genuine imperative for business associations of all kinds. Those needs are hardly monolithic, however, even within individual associations and certainly not across different organizations. Even within individual interest groups, segmentation of interests exists. There is, in a sense, a dialogue of expectations among the different interests found within associations. The elected leadership, the professional staff, and the membership at large each has a firm grip on a different part of the elephant; their respective perceptions of what the beast is, or ought to be, vary accordingly.

Those interests may be segmented still further. The members' views and perceptions differ widely according to their individual needs, interests, and positions within the industry. The officers and other members of the board of directors also are often less than unanimous in their points of view. Sometimes the board has a different perception of association needs than the general membership has. And even within the staff, there are likely to be variations in attitude and perception; the organization looks very different to the convention manager than it does to the government relations director.

Disparate views about the needs of segments of the membership and the appropriate role of the association can lead to internal crisis and threaten the viability of the organization, if not well managed. An example occurred some years ago in a trade association whose members produce a popular consumer product.

The industry represented by the association was comprised of over a hundred companies, but five of these controlled well over half of the market at the time of the group's internal dispute. Dues, the association's primary revenue source, were tied directly to sales, so that the "big five" provided the bulk of the funding. However, these five held only a third of the fifteen seats on the board of directors, though on a more or less permanent basis. The remaining ten directorships rotated among the smaller companies, most of them family businesses. The "smalls" thus had political power disproportionate to their financial contribution.

For most of the association's history, this situation presented no great problems. The issues the association dealt with were seldom controversial within the board, and decisions were normally reached by consensus. The crisis arose when the industry's sales flattened. The large firms responded by more aggressive marketing. Total industry sales stayed fairly constant but several of the big companies were able to increase their market share, partly at the expense of the other large competitors but mostly by taking business from the small firms.

The association's executive director responded to this situation by developing an export promotion program largely centered around group sales missions abroad. Exports of this product had never been substantial, in part because it had never been as popular overseas as in the United States but also because what markets did exist in other countries were adequately served by local manufacturers—many of them affiliates of the same multinational corporations that controlled several of the large U. S. producers. The association's program, at least in theory, was intended to increase the total international market as much as to promote exports.

The program had little appeal to the "big five," but was pushed through the board by the "smalls," among which it was quite popular. This popularity continued even though the program had little sales impact. The large companies then attacked it, claiming that the semi-annual trade missions were little more than vacation junkets financed by their dues.

The small manufacturers responded that the association had long had a regulatory compliance program to which they had never objected, even though it benefited primarily the large companies. The "bigs" countercharged that they were doing most of the compliance work in-house and that the association's role was merely that of a coordinator and spokesman.

Finally, the major producers tried to force out the executive director, the architect of the export program, with complaints about his high salary, perks, and lack of attention to their needs. They threatened to resign from the association if he were not removed. They failed in this effort, and the three largest members did actually quit, precipitating a revenue crisis.

The executive director and one of his subordinates responded by developing proposals for new, non-dues revenue sources. The subordinate proposed that the necessary seed-money be obtained by diverting it from the regulatory compliance program. The program manager protested and later resigned when the executive director overruled his protests. The program was then disbanded and taken up by the large companies, which formed a coordinating committee for the purpose. The new revenue programs turned out to be no more successful than the export promotion effort. The association shrank its programs and staff, but continues to exist.

Ultimately, a new association was formed by the "bigs," some of the "smalls," and a group of distributors and suppliers. Both organizations coexist, not always peaceably. The executive director of the older group retained his position and now also manages several other small associations through a multi-association management firm that he started.

The problems that beset the original organization resulted partly from its structural imbalances, but mainly from the gaps in expectations among membership factions. Rather than seek solutions to unite the membership, the executive director played to the group that controlled the board, exacerbating the problems. He was able to preserve his job, although in a shrunken association, by forcing out subordinates with different points of view. In the end, nothing was gained by either segment of the membership.

The blame for this situation must be shared by a manipulative executive director and a membership that allowed itself to be exploited. The lesson is that effective participation in associations requires an investment by their members in understanding both the organization and its key elements—not only to avoid negative situations but also to maximize positive benefits.

An analogy can be drawn with the techniques that business people use in sales and purchasing. Effective purchasing necessitates a keen understanding of potential suppliers, just as successful selling requires research and analysis of the market. In the same way, the association's clientele, the members, need to know at least as much about the organization they belong to as the group knows about them. Effective membership that is capable of minimizing the downside and maximizing the advantages requires a grasp of the association and the elements that comprise it: other members' needs, governance, staff, financial and other resources, organizational culture, and inner politics, along with programs and effectiveness.

EVALUATING ASSOCIATION STRENGTHS AND WEAKNESSES

Business executives sometimes confuse two kinds of non-profit organizations that they support financially, often in the same budget item. The first type includes groups like hospitals, universities, the Boy Scouts, the United Way, and so forth. These are charitable organizations to which contributions are made because they are worthy causes that enhance the well-being of the general community: Donors do not usually expect direct and specific benefits from these charities.

Let's call such institutions *"the care-givers."*

The second type includes organizations that businesses and professionals support for very concrete reasons. These groups are expected to produce specific results and benefits in return for the dollars paid them.

These organizations are *"the bacon-bringers"* and should not be confused with "the care-givers." The business associations discussed in this book are bacon-bringers. Associations have an obligation to meet their purposes and objectives, to produce results for the membership, to satisfy their clientele.

In its excellent 1925 analysis of trade associations, the National Industrial Conference Board (today known simply as the Conference Board) recorded the astute observation quoted in the headnote at the beginning of this chapter.[2] This point merits some elaboration, not least because some other studies of associations have come to rather naive, and therefore unfair, conclusions about associations.

One study, for example, evaluated trade and professional association activities "in the light of the impact of these activities on the American Heritage . . . defined as a dedication to the inherent worth of the individual." At the end of 150 pages of analysis, the author came rather lovingly to the conclusion that "The activities of national trade associations and national professional business societies are in harmony with the aspirations of a free society.[3]

True enough, but business associations do not exist for the purpose of promoting civic virtue. Their sole purpose is to make life easier for their members. This is not to deny that society gains from the activities of business associations; unquestionably, it does. A new report by the Hudson Institute documents the economic and social contributions of associations through the development of ethical, professional, product, and safety standards; through educational, research, and statistical activities; and through economic, political, and community service.[4]

Valuable to society though such contributions are, they are by-products of fundamental association purposes. As the Hudson report is careful to emphasize, the public value of associations derives from activities carried out in their collective, enlightened self-interest. Thus, when standards upgrade the quality of products or professional services, when conventions and other association activities create local jobs, or when research and education enhance knowledge and public understanding, there is a gain to society as well as to the organization's members.

Associations, however, are not primarily public service organizations, nor for that matter is any other policy advocacy group, whatever its pretensions. Interest groups exist to serve *private* interests and points of view. To achieve that objective, business associations will do whatever the law and society permit.

As the review in chapter 2 of the development of associations makes abundantly clear, business associations have sought to regulate prices and competitive conditions for their industries wherever and whenever they could. Despite the fact that the practice has seldom proved effective, many of them would undoubtedly try to do so in contemporary America, were it not prohibited by the antitrust laws. Indeed, absent that ban it would be a wholly legitimate activity!

The point is that associations do whatever they can and must to "enhance efficiency and circumvent barriers." Given their voluntary nature, one imperative governs the world of associations: They either successfully market to and satisfy the needs of their members or they fail as organizations.

Associations use a variety of formal and informal survey techniques to determine what their members want. These wants are typically expressed qualitatively and even intuitively. There is, however, a procedure by which association members can determine exactly what they want from the organization and whether they are getting their true money's worth from participation. That process requires an understanding by the members of the strengths and weaknesses of business associations. A summary of those assets and liabilities is a useful prelude to a discussion of this value-oriented analysis of needs and performance.

Assets of Associations

Institutions and individuals create or join business associations for several reasons.

1. To engage in activities that are more efficiently conducted on behalf of the group than alone. No business is wholly unique. It shares common characteristics with the other firms that make or sell the same or related products, that use the same raw materials, that offer or utilize similar services, that suffer from identical or comparable problems, or that otherwise have similar needs. It deals with these needs by joining trade and umbrella associations. It also shares other kinds of needs and characteristics with enterprises in the same locality, whether or not it competes with them, and therefore joins chambers of commerce and other community organizations. Many of its executives and professionals identify requirements and personal traits that they have in common with their individual counterparts in the same calling or line of work who are employed elsewhere; for that reason, they join professional associations.

A company may feel a need for standardization of products, services, or nomenclature within its industry, in order to elevate those standards in ways that are legal and will not put it at a competitive disadvantage; to obtain economic and trade data specific to it and its commercial rivals; to exchange information on better ways to do business; to improve the business climate within its community; to alter government policies that restrict profitability or hamper expansion; to enhance the public's view of the products or services that it and its competitors offer; or to get to know the people who manage competitive or neighboring enterprises, as well as potential customers and suppliers.

These are needs that the firm cannot satisfy by itself or meet as efficiently alone as in combination and cooperation with others similarly situated. Much the same is true of individual practitioners in particular professions or occupations. Trade and professional associations, as well as chambers of commerce, provide the means to fulfill those needs.

2. To engage in activities that individual members consider necessary but which they would prefer not to perform themselves. Companies or individual practitioners have needs whose satisfaction might have adverse or expensive consequences. They may wish to oppose a popular piece of legislation, for example, without suffering the consequences of doing so in public. Similarly, they may find it preferable to negotiate a labor contract as a group rather than enable the union to attack each individually. Business associations can provide a shield behind which such needs can be met.

3. To obtain essentials that can be procured more cost-effectively from a membership organization than from commercial sources. The company or individual may have a need for services that can be purchased or provided less expensively on a group basis than if purchased individually. Insurance of various kinds, accounting or data processing services, certain types of equipment, educational training, and government relations are all examples of services or products that business associations can frequently provide on a more economical basis than their members can obtain individually in the marketplace. In unity there is not only strength, but cost efficiency and a common defense.

Liabilities of Associations

Associations also have inherent costs and drawbacks. For one thing, there is the expense of membership. This includes not only direct outlays for dues and service purchase fees (for example, meeting registrations), but also indirect expenses that are frequently quite substantial. Such indirect costs include travel to meetings and the expense of executive time and associated overhead. In addition, a number of other potential problem areas may be associated with membership:

1. Legal Questions. There are unquestionably legal risks in association membership. Prominent among these is the hazard that the association may venture into forbidden activities, most notably in the antitrust arena. Even if the association avoids transgressions, some of its members may not. Illegal behavior need not be complex or even deliberate. A casual comment—"We're raising widget prices next month, thought you'd like to know"—can bring down prosecutorial wrath. Both the association and those members not party to the conversation may end up having to show that they were not involved.

Moreover, the association may be liable for the acts of individual employees even if the group's elected and staff leadership is unaware of those actions. Illegal political or lobbying actions by an association can likewise create unwelcome problems for the members, as can activities that run afoul of the tax code and jeopardize the deductibility of membership dues.

Most associations today provide liability insurance for members of their boards of directors to protect them should members or others challenge in court their actions or those of the organization. Legal issues for business associations are discussed in more detail in chapter 9.

2. Embarrassments. Associations may also engage in activities that, if not illegal, could prove awkward for their members. Erroneous information provided to government officials, inaccurate or tasteless industry advertisements, and ill-considered public or personal attacks that exceed reasonable limits are behaviors that may be identified with a particular association and make individual members wish that they had not paid their dues that year.

3. Free-Riding. In fact, there are some who choose not to pay dues, that year or any year. In any industry, community, or profession, there are always potential members who prefer to remain just that, eternally potential. These "free riders" happily enjoy the benefits of certain association services, such as public and government relations, while foisting their share of the burden on those competitors willing to pay the costs of membership. Small companies seem particularly prone to let the "big boys" in their industry shoulder such costs in the knowledge that they will do it anyway.

4. Ineffective Decision Making. A different kind of liability is inherent in the nature of associations. While in theory most associations make policy and other decisions by majority vote, in practice all prefer membership consensus whenever possible. Very frequently, that preference produces decisions that are at the lowest common denominator of member interests and that may only partially meet the needs of some members. The larger and more heterogeneous the organization, the more likely it is to make decisions at the lowest common denominator.

The difference between what the individual member desires and what the association as a group will accept presents the member with Hobson's choice: The member must either swallow and accept the difference or take independent action to get all he or she wants. Both options may be unpleasant and possibly expensive.

5. Conflict within associations. At the opposite extreme from ineffective decision making is intra-association conflict. Differences arise from time to time in every organization, from the smallest local chamber of commerce to the giant umbrella organizations, concerning programs, priorities, policy, and politics. If these differences are substantial and irreconcilable, they can have adverse consequences for the association and for its membership.

The conflicts may drive a minority within the organization to take independent action. If that action is public, it can prove embarrassing for the association and the majority. Ultimately, it may result in the secession of a disgruntled faction and the creation of a rival association. These situations may also pose an employment danger for the staff.

Some years ago, the C.E.O. of a major corporation was asked by the White House to support the president's position on an issue that was quite controversial within the business community. The corporate exec-

utive agreed to the president's request. At the time, the executive was
serving as chairman of the board (the top elected position) of the U. S.
Chamber of Commerce, an organization that had adopted a policy opposed to the White House position.

Although some members of the Chamber's board supported the chairman, many others did not. The organization's president (the senior staff
executive) felt that the chairman's actions undercut his own position as
well as the Chamber's. He became so personally involved in the contro-
versy that the disagreement ultimately became a power struggle between
the association's top elected and staff officers. When the conflict esca-
lated onto the front pages of national newspapers, it was clear that one
or the other of the group's top two leaders would have to go.

After much contentious campaigning the board of directors voted to
support its staff chief and retain its existing policy on the issue. The
chairman soon departed from both his company and the Chamber to
accept a major presidential appointment.

The outcome was unusual. As a rule, association boards are more
prone to side with the top elected officer—one of their own, after all—
than with what some tend to see as the hired help. Although the battle
produced the healthiest result for the organization, washing its laundry
in public embarrassed the Chamber and put its directors and members
in very difficult professional situations.

The outcome could have been much worse, however. Had the policy
disagreement affected vital corporate interests, the organization could
have been faced with massive membership resignations—even the formation of a rival association. Such a consequence would have produced
two weaker associations and seriously diluted the ability to satisfy members' needs.

The Effective Membership Process

Notwithstanding all these potential (or not so potential) liabilities, the
vast majority of companies find the advantages and benefits of association membership and participation more than compensate. Nonetheless,
every company or individual considering whether to join or continue in
a particular business association should constantly balance the association's assets and strengths against the expense and the potential economic, legal, and political liabilities of membership.

That assessment involves appraising the association's value to the collective membership—the industry, community, or profession of which
the individual member is part. At least as important, however, is a cost-
benefit evaluation from the perspective of the member's individual interests, an approach that can be called the Effective Membership Process—
EMP.

The EMP analysis applies equally to companies seeking to evaluate the value of an association to which they already belong or deciding whether to join it in the first place. It produces answers to several critical membership questions:

- How can the value that this association provides to its members be measured in economic terms?
- Above and apart from mere dues, what are the actual costs of belonging to the group?
- What are the *collective* needs of the membership, and is the association meeting them?
- What are the *individual members'* needs, and are they being satisfied by the organization's services?
- What steps can members take to increase the value of the association's services to them individually—that is, to maximize effective membership in each association to which they belong?

Calculating the True Costs of Membership. Like any other business expenditure or investment, association memberships should be evaluated as a function of *value*—that is, assessing benefits relative to costs. Where business associations are concerned, however, the concept of cost may be more slippery than it appears. EMP therefore begins by measuring the true costs of association membership. These costs are of two kinds: direct and indirect.

Direct costs are easily measurable. They include not only membership dues, but also meeting and conference registration fees, contributions to the association's foundation or political action committee, special assessments, and other cash outlays.

Indirect costs are harder to measure. They include members' travel expense to various association meetings and functions, executive time spent on these activities, and correspondence and telephone use on behalf of the association. Office overhead must also be added in, including personnel benefits, secretarial costs, and other office expense. These costs can be quite substantial. For an executive paid $100,000 per year, the indirect costs of attending a single overnight meeting work out to approximately $1300. Total indirect costs of association participation for that same executive, assuming a moderate level of activity, amount to about $12,000 per year.

That is not the end of the cost analysis. Frequently, several executives from a company will participate in the affairs of an association. One may serve on the board and perhaps a committee or two. Others, with an interest or expertise in the work of sundry other association committees, will be involved to varying degrees. Still others may take part in particular projects or conferences. All may attend the annual convention and possibly other major meetings. Consequently, association participation costs must reflect the actual number of people participating and the relative costs of the involvement of each. That analysis will show how large indirect costs can really be.

The *true cost* of belonging to a trade association is the sum of the direct and indirect costs. True costs can amount to several times the outlay for dues alone.

Companies of substantial size generally belong to at least one trade association for each line of business. If a particular line of business or industrial sector is fragmented among several associations, the company is likely to have multiple memberships. A food manufacturer, for example, is likely to belong to the Grocery Manufacturers of America or the National Food Processors Association, or both. It also probably belongs to at least one national trade association for each of its product lines. In addition, it may be a member of associations representing users of its principal agricultural raw materials and of other groups representing particular marketing or regulatory concerns.

Companies in other industries may belong to more or fewer national associations. State or local trade associations are also prevalent in certain industries. Their members include companies with operations in those locales, whether they are headquartered there or elsewhere.

These enterprises usually belong to at least one of the national umbrella associations as well, and sometimes to two or three. Likewise, they tend to join state chambers of commerce or other umbrella associations in the states where they operate and commonly participate in local chambers in every community where they have some kind of significant facility.

One such company, by no means one of the largest, is a member of seven national trade associations, the U. S. Chamber of Commerce, and the NAM. It belongs to about twenty-five state chambers of commerce, state manufacturers' associations, state trade associations, and over twenty local chambers. This particular corporation estimates that its membership dues to these organizations total over $400,000. The company's level of activity and involvement varies from association to association. Its executives serve on committees and boards of directors for many of these groups, maintaining a nominal membership in a few.

This corporation has computed its participation costs in one of its national trade associations. The direct costs include dues ($25,000) to the association, contributions to its foundation ($8,000), and meeting registrations and miscellaneous direct expenses of $6,300, for a total of $39,300.

The indirect costs add up like this:

The C.E.O. of the company, paid $300,000 a year, is on the association's board of directors, the executive committee, and the finance committee. His involvement in these groups requires attendance at twelve overnight meetings each year. Three vice presidents of the company, paid an average of $150,000 each, serve on the association's government relations, standards development, and marketing committees. The government relations committee meets six times a year; the other two committees meet quarterly.

All four executives regularly attend the association's annual three-day convention and its two-day mid-year conference. They also spend considerable time in their offices on association-related reading, correspondence, and telephone discussions. Four other managers, paid an average of $75,000 each, also attend the convention but no other meetings.

This company's indirect costs of association participation, including the salaries of these executives and those of support personnel, office overhead, travel, and related expense work out to this:

C.E.O.	$60,000
3 vice presidents	62,900
4 managers	12,000
Total, indirect costs	$134,900
Total, direct costs	39,300
Grand total (true costs)	$174,200

The true cost of this company's participation in this one association—almost $175,000—is a large multiple (4.4 times) of its dues and other direct outlays. Even allowing for the fact that its levels of activity involve more executive time in some associations and less in many others, this company's dues outlays of $400,000 extrapolate to an aggregate true cost of approximately $1.75 million a year. This number is completely exclusive of dues and participation costs in the many professional societies (such as technical, accounting, and bar associations) to which its executives belong.

Large, multi-divisional corporations are likely to spend several times these sums on their association activities. A company deeply involved in federal and state government relations or other time-consuming association-related activities (standards development, for example) is likely to find that the amount of time expended by the executives in the illustration above is quite conservative and understated. One executive calculated that, during a particular week, she spent 70 percent of her time on matters related in one way or another to her company's business associations.

The essential point of this exercise is that the value of the association to the company is unknowable unless the true cost of membership has been measured. Unless individual companies take the trouble to measure true costs, they have no meaningful way to judge the real value of their associations or their membership in them.

It can be argued, of course, that executives active in associations know intuitively whether their companies are getting their money's worth out of these groups, so that it is not useful to bother computing costs. This overlooks several important factors:

Intuition may not be a good guide. Often, business people active in an association develop a loyalty to it that clouds their judgment of its benefits. Even if this does not occur, feelings and intuitive beliefs are not a sound basis for business decisions, any more than they are in other areas of corporate expense. Moreover, in the case of associations in which a company does not have its people currently active, there is little basis, intuitive or deductive, upon which to make judgments about the value of membership.

As in other areas of business decision making, there is simply no adequate substitute for a cost-benefit analysis of association memberships.

Assessing Members' Needs and Association Effectiveness

Once true membership costs have been calculated, the next phase of the EMP analysis involves assessing the benefits of participation in the association. In making that evaluation, it is important to understand what the association does as well as what the individual member wants it to do. The effectiveness of each association therefore must be measured against two standards: How well it is doing against its own goals and how well it is doing against that member's objectives for it.

It stands to reason that association leadership and management should be fairly evaluated against the group's own goals and priorities. But each member-company also needs to have a clear focus on what it wants from its associations. The company has to know what it wants before it can go about getting it.

That involves determining what the member's needs are for the kinds of services that associations provide. Chapter 4 contains summary descriptions of the most prevalent economic and informational services offered by business associations. These descriptions can be used as a checklist to ascertain most companies' needs. Each member knows best what additional, specialized services it may require.

The company's needs should be enumerated in light of both its long-term strategic and tactical goals and its current business plan. For large firms, this analysis should be conducted by business or operating units as well as at the corporate level. The needs list should be as specific as possible: *Not* "productivity information" or "customer contact opportunities," *but rather* "proven techniques to obtain specific sales productivity improvements particular to our marketing situation" and "programs that will allow us to strengthen personal relationships with the following existing or potential customers.''

A needs analysis in the area of government relations and public affairs services (discussed in chapter 5) may be more complex. It is likely to involve answering questions like these: What pending issues or proposals would increase our costs or restrict our operations, marketing, and profitability? Are there changes that could be made in public policies that could lower our costs, remove restrictions, or expand our marketing opportunities? Can we foresee possible shifts in the public environment that might alter, positively or negatively, the climate for our business?

The company should prioritize its list of basic needs. Needs are not of equal importance, either to the member or to the association. An analysis that compares the member's requirements with the association's ability to satisfy them has to take priorities into account.

Another important factor in association assessment is the application of its various resources. These include not only its financial management but also its effective utilization of staff, leadership, and membership. The staff provides continuity and expertise. The leaders and members provide objectives, policies, program guidance, and at least some of the money. They interact on program implementation. (These subjects are discussed in detail in chapters 6, 7, and 8.)

Having calculated its true costs of association involvement and assessed its needs and priorities against the association's services, the member is now in a position to determine the value of its membership. Value is the outcome of an equation that measures cost-effectiveness: What is it costing us to satisfy our requirements? Do the services justify the expense? This leads logically to another critical question: What can we do to get increased value from the association for the dollars and executive time we are putting into it?

If the member is dissatisfied with the association and feels unable to alter the current state of affairs, it should consider leaving the group and exploring other options that will meet its needs. The alternative is to develop an action plan to increase its influence. It is a pointless waste of money to remain an impotent member.

Dispelling the Influence Myth

On the assumption that the situation can be changed, which is almost always the case, an action plan should be developed with the goal of making the company a center of high influence within the association.

It is essential at this point to address a virtually universal myth about business associations. The myth holds that the largest members in any association will always dominate it.

The *truth* is that other members can indeed develop and wield significant influence—if they go about it correctly.

Associations are often accused of being run by a clique of "insiders." The charges of course come from the self-perceived "outsiders." In most membership groups, one group indeed tends to have the dominant voice on boards of directors and key committees. Often, but by no means always, this group is comprised of the larger members.

A statistical principle, Pareto's Law, describes situations like these, in which most of the work is done by a small percentage of the members—the so-called "80-20 rule."[5] In the case of associations, the ratio is probably closer to 90-10 or even 95-5; that is, 5 to 10 percent of the members provide 90 or 95 percent of the effort and leadership. It is probably safe to say that the larger the association, the smaller the percentage of members who make up the leadership cadre.

Nevertheless, there are almost always measures that any member, regardless of size, can take to break into the leadership. Active contributors of ideas and effort tend to be drawn inexorably into the group that exercises the greatest influence on association policies, programs, and activities.

Two pre-conditions exist for a member-company to work itself into the inside group: First, development and implementation of an action plan to gain influence and power in the association; second, strong motivation to succeed.

An action plan includes elements such as the following:

1. *Cultivate the staff.* No other element in the association can do more to help a member achieve its aims than the staff. Whether one person or ten, staff personnel always have more on their plates than they can ever digest. Volunteering to be a truly helpful resource is the best possible way to win goodwill and become influential. Make known the company's new interest in becoming active. Find ways to help the staff achieve its objectives—raising money for the political action committee, signing up new members, participating in an important project, or implementing some neglected goal. Supporting the staff executive to win approval for a budget or get a raise are superb techniques!

2. *Place key people on key committees.* It is not enough simply to have representatives on committees and boards of directors; they must be people knowledgeable on the issues and able to speak with authority for the company. Avoid sending note-takers; notes are all they will bring back, not helpful decisions. The company's board representative should be the most senior executive who has direct profit-and-loss responsibility for the products or services affected by the association. Only top-quality people can produce top-quality results.

3. *Help shape meeting agendas.* By working closely with staff and committee or board chairmen, it is often possible to have significant in-

put into meeting agendas. This will assure that issues important to the company come up for discussion and decision when they should.

4. *Be expert on the subject matter.* It is important, of course, that the right company executives be placed on the board of directors and key committees. The key to influencing and even dominating a policy meeting, however, is to know more about an issue than anyone else there. Deferring advance reading until the night before the meeting is no way to insure that decisions go in the right directions.

5. *Set your own meeting objectives.* The member-company must set specific goals for the meeting if it is to get the results it wants. As one veteran participant in associations has put it, "Write the minutes *before* you go to the meeting." The member who is effective in shaping the agenda and participates knowledgeably and persuasively at meetings soon finds influence and leadership flowing his or her way.

6. *Stay involved.* Regardless of the outcome on short-term objectives, hard-won influence should not be dissipated by dropping back in activity. There will be other issues, other needs, for which the association will be an important, continuing resource.

None of these measures will be effective, or even undertaken, if the member-company does not have strong reasons for wanting to become a powerhouse in the organization. Re-evaluating the original reasons for joining the association is an important element in regular assessments of the company's trade associations. If a firm goes through the process of identifying its needs and ascertains that the association is meeting them, then no change in membership or level of participation is required. But if there is dissatisfaction with the extent to which the company's priority needs are being met, then it may want to increase the effectiveness of its participation in order to satisfy its unmet needs.

State and Offshore Associations. Of course, levels of motivation depend both on the importance of the member's needs and on the nature of its business in a geographic area. A company that has substantial physical operations in a particular state or foreign country has obvious on-going legislative and regulatory interests there. But any company that engages in interstate or international marketing of products or services does business in many states or countries in which it has little or no operational presence.

One would think that the experience of decades of tax, consumer, environmental, and other issues affecting companies based elsewhere would long since have led interstate and international marketers to develop resources to protect their interests, should problems arise. Most such firms rely on associations and commercial or consulting services to monitor issues, but even sophisticated companies tend to wait until a governmental crisis develops before actively seeking help. At the last moment, they turn to an association on the scene to which they have been passively paying dues, only to be surprised by the association's failure to alter the priorities of its long-involved members in favor of the precinct just now reporting in.

A company that has treated its overseas or out-of-state associations as essentially subscription services for issues monitoring will rarely get the favorable treatment accorded members who have taken the trouble to play a dynamic role in the organization. This is why it is so important to become involved ahead of time in associations active in those states or countries where companies suspect serious problems could develop in the future.

This approach takes a degree of foresight sadly absent in many corporate managements. The attitude that "it won't happen to us" or "I won't worry about it until I have to" may turn out to be valid. If not, it may well be too late to develop the necessary resources.

Business associations—whether national, international, state, or local—provide valuable insurance against such contingencies, but only if the member-company makes sure it is getting its money's worth and pursues its investment with vigorous and effective participation.

THE UTILIZATION OF ASSOCIATION SERVICES

The range of services differs widely among associations. Even the largest will not offer all of them. Small groups may be engaged in only a few.

The company trying to decide whether to join a particular association or to take better advantage of one to which it already belongs should carefully analyze its own needs and the best means of satisfying them. Some companies, particularly large ones, may well opt to develop their own internal series of educational seminars, for example, in preference to those of the association. Small and mid-sized firms, by contrast, are less likely to have the resources to undertake their own educational programs.

Cost-effectiveness ought to be a primary criterion in assessing which association services the member needs to utilize. The steps in this assessment parallel those in the EMP evaluation:

1. List the company's needs and the kinds of services or information required to satisfy them.

2. Catalog the alternative sources available to furnish those services. Some of these sources will be particular trade or other business associations. Alternatively, services may be obtained internally, through outside consultants, or from other external commercial sources. Assess the likely *quality* of the service that each alternative source can provide.

3. Determine the *true* costs of each alternative, not only direct costs but also marginal overhead and other indirect or hidden expenses.

4. Then decide among these options by evaluating cost-effectiveness—that is, the true costs relative to the quality of the service in terms of internal needs: Who can provide the optimum quality of service to meet requirements at the lowest possible true cost?

In many cases, an association will turn out to be the best choice to provide the service in question. If the association already offers the service or a similar one, it is an elementary matter to take advantage of it. If the association does not currently render the particular service, then the company may want to develop and act on a plan to persuade the group to do so. That may be as simple as a telephone call to the association's chief executive. But if it meets resistance, the company will need to work through the association's committee and board policy-making structure to get the decision it wants.

WHICH GROUP TO JOIN?

Companies frequently face confusion about whether to join particular associations. The decision to join or not should follow much the same process used in evaluating existing association memberships. More reliance, however, will have to be placed on the cost estimates and judgments of others, rather than on the firm's own experiences. There are several steps in the process.

1. Choosing the association. With respect to single-industry associations—whether international, national, state, or local—the choice is not likely to be wide. Where more than one association exists to serve the same industry, consultations with others in the industry, related associations, legislators, local lobbyists, and others familiar with the situation can provide useful inputs about effectiveness. The company should verify this information to its own satisfaction through interviews with association staff and elected leaders.

Where only a single association exists to represent the industry, the choice is limited to whether or not to join at all, the alternative being reliance on outside economic consulting firms or other providers of the economic services required. For government relations services, the alternative is the use of local independent lobbyists or the development of in-house government relations staff specialists.

Regardless of the number of associations being considered, their staffs and leaders should be carefully interviewed. These interviews should focus on the association's willingness and ability to deliver for the company on its high-priority needs, needs that may not be universally shared throughout the industry. Data necessary to estimate true membership costs should also be obtained.

In addition to single-industry groups, the company should consider joining national and state umbrella associations that generally provide a valuable supplement to the services of single-industry trade associations. The existence of competing associations is fairly common among state umbrella groups and should be taken into account. All these organizations are active in government relations and are generally good monitoring sources. Because they tend to focus on broad business issues (such as labor and taxation), however, they may not be able to give adequate attention to the company's priority problems, particularly regulatory ones.

2. *Judging costs and benefits.* Even though the company may not have its own on-site experience to go by, it still should make every effort to estimate the likely true costs and benefits of prospective membership. The information obtained through interviews, especially those with association personnel and other industry members, will provide a good basis to determine how active it will need to be to gain what it wants from the association. This knowledge will facilitate an informed estimate of probable true costs and benefits and is necessary for making a decision about membership.

If the results of this analysis do not dictate a clear decision, the benefit of the doubt should be in the direction of signing up. That choice should be reassessed after two or three years of concrete experience.

NOTES

1. Hudson Institute, *The Value of Associations to American Society* (Washington: Foundation of the American Society of Association Executives, 1990).

2. National Industrial Conference Board, *Trade Associations: Their Economic Significance and Legal Status* (New York: 1925), 288.

3. Joseph F. Bradley, *The Role of Trade Associations and Professional Business Societies in America* (University Park, PA: Pennsylvania State University Press, 1965), 149.

4. Hudson Institute, *Value of Associations.*

5. More precisely, Pareto's law (enunciated by the Italian social scientist, Vilfredo Pareto) describes phenomena in which a small percentage of a population accounts for a large percentage of a particular characteristic.

4

Economic and Communications Activities

It is because of our system's complexity that associations have such a potentially useful role to play. They can educate and inform, they can improve the quality of decision-making by their expertise, they can be advocates for a position or an approach to issue.

Ronald Reagan

Associations provide a variety of economic and communications services to their members. The range of economic services varies broadly, according to the nature of the association and the needs of its membership. At the same time, communications and information services, especially association meetings, are virtually universal. Almost every association holds at least one major meeting a year, and smaller meetings are ubiquitous. Association publications also appear with great frequency.

Associations typically offer basic services to dues-paying members without additional charge. Non-basic services are available by payment of additional fees and charges. For example, associations usually provide their members with subscriptions to at least their principal publication as a basic dues-funded service; by contrast, most groups levy registration fees to attend conventions and some other meetings, although at a lower rate than non-members are charged. Associations generally allow non-members to purchase certain non-basic services (such as publications, audio-visual materials, educational programs, insurance, and convention registrations), usually at rates about a third higher than members pay.[1]

The member that wants to maximize the benefits that the association has to offer must understand all its programs and services, not just the one or two that may attract immediate interest. This chapter deals with the range of association economic and communications services. Government relations and related activities (typically considered basic, dues-funded services) are discussed in chapter 5.

ECONOMIC SERVICES

Historically, U. S. trade associations have concentrated their priorities on economic activities and information, as local chambers of commerce also do. As a group, professional societies have not placed heavy stress on economic activities, focusing more on member education.

As membership needs have changed over time, so have the economic services that associations offer. In some cases, the need has largely disappeared or been legally discouraged. In other cases, individual companies have chosen, for competitive or other reasons, to carry out these activities themselves. Thus, association involvement in such fields as industry-wide collective bargaining, traffic bureaus, and credit information exchanges is today rare at best.

Other services with a long history of association involvement, like standardization, compilation of economic statistics, and cooperative purchasing, have continued and evolved in many industries. Still other areas, like travel services and data processing for members, are comparatively new.

By their very nature, specific economic activities differ substantially from association to association, depending on the particular needs and interests of the individual industries or communities they represent. The following are among the more widespread services:

Accounting and Finance Services

About one trade association in six provides some form of financial service. The most common of these are accounting manuals for the industry. Many associations also publish comparative financial classifications and data, including certain kinds of costs. Some trade associations offer data-processing support, supplying their members with accounting services in such areas as billing, payables and receivables, periodic income statements and balance sheets, payroll and personnel data, and the like. Financial services of this sort are typically provided on a fee basis.

Advertising Programs

About a third of trade associations and many chambers of commerce engage in advertising services to promote the activities or merits of the industry or community. Associations purchase advertising, for example, to elevate public consciousness about aspects of the industry's record, using an image advertising campaign in the public media, electronic as well as print. Just as individual suppliers advertise to potential customers, so might their trade association in order to promote the benefits of the entire industry relative to its competition. For instance, the advantages of steel and aluminum as commodities were widely advertised against each other by their respective associations (or by captive foundations) for a number of years; the advantages of glass over other container materials have been advertised by the glass packaging industry.

Advertising may be used in a number of other ways. In some instances, when an association wishes to place advertising in another publication, perhaps as a public service message or other communication, industry suppliers may pay for the advertising costs in order to reap the benefits of goodwill and improved trade relations. State and local chambers often place economic development advertising in out-of-state publications to attract new industry, thereby expanding local employment and business opportunities. Some associations serve as industry clearinghouses for customer requests for information or product samples. Others provide their members with point-of-sale and similar materials. Still others prepare advertising materials for individual members.

Advertising Sales

A great many associations and chambers sell advertising space in their publications as a major source of income-generation. Over half of associations of all kinds accept advertising in at least one of their publications. Suppliers of goods and services to an industry's member-companies frequently find association publications a highly targeted and cost-efficient method of reaching their actual and potential customers, which also strengthens trade relations. Many groups use their own employees to sell advertising space, while others utilize outside sales agencies.

Cost Control

Many organizations sponsor services to help members reduce expense in particular fields. Typical areas of cost-reduction consultation include unemployment compensation, worker's compensation, insurance risk management, telephone and computer usage, real estate and property tax assessments, sales tax audits, and other broad business costs. The most common means used to offer this benefit is through group sponsorship of a commercial consulting service that offers lower rates to members of the organization than they could get individually. The association or chamber usually receives a fee or commission from the consulting firm in return for the sponsorship.

Economic Analysis

Some large associations offer sophisticated economic research and forecasting activities. This is particularly important in those industries that tend to be highly cyclical or otherwise dependent on particular economic factors. The ability to obtain accurate forecasts of future interest rates, for instance, is quite important in the housing and financial industries. Large umbrella associations, such as the U. S. Chamber of Commerce and the NAM, also provide economic analysis services.

Many associations refine and analyze data collected by others, usually government agencies, but some also compile original economic data. For instance, surveys of purchasing agents on buying decisions and inventories, conducted monthly by the National Association of Purchasing Management, are considered an important and widely published indicator of the condition of the national economy. Extensive surveys by the National Federation of Independent Business on sales, inventories, capital expenditures, business conditions, and the plans of small enterprises are a unique source of information.

Economic Development

State and local chambers of commerce often have aggressive programs, generally in close cooperation with governments in their locales, to attract new industry. These campaigns are commonly quite competitive, seeking not only to encourage the in-migration of employment opportunities from brand-new enterprises, but also to lure existing facilities away from other regions of the United States. The Sunbelt states of the South and West have been particularly successful in recent decades through chamber-government offensives that stress lower labor costs, better climates and transportation systems, and more favorable tax treatments.

Another major target of economic development programs has been those foreign countries whose companies have been investing in new plants and facilities to strengthen their expansion into American markets. A number of chambers employ representatives who travel abroad to solicit investment in their communities by major European and Asian companies.

Export Promotion

Cooperative programs to promote foreign sales of members' products are not the association priority that they once were. It is not that the advancement of exports is unimportant to companies; on the contrary, it has grown to such importance that most firms now prefer to do their own overseas marketing. Consequently, Webb-Pomerene organizations (trade associations partially exempted from antitrust limitations for export marketing purposes) have been declining in number. Some other associations do sponsor sales promotion trips to other countries, sometimes in cooperation with a federal agency or a specialized private organization.

Far more common are association efforts to advance their members' business opportunities abroad through government relations efforts to reduce trade barriers. These include lobbying target countries directly and, more frequently, through the U. S. government. Some trade associations maintain branch offices abroad, particularly in Japan and the European Economic Community. Although direct overseas marketing is unlikely to be a major activity for most associations, the lobbying aspect of this function will continue to grow in both scope and sophistication in future years.

Insurance

A majority of trade associations and chambers of commerce offer group insurance programs, usually at discounted rates. Life, medical, disability, accident, and dental insurance are the most common forms, but many organizations also offer worker's compensation, liability insurance (business, personal, and professional), and retirement benefits. These programs are frequently marketed to both members and non-members, the latter usually being charged higher rates. Thus, the association can use its insurance program as an incentive to increase membership.

Most groups simply endorse insurance programs operated by commercial insurers, but some administer their programs directly (or through an association or chamber subsidiary) and process claims themselves. This can have its risks; one state association almost went bankrupt when the liability insurance field went through one of its cyclical crises. Generally, though, associations have found insurance services a good, steady revenue source as well as a popular member benefit.

Labor Relations and Personnel

Even apart from lobbying on labor issues (which, along with taxation, is the most widespread subject of association government-relations activities), labor relations services are offered by a substantial number of associations. Many conduct surveys of industry practices concerning wages, benefits, workplace safety, position evaluation processes, personnel policies, and the like. Generally, they also keep abreast of the specifics of labor negotiations and agreements.

Multi-employer collective bargaining, once a frequent association service, is relatively uncommon today but is still found occasionally in particular industries and geographic areas. However, a substantial number of associations provide expert advice and counsel to members on labor matters. Others sponsor or operate mediation or arbitration services in labor disputes. An even larger number offer arbitration programs for general contract disputes.

Some associations also provide job placement or referral services for executives or other personnel. This must be managed with considerable care, lest the association be accused of raiding the employees of one member to benefit another.

Purchasing

A small number of associations offer their members group-purchasing programs. Business forms, equipment, and materials—even magazine subscriptions—are provided at discounted or wholesale prices. Credit cards at discounted fees or interest rates are an increasingly common benefit. Some associations make loans to their members, sometimes directly, sometimes through a credit union.

Research and Statistics

For a substantial number of associations, especially large ones that deal in technical areas, research projects are an important activity. Research on safety or health matters—both consumer and workplace—can broadly benefit the members of many organizations. In mature industries, where processes are likely to be quite similar or even generic among members, improvements in process technology can be a valuable support.

Many associations also conduct or sponsor a variety of studies intended to enhance the quality, effectiveness, or efficiency of members' services or products. In the past, some trade associations actually developed new products for their members. Today, this is almost always an activity of individual firms. Some associations have sponsored research on subjects to advance management productivity. Others do studies on personnel performance or other human relations matters. For example, the American Institute of Physics compiles data on scientific manpower.

Associations often sponsor technical research geared to their regulatory or legislative concerns. These include, for example, the Cosmetic, Toiletry and Fragrance Association on ingredient safety and the Chemical Manufacturers Association on environmental and health issues. Other associations, while not sponsoring or undertaking their own research projects, provide their members with advice or assistance in obtaining research funding from government agencies, foundations, or other sources.

Two-thirds of associations compile and publish a variety of statistical data on topics important to their members, including economic analyses and some of the other services and subjects described elsewhere in this chapter. Some organizations collect and disseminate the data of others, particularly government agencies, sometimes performing additional analysis on subjects important to their industries. Others compile data from their own members on such topics as sales, production, employment, inventories, financial operating ratios, profits, construction, workplace safety, and so forth.

These statistical compilations are frequently of great value, not only to the members of the association's industry or profession—for example, by providing benchmarks by which to compare a member's performance with that of the group as a whole—but also to government, the press, and economists, among others. All told, associations spend over $2 billion a year on their research and statistical programs.

Standardization

The development of product standards is a major function of many associations. About 50 percent of trade associations engage in standards activities. Product standards typically deal with such matters as consumer, environmental and occupational health and safety matters; product performance; grades, sizes and other characteristics; manufacturing processes and technology; terminology; measurements; testing and evaluation procedures; materials and components; design criteria; simplification programs; and so on.

Association standardization activities are often coordinated through specialized organizations, such as the American National Standards Institute, the American Society for Testing and Materials, and the American Society for Quality Control.

Associations spend a large amount of money on standards development and compliance: $345 million of their own funds, plus an additional $14.5 billion annually by association members.[2] Standards benefit business by promoting economies, efficiency, and technical developments, and by generally upgrading products, services, and professional performance. They benefit consumers by enhancing safety and quality. They also provide a basis for the evaluation of advertising claims and price comparisons.

Standards developed by associations are voluntary, except in those cases in which they have government sanction. Individual companies are free to adopt or reject voluntary standards. In many cases compliance comes about through customer and competitive pressures, as well as the firm's own self-interest in participating.

In addition to association activities, a number of government agencies are also in the standardization business. Some agencies develop standards that may or may not be voluntary, such as those of the National Bureau of Standards. Others, like the Food and Drug Administration and the Department of Labor, publish standards that are generally mandatory. In either case, trade associations play an important liaison role with the agencies in developing standards, disseminating information, and promoting compliance among their members.

Many government agencies also develop standards for the products and services that they purchase from the private sector. The federal government's General Services Administration, as well as departments and agencies involved in national security, transportation, and aerospace, are extensively involved in such activities, as are many agencies of state and local governments. Associations representing supplier industries are frequently active in coordinating with government officials on procurement standards; they keep their members informed on what can often be frequent and complex changes in requirements.

A number of associations sponsor quality seals and product or service certification programs that publicly attest that certain brands, models, or types meet established standards. This information is intended as a guide to consumers and industrial purchasers.

Professional societies and some trade associations engage in programs to standardize, measure, and upgrade the quality of individual practice. "Certification" and "accreditation" are typical terms used to describe these activities. They generally involve specialized education and training, followed by passage of an examination or some other evaluation of individual performance against standardized professional criteria. Nearly a quarter of trade and professional associations offer professional standards programs, and 31 percent have ethical standards or codes to assure fair dealing. In the aggregate, associations spend $275 million per year on these programs.

Trade Relations

A number of associations provide services or activities intended to strengthen relationships between their members and major customers or suppliers. These activities may include expositions or trade shows, advertising programs, working committees that focus on specific topics of mutual interest, and typically a large number of social functions for developing personal contacts. In the food industry, for example, the cooperative trade relations activities of several associations resulted in the development of the universal product code that now appears on all grocery packages and that is "read" at retail checkout stations by computerized optical scanners.

Travel Services

Package tours and other travel services are offered by some associations. A few even operate in-house travel agencies. Automobile rental companies routinely provide discounts to association members, the size of the discount usually varying with the size of the membership. Some hotel chains also provide association members with discount programs.

Miscellaneous Services

The foregoing list hardly exhausts the scope and volume of association activities. There is a wide range of other economic services that associations provide their members. Some engage in transportation coordination and traffic analysis. Others provide members with factoring services, such as purchasing certain kinds of receivables at discount (for example, retail food store coupons). Still others offer group legal services. The extent of these services is limited only by the needs of the members and the ingenuity of association executives.

COMMUNICATIONS ACTIVITIES

In the broadest sense, the core business of associations is communications. Through a variety of media—print, visual, electronic, and meetings—associations are constantly involved in communicating with their various audiences. The most important of these audiences, of course, is the membership, but associations also communicate with other interest groups, intellectual and academic institutions, the press, the general public, and government.

Public Relations

Too often executed *ad hoc,* association public relations and other communications benefit greatly when they are part of a well-thought-out comprehensive strategy. An association's communications/public relations strategy should serve its overall organizational goals and address the specific ways in which it will advance them. It should also address the target audiences it needs to reach and the image it wishes to cultivate, overall and within each individual audience.

The communications strategy should cover the association's public relations philosophy as well—whether and when to adopt a high or low profile and the extent to which the needs of the group and its members compel or restrain the association from speaking out. In particular, the association must coordinate its public voice with members' own public communications on parallel subjects. A public relations/communications strategy should identify both the chief spokesperson for the association and also others on the staff or in elected leadership positions who will speak out on specific topics for which they have singular qualifications.

Decisions on these matters depend on the association's needs, circumstances, and culture; patterns vary widely. Among professional groups, for instance, the chief elected officer is more likely to be the designated spokesman than is the top staff executive. The same is true of local chambers. Among national and state trade associations, the reverse is more often the case; indeed, many such organizations increasingly place communications skills high among the qualities that they seek in a chief staff executive.

Associations frequently undertake public relations programs to enhance their image and that of their members with other important interests, with key opinion leaders, and with the public. These may take many different forms.

- A major trade association in the retail food industry, the Food Marketing Institute, has subsidized the publication costs for an important consumer activist organization and often invites consumer spokespeople to address its meetings.
- The Association of Home Appliance Manufacturers maintains a clearinghouse for consumer complaints about its members' products.
- Many associations undertake image advertising or public information programs to strengthen knowledge, understanding, and support for their industry among the consuming public. Examples include associations in the food, home heating, motion picture, and public utility industries, among many others. Some professional societies provide parallel services for their members.
- Several packaging industry associations have provided extensive support for community litter control organizations and recycling programs.
- A number of associations have had active programs to promote the hiring and advancement of women, minorities, and the physically handicapped.
- Associations particularly sensitive to their members' image among intellectuals maintain programs for financial and other support of the arts.
- Other associations and many chambers of commerce have long histories of support for particular programs in secondary and higher education to strengthen the skills of present and future employees. Several retail associations provide technical and financial support for distributive education. Other associations have provided grants to academic researchers.

None of these association programs is altruistic, nor should it be. The programs further particular needs and goals of the association, its industry or community, and its members—whether those needs are to increase goodwill among certain potentially or actually antagonistic groups and individuals, to build a stronger base of future employees, to undercut long-term pressures for unfavorable legislation, or simply to enhance the association's image with the general public.

Conventions and Meetings

The gathering of the faithful is a major element in any organization's communications program. A veteran association staffer likes to ask audiences, "Do you know the difference between drunks and alcoholics? Drunks don't have to go to all the meetings." The line invariably gets a roar of appreciative laughter from both association executives and their members.

About 95 percent of all associations hold at least one convention or conference per year to which all members are invited; some groups annually organize three or more such gatherings. The number holding smaller meetings of some kind is undoubtedly 100 percent. Associations spend over $870 million a year on conventions, the Hudson report estimates. The total spent directly by their members to attend must surely run well into the billions.

Convention-type meetings are held for a variety of purposes: to furnish information on the state of the industry and its economic and political environment; to offer educational programs; to afford members contact opportunities with peers, suppliers, or customers; to promote other association services; and to increase the membership's sense of unity and togetherness through the association. These meetings provide opportunities for members to learn of new developments, techniques, and ways of doing business. They allow members to strengthen old relationships and build new ones. Good conventions are convivial places indeed; social functions are a major part of the schedule, and cocktail parties and corridor conversations are important ingredients.

Some 80 percent of association conventions build an exposition or trade show into the program; many local chambers, particularly in larger communities, also sponsor trade shows. These are mainly opportunities for vendors to display their products or services to association members, but demonstrations of members' own wares are not unknown. Expositions are often quite popular among members, and some have been known to comment that the annual trade show is itself worth the cost of membership. Trade shows are often lucrative sources of association revenue. A few associations also have organized industry shows for consumers, some with great success, others with very little.

Over and above all this are the many smaller gatherings that associations organize each year. These may range from educational seminars and sessions on specialized topics, to the board and committee meetings that form the backbone of association governance and policy-making (see chapter 7).

Information and Education

Most associations offer their members formal or informal reference-services. This is an almost inevitable service, because members turn to their associations with great frequency for answers to a wide variety of questions directly and indirectly related to the association's mission. Close to two-thirds of associations of all kinds maintain a formal information service or reference library, generally as a basic benefit, although a few charge for it. Association-sponsored foundations often offer reference and information services to the general public as well.

As commercially available on-line and data-base information services become more prevalent, the demand for general information services by associations could well decrease, unless associations develop their own specialized data networks that any member with a personal computer and a modem can hook into at will (see chapter 13).

Educational Offerings. Almost 90 percent of associations offer educational programs to improve the professional knowledge or skills of members or of certain groups of their managers and employees. Associations spend $1.4 billion a year on educational services and their members another $5 billion, according to the Hudson study.

Among professional associations, member education is typically a primary purpose, frequently the principal one. Like the economic functions of trade associations, the content and focus of educational services vary with the particular needs and interests of the profession served by the society. The educational programs of these organizations commonly deal with such subjects as new developments in scientific research and discovery; technological innovations; improvements in process, management, marketing, and delivery of services; professional standards; changes in licensing and regulatory requirements; and so forth. These or other topics that must be mastered to attain professional accreditation or certification are generally an important part of the educational subject matter among professional groups.

Among trade associations, the range of topics on which a given association may offer educational services is likely to be as broad as the industry's own long-term and current interests.

- For instance, a manufacturer's association may offer courses or workshops on new production technology; techniques to improve plant productivity or safety; "just-in-time" inventory management; and recent technical or regulatory developments in the transportation of raw materials or finished goods.

- A commodity association might conduct seminars on materials handling and storage; prospective economic changes affecting commodity prices and futures markets; recent scientific discoveries in gene technology to eliminate plant pests and lengthen growing seasons; and new policies of the U. S. Department of Agriculture or European Economic Community affecting commodity transport.

- A retailing association could offer courses on employee and consumer relations; recent innovations in computerized inventory management and point-of-sale technology; better cash management; successful marketing and merchandising innovations; and new ways to reduce "shrinkage" of store inventories and to strengthen security against shoplifting and employee theft.

Many associations, the American Booksellers Association among them, provide training to help independent members get started in business and grow. Others, such as the Food Marketing Institute, whose members are supermarket operators, offer education in a wide range of technical subjects covering all aspects of store operations. The Hotel Sales and Marketing Association teaches its members how to do market research, analyze data, and communicate effectively.

Educational formats are also varied, although the seminar or workshop continues to be the most popular approach. Virtually all associations include educational programs in their convention schedules. Most also sponsor additional, free-standing seminar programs ranging in length from a half-day to a week or even two, sometimes in cooperation with an educational institution. Speakers or seminar leaders are often outside consultants or academicians with particular knowledge of the subject, but sometimes they are experts among the membership or on the association staff.

In addition to the seminar approach, a number of associations offer manuals for self-study programs. Many are also making increasing use of self-study diskettes for personal computers. Video tapes and multimedia visuals are widely used in seminars. Teleconferencing via real-time satellite transmissions is expanding although costs and a lingering preference for face-to-face personal contact with speakers continue to hamper the rapid growth of this medium.

Publications

Members of business associations need never feel lonely. In between the ubiquitous meetings, the mail brings frequent greetings—sometimes so frequent and voluminous that members complain about the sheer quantity of reading matter. One large national association sends its members a weekly packet of materials measuring a quarter- to a half-inch thick!

Publications of different kinds are the most visible means by which organizations communicate with their members and other constituencies. Over 90 percent of chambers and associations publish at least one periodical newsletter, newspaper, or magazine; the remainder undoubtedly issue frequent non-periodical bulletins.

These publications primarily keep members informed about important external, industry, or area developments, generally emphasizing legislative and regulatory news and analysis. Specialized publications are often issued for particular classes of members; for instance, marketing managers, financial executives, and in-house attorneys might each be furnished special bulletins or newsletters by the same association. Professional societies commonly publish learned or technical journals and similar publications to keep members abreast of relevant developments in the field.

In addition to periodicals, associations and chambers often publish books, directories, technical manuals, explanations or digests of pertinent laws and regulations, and other materials. Most are for member use but some are for government officials, the general public, or other external constituencies.

Associations are also making increasing use of non-print media. Computerized messaging is a growing medium of information. Educational materials now come in audio and video cassettes in addition to traditional print formats. Some associations also use video cassettes and closed circuit television to promote and retain memberships and for informational purposes. Cable television is coming into wider use to communicate not only with members but with other audiences as well. The most advanced use of television by associations is BizNet, the U. S. Chamber's network, which uses satellites to transmit programming to commercial cable television outlets across the country.

HOW TO TAKE ADVANTAGE OF ECONOMIC AND COMMUNICATIONS SERVICES

Individual companies commonly select those association economic services that they find useful on an on-going basis and ignore the rest. Sometimes, however, services not typically utilized can be viewed as occasional alternatives to those available internally or from consultants. The following illustration shows how the process can work.

Let us say that a manufacturing company has developed a new product line that it wishes to market to a very select group of retailers. The company, having analyzed particular issues related to its business plan, determines that it has three marketing needs:

1. Statistical data relating to supply needs and potential competitive sourcing among the target customers;

2. A training program to educate its sales people about the economic environment and conditions in that customer industry, as well as the retailers' particular supply requirements that the manufacturer wishes to meet; and

3. Improved opportunities to establish good personal relationships between company executives and those of its potential retailer customers.

To meet these needs, the company takes the following steps.

1. The company's market research staff finds that the statistical information can be obtained in raw form from a government agency, but will need extensive manipulation to be usable. Several economic consultants could provide the necessary data refinements on an exclusive basis but at high cost. The company's trade association has a research department with the capability of refining the data at lower cost than the consultants, but will have to make its findings available to all industry members and not just to a single company.

The manufacturer decides that only a few competitors are likely to be able to supply the potential customers with the new product line and that it probably can obtain a very satisfactory and profitable market share. A letter and a couple of follow-up telephone calls are sufficient to persuade the association to provide this statistical service for a modest fee.

2. The training programs could be developed internally with the assistance of sales consultants, but at considerable expense. The trade association is willing to offer this training (provided, of course, that it is equally available to all its members), but for reasons of cost-control wishes to hold the seminars at its headquarters location.

After factoring in travel and other indirect costs, the company's executives find that it will be less expensive in the long run to use consultants and develop its own training program.

3. None of the trade associations to which the manufacturer now belongs has any members from the customer industry. However, a trade association of retailers admits certain supplier firms as associate members, and this company qualifies. Moreover, the retailers' group offers a comprehensive trade relations program that would provide the company with extensive personal contact opportunities and with trade shows where it can demonstrate its wares to just the people to whom it wants to sell. Participation costs in this program would be expensive, but no more so than the fees of the marketing consultants who could provide the contact opportunities without the trade show. The company thereupon joins the retailers' association as an associate member and signs up for its trade relations program.

The point is that associations provide a range of services whose usefulness may not always be foreseen by its members. Moreover, there may well be associations with which the company would not ordinarily affiliate that engage in activities that meet a firm's particular needs for economic services, education and training, or information. A little research can often turn up an association that meets a special need on a basis more favorable than the obvious alternatives.

NOTES

1. Sources for data in this chapter include two books by the American Society of Association Executives: *Association Activities* (Washington: 1985) and *Policies and Procedures in Association Management* (Washington: 1987).

Other relevant, though not particularly contemporary, sources include: Walter Mitchell, Jr., *How to Use Your Trade Association* (New York: Prentice-Hall, 1951); U. S. Department of Commerce, *Trade Association Activities* (Washington: various editions, the most recent published 1947); and National Industrial Conference Board, *Trade Associations: Their Economic Significance and Legal Status* (New York: 1925).

2. Hudson Institute, *The Value of Associations to American Society* (Washington: Foundation of the American Society of Association Executives, 1990).

5

Public Affairs and Government Relations

An association for political, commercial, or manufacturing purposes, or even for those of science and literature, is a powerful and enlightened member of the community, which cannot be disposed of at pleasure or oppressed without remonstrance, and which, by defending its own rights against the encroachment of the Government, saves the common liberties of the country.

Alexis de Tocqueville

A major purpose of business associations is to enhance the climate for commerce within which their members must operate. This activity includes the representation and advocacy of the members' collective needs, both broad and narrow, with all those in a position to influence the destiny of the industry or local business community. While government is far and away the most important of these, efforts to affect official policy are most effective when they extend beyond national and state capitals to the far reaches of public influence.[1]

The legislative and regulatory activities of governments at all levels continue to have an increasingly pervasive and often costly impact on businesses. Because these activities generally affect entire industries, business sectors, or professions, associations and chambers are the first line of defense for their members. Sometimes industries and professions choose to initiate legislation to alter government regulation—to allow them to expand into previously restricted markets or perform other activities, for example. If the proposal would affect a group of companies and not just one or two, then associations are likely to be the prime instruments of member reliance.

Representing the needs and interests of the members with respect to government is certainly not a new challenge for business groups:

The great accumulation of public measures of direct or indirect economic significance, and the constant agitation for their radical change or tentative modification which characterizes the current political ferment, are of continuously vital concern to the business world. The unexercised possibilities of governmental power are fraught with even more far-reaching consequences, good or ill, both for specific trades or industries, and for the future status of the prevailing economic order.[2]

That statement was written 65 years ago, well before the onset of the Great Depression and the impact of the New Deal on business regulation.

A quarter-century later, another observer of the trade association world wrote:

With every turn of events in the past 50 years, American industry has been subjected to increasing government control or interference. It is only natural for industrial management to wonder whether these developments are directed by some unseen and malevolent genius. . . . Must this trend be fought, or lived with, or both, and how? . . . Good trade association leadership can retard this trend by eliminating the excuse for it.[3]

That last sentence, written in 1951, may have been a trifle optimistic and premature. The need for effective business-government relations has continued to rise ever since, even during the Reagan and Bush years, undoubtedly the friendliest period for business since Herbert Hoover departed the White House.

The fact is that government relations is the most significant function that business associations now perform, whether in Washington or in the state capitals. Indeed, for many associations, public affairs and government relations are today their principal reason for existence. One indication is the steady migration of national associations to Washington. Twenty years ago, less than 20 percent were headquartered in the nation's capital. Today, over a third are, and the number grows every year.

Despite the importance of the federal government, it is at the state level that government relations activities are booming. In consequence, state associations are more likely than national groups to have a full-time government relations staff professional and more than twice as likely to have a registered lobbyist on staff.[4]

At least 85 percent of trade associations at all levels and 70 percent of professional associations report involvement in government relations activities of some sort.[5] Among national and state umbrella associations, the number is virtually 100 percent. Local chambers of commerce are also involved, with a commitment to government relations approximately proportional to the size of the group. Among chambers in smaller communities, 70 percent claim a government relations program; the percentage rises to 90 percent among chambers in the mid-range and to 95 percent in the largest cities.[6] These high numbers reflect the steadily growing importance that associations and their members place on the need to stay abreast of governmental activities affecting business, even if such self-reported data are overstated.

A hint of that overstatement is that only a third of trade associations and not more than a quarter of professional societies employ a full-time government relations staff executive. Many associations would undoubtedly protest that government relations is a major part of the chief staff executive's job, but the individual charged with managing the organization overall clearly has many other tasks that inevitably take time away from lobbying. A further indication that government relations may be discussed more than implemented is the Hudson Institute's estimate that only 10 percent of trade association expenditures (2 percent for professional associations) support political and public policy activities.[7] Nonetheless, given the stress that their members place on government relations, few groups are likely to confess in this day and age that they perform below par in this critical field.

All association government relations programs engage in essentially similar activities. They monitor relevant issues and report to their members on developments. They take positions on the issues through fairly standardized procedures, and they implement those positions through a wide array of government relations techniques.

INFORMATION MONITORING AND REPORTING

Business associations keep tabs on a broad cluster of pertinent issues, generally many more than those on which they actually take positions or lobby. There are two reasons why these groups cast a wide monitoring net. First, only a fraction of public policy proposals are ever acted upon; the trick is to understand which issues are truly important and to be alert for movement. Second, not every issue affects an association's membership powerfully enough to warrant action on its part.

It is not surprising to find that national associations focus on national issues and that state and local associations concentrate on issues at their own governmental levels. What *is* surprising is the interest that associations take in developments elsewhere. About half of national associations monitor not only federal issues but those in the states too; a fifth also watch issues at the local level. An even larger percentage of state associations keep an eye on federal issues as well as on state and local ones.[8]

The analysis of current issues is the most prevalent form of monitoring. Some organizations, probably not a large number, also study trends with the objective of identifying emerging issues; that is, issues still a few years away from becoming current.

Current Issues Analysis

Associations use a variety of sources to obtain information on legislative and regulatory issues affecting their members.

Networking. Association staff professionals develop networks of personal contacts with whom they stay in close touch to learn of new issues and developments. These include legislators, executive and regulatory officials, and particularly issue experts and specialists on governmental staffs; researchers with policy research organizations ("think tanks") and academic institutions; and government-relations personnel in other business associations and, less often, in non-business organizations (such as labor unions, consumer and environmental groups). Sometimes, association members with their own contacts are also good sources.

Published Sources. Various print and computerized services report in extensive detail on federal and state legislation, as well as on executive and regulatory developments in Washington and the fifty state capitals; information on issues in local government is far less abundant. Some of these services and publications are available from governmental sources; others come from private firms.

Many specialized periodicals, trade journals, newsletters, almanacs, and directories are also extensively utilized for information on issues and political developments, lists of legislators and officials, and so forth. And, of course, national newspapers and those in state capitals provide timely if not always detailed information.[9]

Back-Channel Information. Some of the most critical issue information that associations collect is political intelligence compiled by the association's lobbyists. Gathering and exchanging information typically occupies substantially more of lobbyists' time than does the advocacy of association views on issues. Intelligence relating to the political outlook and prospects for issues, timing, strategy, and tactics is often confidential and sensitive, but always essential both for monitoring and lobbying. Because of its nature and the necessity to protect sources, this kind of information is reported to association members with great care and sometimes cannot be communicated at all.

Analyzing Emerging Issues

Most legislative bills and proposals for regulatory action never advance very far beyond the idea stage. Legislative and governmental policy processes are deliberately so complex that only a small fraction ever successfully navigate all the hazards to final adoption. It is therefore difficult to know which initial current proposals will receive active consideration.

Even more difficult is the identification of future issues. Nonetheless, successful analysis of emerging issues can be invaluable for association members because it can facilitate forestalling adverse issues or advancing favorable ones. Unfortunately, few associations devote the resources necessary to focus on issues unlikely to be active for another three to five years.

The identification of tomorrow's issues involves determining the leading indicators of potential problems; tracking their evolution through analysis of the content of particular publications and of the agendas of particular activist interest groups; expert forecasting of conditions and trends; and monitoring developments by certain innovative governments, state and foreign. The analytical process also involves cross-plotting the emerging issue's potential *severity* for the association's members against the *probability* of the issue's emergence in order to develop a guide to the need for action.

This process is critical because issues are most malleable and responsive to change and influence before the positions of interest groups, the public, and governmental policymakers have hardened. This is a field of government relations to which associations should devote considerably more effort than they now do.

HOW ASSOCIATIONS SET POLICY POSITIONS ON ISSUES

Associations utilize a fairly uniform procedure to adopt positions on issues. Typically, the process involves staff research on the issues and their probable impact on the membership, an assessment of the legislative outlook, and recommendations from the staff or a committee to the board of directors, which makes the final policy decisions.

Researching the Issues

The research function is the most important of these stages because decisions at every other step are based on it. Regrettably, not every organization is meticulous in researching issues, and sometimes poor decisions result. The optimum association research process should develop answers to the following questions:

What is this issue all about? How will it affect our members? Will it increase their costs of doing business or add to their burdens in some other fashion? Alternatively, will it remove restrictions on them or open up new marketing opportunities? What hard data support responses to these questions?

What is the rationale for this proposal? What are the arguments in its favor? Who would benefit?

What are the arguments against it? Who would be harmed?

What key legislators or other policy officials might support our likely point of view?

Who is on the other side—which specific interest groups, legislators, or government officials?

Has a specific bill or regulatory proposal been introduced? What is its number or other identification? What is the history of action on this or similar proposals?

What is the probable timetable for this issue? If it is a current or even immediate matter, how soon will action take place? Will public hearings be held? If so, who will testify, and what are they expected to say? If the issue is longer-term, how soon is it likely to become current?

What additional information do we have concerning the political factors surrounding this issue?

Are there other associations, companies, or non-business organizations that share our stake on this issue? Is a coalition with them feasible? Should we take the lead on this issue, or does it make better sense to defer leadership to another group?

Are there alternatives, governmental or voluntary, that provide a preferable method of dealing with the problem underlying this issue?

What are our realistic options: Support? Oppose? Support or oppose with particular changes? What are our fall-back options if we cannot prevail in our original position?

What priority should be assigned to this issue, based on its probable impact and degree of immediacy?

Based on that priority, what lobbying actions should be considered?

Adopting Positions

An options paper provides associations with a handy format in which all this information can be pulled together to facilitate recommendations and decisions for positions and action. This options paper, together with any supporting documents, is generally prepared by the staff and submitted to the appropriate association committee. This may be a government relations committee or a group concerned with issues falling within a designated subject area (for example, Tax Committee, Environmental Issues Task Force, Working Group on Housing). After discussing the impact and ramifications of the issue, that body then makes its recommendations to the board of directors for final decision.

In many associations, particularly small and mid-size groups, recommendations on issues come to the board directly from the chief staff executive or, less often, from the government affairs director. Sometimes the issue will be processed by the executive committee before going to the board.

Adoption of formal positions should not be the only decision the board is asked to make. Because direct lobbying is a negotiating process, consideration should also be given to fall-back positions, which are more important than most boards realize. In the heat of negotiations, lobbyists are often asked by legislators if certain amendments are acceptable. Sometimes there is time to check with the board, but sometimes not. Authorizing the staff to make such decisions is not only good lobbying practice, but also a sign of an effective association.

The decision making process is not always wholly dispassionate. Many issues generate strong feelings on the part of members and elected leaders, and these emotions frequently distort the association's decision making and plans for action. This is almost always a trap that should be avoided. When committee or board members start making statements like, "I don't care what the research says, this bill will kill us" or "We've got to fire all the torpedoes on this one right away, whatever the political consequences," that is almost invariably a signal that ill-considered decisions that the organization may come to regret are being made. Good decisions are made in the presence of light, not heat.

Boards and committees are quite often accused of adopting association policies and positions at the lowest common denominator of membership views. The larger and more diverse the organization, the more probable it is that these situations will arise. They occur not only because companies have different interests and points of view, but also because associations have a strong impulse for consensus. Policy debates in boards or committees tend to end with a position everyone can live with—a consequence that achieves the desired unanimity but possibly at the cost of taking issue positions that do not square with political reality.

There are no easy answers to the lowest-common-denominator problem. Association executives often surrender to it in the belief that the solidarity of the organization is more important than the position adopted on any given issue. Yet, this choice often diminishes the group's legislative effectiveness on the issue in question and sometimes on the totality of the organization's government relations—presumably exactly the opposite of what the members responsible for it intend.

An observer attending board or committee deliberations occasionally gets the impression that the participants think that they themselves are actually legislating on the issues, instead of merely taking advisory positions on them. They seem to forget that these are steps in a process that will ultimately be resolved by elected officials. The most effective contributors to association policy discussions maintain a realistic perspective about their role in policy-making and the role of the organization in the legislative process.

Closely related to the lowest-common-denominator problem is the reactive-proactive dilemma. Confronted with an emerging public problem that may prove costly to the membership, associations often have a window in time in which to develop a proactive solution. However, that solution may involve voluntary action or a legislative alternative that not all members are willing to support.

Members unwilling to incur the costs of either proactive alternative argue, not without reason, that the issue may be defeated or just go away. Sometimes they are correct. The result can be expensive when they are not, however, particularly if the final legislative outcome turns out to be more onerous than the earlier alternatives. Nonetheless, the lowest-common-denominator factor helps the nay-sayers prevail more often than not.

Situations like these point up the importance to member-companies of being represented in the association policy process by individuals able to take a broad view of the interests of their own companies, as well as those of the organization's membership at large. Member-companies also need their own internal mechanisms to grapple with these problems in advance of the association's deliberations.

Boards of directors and their subordinate committees do not always see eye to eye on policy matters. For one thing, boards usually consist of more senior executives than the committees do. Their perspectives are therefore likely to be different. For another, the mix of companies represented on the board probably differs from that on committees, especially in mid-sized and large associations. In addition, there is the human factor: individuals from the same enterprise do not always have the same point of view. If differences have not been resolved as a matter of corporate policy beforehand, they may spill over into association deliberations.

One large national company, which did not have a formal internal process to establish public policy positions, was represented by two executives of quite different political philosophies on separate committees of one of the umbrella organizations. Their frequently conflicting opinions on issues led association staff people to complain that they did not know whose views actually represented those of the member-company. Such situations can mislead the association and reflect poorly on the company's management.

The purpose of the association policy process is to take positions that reflect the best interests of the constituent membership as a whole. Each member will, very properly, consider its own needs paramount, but those needs should also take into account the member's extended interest as a constructive member of its industry, profession, or local business community as well as the narrower interest reflected in the issue immediately at hand.

Well-constructed options papers support sound policy debates. A good options paper assures that committees and boards have all the relevant data, including essential political background information, necessary to adopt positions that reflect the members' long-term interests as well as their immediate ones.

GOVERNMENT RELATIONS TECHNIQUES

Once the association has established a policy on an issue, two documents should be developed—a position paper and an action plan.

Position Papers

Associations utilize position papers to communicate their views on public policy matters to legislators and government officials, the press, allies and other interested groups, and, of course, members.

Position papers are one- or two-page, clear, factual statements of the association's views on a particular issue or, occasionally, groups of closely related issues. A typical position paper describes the issue, explains how it would affect the association's membership and, as appropriate, the public. The paper states the association's position, together with readily understandable supporting arguments and substantiating documentation. In addition, position papers often summarize the arguments of the other side, together with the association's rebuttal arguments.

Associations also mine position papers for their membership value. They are a valuable way to show current members what their association is doing to protect and advance their interests. They can also be used to help persuade potential members to join up.

Associations sometimes publish "white papers," which are somewhat fuller and more detailed versions of the position for dissemination to legislative or agency staff specialists and analysts, as well as to private-sector audiences with an interest in a thoroughly substantiated statement of the association's position.

A few associations are starting to make use of video cassettes to present their position papers in a visual, often dramatic, format.

Lobbying Action Plans

Associations utilize any or all of a variety of lobbying techniques to implement their positions on particular issues. An action plan is a blueprint of the strategy and tactics that the association expects to use to prevail on the issue. Its elements will include one or more of the following:

Direct Lobbying. The most prevalent and best known form of government relations—direct lobbying—generally involves personal, face-to-face advocacy of a point of view with individuals in government who are in a position to influence public policy. Those individuals may be legislators, regulatory or executive officials, or key staff aides.

Lobbyists for business associations really perform four different functions:

1. The cultivation of relationships with those individuals.

2. The communication of factual information to policymakers—the needs and problems of the industry, profession, or region the association represents; specific issues; or any matter on which the association has expertise or data to share.

3. The compilation of political intelligence or other information that the association needs to carry out its government relations or other programs.

4. The advocacy of the association's position on issues of concern to it, together with supporting data and arguments.

Although this last function is what the general public thinks of when the word "lobbying" is used, in reality it consumes a far smaller share of lobbyists' time than do the first three. Direct lobbying can take place with respect to pending bills or other legislative matters, regulatory proposals of various kinds, the policy proposals of elected or appointed executive officials, or the implementation of existing law.

Business associations contest each other on legislative issues more often than might be supposed. There is a common attitude that business groups operate with considerable solidarity on issues, in opposition to labor, environmental, or consumer organizations that are similarly monolithic in their views. The fact is that trade associations and other business organizations frequently have opposing interests that put them at odds with each other. Associations of transportation companies may have positions that conflict with transport user groups. Associations of manufacturers and retailers are sometimes on opposite sides of the fence. Banking, insurance, and securities industry associations have been known to claw vehemently at each other when their respective interests conflict.

The same state of affairs sometimes occurs among non-business groups. On some issues, in fact, these groups may splinter, with some of them forming coalitions with business associations (see below).

Grass-Roots Lobbying. This activity is sometimes called "indirect lobbying" because it involves asking intermediaries to communicate the association's views to governmental policymakers. In the case of associations, those intermediaries are their members.

Those members possess a political asset that the staffs of their associations, with all their skills and resources, do not. Association members (or their managers and employees) are citizens who live and vote in the constituencies of elected legislators—local, state, and federal. Because those lawmakers are keenly responsive to the informed and knowledgeable views of their constituents, grass-roots communications can be a highly influential force in the lobbying process.

Recognizing this, many associations have developed programs to mobilize and train their members in effective grass-roots lobbying communications. Most of these programs involve the use of written or telephone messages to legislators and other elected officials. Even more effective are programs involving membership visits to legislators, but these activities involve more training and administrative expense for the association, as well as higher costs in dollars and time for the members, and are therefore less frequently used.

Associations whose members are national companies have the most difficulties in recruiting large numbers of individual participants for grass-roots legislative networks because (a) their prime company contact is often not the optimal person to solicit participation and (b) individuals who have an interest in local politics and government are not frequently involved in national trade associations. Associations with individual members have fewer problems of this kind.

As a generalization, however, state and local associations and chambers often develop the most effective grass-roots programs. Their staffs tend to be personally closer to their members and are in the best position to know the most promising participants. Not only do these associations frequently have excellent relationships with state and local legislators, but they are also in a good position to reach members of Congress from their states.

For that reason, national associations often try to utilize state and local associations in their own or allied industries in their grass-roots efforts. For example, two national food retailing associations, the Food Marketing Institute and the National Grocers Association, not only try to stimulate grass-roots lobbying on the part of their own members, but also invest considerable effort in cultivating state and local retail associations to win their assistance on federal food issues. Moreover, the Grocery Manufacturers of America, which lacks significant local or state counterparts, also works with the same state and local retail groups whenever it can enlist their support. Other national associations, for example, the Chemical Manufacturers Association, have stimulated the formation of state groups in their industries.

Alliances and Coalitions. Alliances of different kinds are increasingly important in association government relations efforts. Associations are no strangers to this concept, since an association is really a permanent alliance among its members.

The impact of many public policy issues is often shared by a number of associations. These groups frequently create coalitions through which they cooperate to accomplish their common objectives. If the issue is broad enough, the umbrella associations will take an interest, usually acting as the lead organization among coalition partners. The U. S. Chamber of Commerce, for instance, is involved in ninety coalitions of this sort, often providing them with staff support.

There are many other coalitions, however, in which the umbrella organizations play only a marginal role or none at all. The American Society of Association Executives has cataloged over a hundred working groups on various national and state issues, ranging from the Cemetery Group to the Sport and Entertainment Business Tax Coalition, and from the New Hampshire Highway Users Conference to the Association for California Tort Reform.[10]

Business associations are far from the only participants in these ad hoc organizations. Many individual companies also choose to involve themselves directly in issues of importance to them. Significantly, many non-business organizations also take an active and cooperative role on issues in which they share a common stake with business groups on specific issues.

Considerable effort is needed to make such "mixed coalitions" work. The business groups may have a credibility problem with the non-business members, and vice versa. Moreover, many members of business associations are suspicious of dealings with organizations that have opposed them on past issues and may well do so again in the future.

On many other issues, coalitions of non-business groups exist, often in opposition to trade associations and companies. Labor unions and environmental and consumer groups frequently work together closely on particular issues of concern to them. Narrower issues produce narrower coalitions, as they also do among business groups. Working alliances like these are becoming increasingly prevalent in Washington. These patterns are widely duplicated at the state level and, less often, locally.

Coalitions cooperate with varying degrees of intensity on their common issues. Many times, the coalition's activities are limited to the exchange of political intelligence. Other coalitions divide direct and grassroots lobbying assignments, coordinating their efforts for the most effective use of their combined resources. The objective, not always attained, is synergy—to get the most that each partner has to offer while maximizing what the coalition as a group can produce.

It is not always possible for associations to cooperate with each other. Many times, even associations with similar memberships adopt incompatible or opposing positions or strategies, making common effort impossible. In other circumstances, rivalry among competing associations frequently hampers or prevents close cooperation, even when they have identical positions, since each is seeking credit among its own members. Often both factors are at work: Conflicting positions sometimes are a direct result of competition between associations with a shared membership base.

Litigation. Judicial challenges are another tool of government relations that associations are using with increasing frequency. Associations are going to court to challenge the constitutionality of laws enacted over their objections, to dispute the legality of regulatory policies and enforcement, and to attack the legitimacy of other actions taken by executive agencies to implement existing law.

The weapons of legal action have long been available to American business groups, of course, but their popularity increased substantially after business observed the successes that civil rights, environmental, and consumer organizations have obtained in the courts after frequent failures in legislative policy arenas.

Litigation is not without its problems as a government-relations tactic. For one thing, it is expensive, and financially strapped associations may not be able to afford it. For another, suing a government agency does not contribute to cordial relations and may be inconsistent with an association's posture of friendly cooperation. Still, even in defeat, litigation can increase respect for the association as a tough player not to be pushed around.

Communications. Communications and public relations on issues and other public policy topics are an important element within the larger government relations strategy, coordinated as necessary with the communications strategies discussed in chapter 4. In government relations, communications are a means to an end, not an end in and of themselves.

On many issues, associations find it valuable and often essential to support their positions with messages tailored to various target audiences. If the group believes that a moral principle is involved in a particular issue or that it will have a public economic impact, it will want to carry this message widely to the public or to other singularly affected interests, such as consumers.

External public relations can contribute significantly to the association's government-relations goals. It can place public pressure on government policymakers in support of the association's position. It can enhance enthusiasm among members, especially those involved in grassroots lobbying. And it can help strengthen relationships with allies in a coalition and perhaps deflate the morale of opponents.

Sometimes, however, the tail has to wag the dog. An association whose industry is in low public esteem will generally find it prudent to avoid speaking out publicly on individual issues until it can take action to improve its overall image. If the association's stance on a particular issue is essentially one of narrow self-interest without elements of larger public benefit, then silence is undoubtedly the soundest communications tactic. Large public events also can mute an association's desire to publicize its issue positions. For example, the American Petroleum Institute's campaign to win support for expanded oil drilling on Alaska's north slope was severely set back both by the Exxon oil spill off Valdez and by revelations of inadequate industry contingency planning for such disasters.

ASSOCIATION POLITICAL PROGRAMS

The association that can alter the political climate is obviously in a stronger position to achieve its public policy objectives. That concept underlies the growth of involvement by business associations in political action programs.

Political Participation

In a sense, President Dwight D. Eisenhower is the patron saint of business political action. His maxim, "Politics ought to be the part time profession of every citizen," inspired a wave of programs to involve business executives in political activity. The political programs of two umbrella associations, the NAM and the U. S. Chamber of Commerce, led to the formation of the Public Affairs Council and the Business-Industry Political Action Committee, groups that have specialized in promoting effective business involvement in politics. Many companies, trade and professional associations, and chambers of commerce proceeded to pick up the political torch.

Initially, these programs encouraged business people to participate directly in three kinds of activities:

1. Involvement in individual political campaigns to help select and aid candidates favorable to business and to influence their issue positions.
2. Participation in the two major parties to affect party platforms and candidate selection.
3. Direct personal commitment to the process by becoming candidates or party leaders themselves.

These programs, though effective, unfortunately began to wane after 1975 when business political action committees were legitimized. Associations in particular found it far easier to gather voluntary political contributions from their members than to motivate them to donate personal time for politics.

Political Action Committees

Associations (and companies) use political action committees (PACs) to aggregate a number of small individual contributions in order to make sizable donations to candidates for elective office and political parties. A single contribution of $1,000 has more impact than fifty of $20 each.

PAC contributions have become a major source of campaign money in congressional races and in elections in most of the states. Associations in many states have been legally barred from making direct contributions out of their own treasuries, but those that have chosen to sponsor PACs have found their legislative influence has increased substantially.

About 40 percent of trade associations and a slightly smaller percentage of professional societies operate PACs. There is a substantial variation among associations of different geographic scope. Local associations are more than twice as likely as national groups to have a political action committee, and state associations are almost three times as likely.[11] Among state chambers, 64 percent operate PACs.[12] Only one local chamber in eight runs a PAC, but the ratio rises to 50 percent among the largest chambers.[13]

Although most associations give PAC dollars to candidates only at their own geographic level, nearly a fourth of state associations report that their PACs also contribute to federal candidates; a slightly smaller percentage of national associations say that their PACs give to state and local candidates. (Cross-giving like this is illegal unless the state organization has also set up a separate federal PAC and the national group has established separate state PACs.)

Though invented by labor, the political action committee has become an instrument of great power in the hands of business organizations. Associations use PAC contributions to support candidates who favor their philosophies of government and positions on the issues; to express their appreciation to helpful and supportive legislators and other elected officials; and to strengthen their access to incumbent lawmakers. Because the latter function has become the paramount use of PAC funds among many business groups, PACs have been attacked as subversive influences on the legislative process, and restrictions are likely. Oddly, there seems to be far less criticism of PACs sponsored by labor unions and cause groups.

Honoraria

Another technique that has long been used by many associations to build relationships and goodwill with legislators is the honorarium. The ubiquitous meetings of associations require speakers, usually on the issues with which the association is concerned. Who better to speak than the legislators immediately involved in those issues? As remuneration for these talks, associations usually pay honoraria to the speakers. Their use, however, will soon be limited to state lawmakers.

Honoraria have been considerably more prevalent among associations than PACs. There are few or no complex organizational, registration, or reporting procedures as there are for PACs. On the other hand, honoraria are at least as controversial as PACs among political reformers. Because honoraria are, at least ostensibly, expenses paid to inform and educate association members on the issues, honoraria can be paid directly out of association funds. Accordingly, critics have charged that these speaking fees are really only disguised political contributions. Associations defend their use as legitimate educational outlays.

Honoraria are still permitted in most states but, at the federal level, the reformers have prevailed. Beginning in 1991, members of the U. S. House of Representatives will no longer be allowed to accept honoraria, and it is quite likely that the Senate will agree to apply the ban to its members as well. Federal officials in the executive branch have long been prohibited from accepting speaking fees. California banned honoraria to elected officials in 1990.

It will be unfortunate if the result of these bans is to cut the number of legislative speakers willing to address association and corporate audiences. Many organizations have found that their members' political sophistication, knowledge of the issues, and grass-roots involvement are greatly enhanced by exposure to the views of legislators. If such genuinely educational opportunities are reduced as the price of reducing outside income for members of Congress, it will be a poor trade-off indeed.

ILLUSTRATIVE APPENDIX

How an Association Processes Issues

Bill Francora, director of government relations for the Institute of the American Cryoptics Industry, was having his usual monthly dinner with Betsy Willard, public affairs vice president of Continental Physics Applications Corporation, to review the agenda for the next day's meeting of IACI's government affairs committee. Willard chaired the committee.

Francora reviewed the status of various federal and state bills on which IACI had taken a position and then turned to new issues. "There are two matters on which I think we need committee recommendations, one state and one federal. Both concern cryoptic lenses. Eleven states still have laws requiring our members to provide consumers with low-temperature storage devices in which to keep the lenses at night. The newest lenses, of course, no longer need overnight reinforcement, and the staff thinks we should make an all-out effort to get those laws repealed."

"Have you got the staff to handle a state legislative campaign?" Willard interjected.

"I've sent in a budget request asking for a new staff person to handle state issues and to hire independent lobbyists in these states, and cleared the idea with Ralph," Francora said, referring to IACI's president and C.E.O., Ralph Philips.

"Let's ask the committee to endorse that tomorrow," Willard commented. "It's time we beefed up the association's state capabilities."

"What's the federal issue?" she asked.

"Senator Fenton is going to introduce a bill denying consumers a tax deduction for purchase of cryoptic lenses," Francora answered. "We're pretty sure he's been put up to it by the makers of more traditional eyeglasses. They're arguing that cryoptics are more cosmetic than medical, and that tax deductibility as a medical expense shouldn't be permitted."

"How can they get away with that?" asked Willard. "We've got FDA approval for safety and effectiveness."

"Some consumer activists are pouncing on that study at Upper Delaware University that questioned FDA's findings and are circulating it around Congress. Our competitors are working with them. We've summarized all this in this options paper we'd like to give the committee tomorrow." Francora handed her a copy, and Willard promised to read it overnight.

"Shouldn't we put this issue at the top of the agenda?" Willard asked. "It's pretty important."

"Potentially, it's dynamite," Francora answered. "If we put it first, it will blow everything else off the agenda. We'd never get to anything else."

Willard agreed, and left the agenda as it was.

The committee met the next morning in IACI's conference room. Philips and Francora joined them. Willard asked Francora to report on the status of the various pending issues that the committee had discussed in previous meetings, and then brought up the matter of the state lens storage controls.

Francora put up a chart that summarized the various state laws and regulations on cryoptic lens storage and said that the staff believed it was time to move on the eleven states with restrictive laws.

Ed Bennington of Amalgamated Cryoptics spoke up: "It seems to me there are several questions raised by Bill's report. First, I'm not sure IACI should scatter its resources by getting into state issues; we've lived with those restrictions up to now and we've got enough problems here in Washington. Second, I don't think there's anybody on staff who has enough state lobbying experience. If we want to do anything on this problem, my suggestion is that we push for a federal pre-emption that would cancel out those state laws.''

Philips responded, ''Several people on this committee have urged us to get deeper into state issues, and some of the members have complained about our absence in that area. The board of directors has never taken a formal position on it, but there seems to be general support for a state government relations program. Bill has asked for funds to do that, and I've agreed to include them when the new budget goes to the board. I'm sure the board will want this committee's views about developing a state capability over and above the question of whether we should tackle the eleven states.''

Willard asked the committee to consider the two points separately. Bennington said he thought it was probably a good idea to develop a state government relations function, provided it did not dilute IACI's federal activities. That view was accepted by the rest of the committee, and a motion to make that recommendation to the board was approved unanimously.

''Okay, now what does the committee think we should do about the eleven states?'' Willard asked.

Jack Cutler of Optic Innovations said, ''I disagree with Ed's earlier comment that we can continue to live with these state restrictions. If we have an opportunity to reduce the industry's costs and broaden our marketing, we should do it. We've sometimes been too reactive in our government relations. Let's take the initiative for a change.''

''Why fight this battle in eleven legislatures when we can fight it in one, Congress,'' Bennington responded. ''Why not go for a federal pre-emption?''

''Well, you can't have pre-emption without a federal law on storage devices,'' Philips put in. ''That issue has never come up in Congress, and I don't know if it would want to pass such a law nor whether it would be better or worse than what we have now. Even with a federal standard, more restrictive state laws could still be allowed. My suggestion to this committee is that you let us take some soundings and put a decision on pre-emption off to next month's meeting.''

Cutler said he thought a pre-emptive federal law was too dangerous, since the result could be stringent regulation nationwide, and that he preferred tackling the question at the state level. Most of the members agreed with him, but several shared Bennington's opinion.

''Let me suggest a middle course,'' Willard said. ''Let's develop some information on congressional opinion on this, but also ask the staff to go ahead on a plan for action in the states. That will give us a better basis for a decision at our next meeting. If that's acceptable, let's move on to a new federal tax bill.''

She asked Francora to explain the Fenton bill and discuss the staff's options paper. Copies were handed around, and he reviewed its major points. "Senator Fenton's staff is still drafting the bill, so I don't have a copy yet. Our information from some friends on the Senate committee, though, is that the bill would deny taxpayers a deduction for purchase of cryoptic lenses on the grounds that their safety and effectiveness are unproven and questioned by the Upper Delaware study, and that people wear them mainly for cosmetic rather than medical reasons. Obviously, such a bill would do our members serious injury.''

"Serious injury!" Bennington exploded. "This bill would put us right out of business. Why weren't we told about this bill before? We can't live with this. Let's drop all this other nonsense and pull out all the stops to kill this thing right away.''

"Ed is absolutely right," said Phil Jarvis of Advanced Optical Research. "This proposal will murder the entire industry. We'll all be out of jobs—including you staff guys," he added ominously.

Willard banged her knuckles on the table. "Whoa, let's calm down. There are a lot of things about this issue we don't know yet. Bill, would you continue?''

"We're well aware that this bill would be a disaster," Francora said, "but it hasn't even been introduced yet, and it's not at all clear that it has much support. We learned about it only a couple of days ago, and we've been digging out everything we can about it.

"We think that our competitors in the other lens industries brought the Upper Delaware University study to the attention of the consumer activists and appear to be using them as lobbying point men on this. We also know that some of the other lens companies are politically close to Fenton.

"However, we do have potential allies," he went on. "FDA, for one, since their prestige is on the line. The medical specialists who prescribe our lenses and their professional society for another, plus the independent research scientists who advised FDA in its pre-approval study. I don't know where the other consumer groups stand on this; most haven't taken a position, and we may be able to neutralize them or get them on our side with hard facts. Finally, Fenton doesn't appear to have any co-sponsors yet, and that indicates his colleagues may want more information before they support him.

"So, we've got a number of tactical opportunities. We will be in touch with other senators, particularly those on the committee, to discourage support and any public hearings. We'll be in touch with the consumer, medical, and scientific groups very shortly, and we've already made contact with FDA on this. Ralph has a meeting with the commissioner next week.''

Cutler said, ''FDA is obviously critical. If they think there's a serious question about cryoptics, they could rescind their approval, even if the bill doesn't pass. I think all of us should get our own in-house scientific people to review the data and come up a solid refutation.''

Philips agreed and promised to call an early meeting of the association's scientific and technical committee.

Francora, in response to a question, said that House support for Fenton's proposal was still uncertain but that he anticipated that a companion bill would probably be introduced.

Harriet Branson, representing the Low-Temperature Technologies Company, asked whether use could be made of each company's warranty lists of cryoptic users to generate consumer support.

''There might be an antitrust question if the lists were pooled,'' Philips answered. ''We'll take that up with the lawyers. Maybe each company could do a mailing to its own list at the right time. We'll explore that and incorporate it in our action plan if it seems feasible.''

''Does anybody have anything else to add?'' Willard asked. ''Even without seeing a bill, we certainly know enough to urge the board to oppose the concept of the Fenton bill. May I have a motion to do that?'' The motion was adopted unanimously.

She continued, ''The staff seems right on top of this, and we'll take a look at the action plan that I'll ask Ralph and Bill to have ready for our next meeting. Of course, they'll be in immediate touch with us if there are any important developments in the meantime. Ed and Phil, is that acceptable?''

Bennington and Jarvis said that it was, provided that the staff gave the issue top priority. Jarvis added that the board should be asked to consider a special membership assessment to fund an all-out lobbying campaign if the bill got serious, and said he would urge his company's C.E.O. to raise that proposal at the board meeting.

Willard adjourned the meeting shortly thereafter.

A few weeks later, IACI's board of directors held its usual quarterly meeting with the government relations committee report a major agenda item. Much of the discussion covered the same ground that the committee had.

Taking up the state government-relations question, the board encouraged Philips to request funds in the budget for a manager of state issues and urged him to start recruiting now. During discussion of the proposal, directors indicated that once the position was created and filled, the new manager should be asked to prepare an overall plan to handle the restrictive state laws, with the matter of hiring state lobbyists deferred until completion of that plan.

The board also adopted a resolution opposing regulation of lens storage devices and expressing support for "legislation at the appropriate level to end these anti-consumer restrictions."

There had been some developments on the tax deduction bar by the time of the board meeting. Senator Fenton had introduced his bill the previous week with only one co-sponsor. Although the bill had been simultaneously introduced in the House, it had equally weak backing there. Philips told the directors that it now appeared the bill would move slowly for at least the rest of the current legislative session.

The board adopted a resolution reaffirming the safety and effectiveness of cryoptic lenses and opposing legislation curtailing taxpayers' right to deduct lens costs. Philips was instructed to continue monitoring the issue closely and to proceed with the development of an action plan, but not to implement it unless the issue heated up. He promised, however, to maintain active communications with various potential allies "just in case."

A substitute motion to develop and implement an action plan on the tax bill as the association's highest immediate priority drew little support and was never voted on.

Commentary. The problems faced by this fictitious association illustrate many often dealt with by business organizations as they wrestle with their government relations concerns. Issues can be contentious within associations, and emotions can run high. A good committee chairman may have her own point of view, as this one did, but still be able to build consensus. Because such problems can be disruptive, agenda placement can be a critical factor.

The question of federal pre-emption is a knotty one for national associations wrestling with state requirements, especially when those requirements differ among the states.

The government relations tactics used or considered by the association demonstrate the inter-relationship of direct lobbying, back-channel information, technical research, grass-roots lobbying, and coalitions. Both allies and opponents may represent mixtures of business and non-business interests and sometimes the public sector as well.

Association boards of directors often modify committee proposals, as this one did in adopting the substance of the recommendations while using compromise language to blur differences and maintain consensus. Similarly, a proposal seen as unlikely to pass may never be brought to a vote at all, in order to avoid embarrassment to its sponsors.

Staff personnel sometimes bear the burden of all messengers—blame for unhappy tidings. They must often walk a fine line, presenting factual information and professional judgments to the members but avoiding the role of advocates for a specific position. At the same time, they often share responsibility for implementation plans with a committee or the board, while generally being solely or largely accountable for the results of those plans.

NOTES

1. Expanded treatment of the material in this chapter will be found in Charles S. Mack, *Lobbying and Government Relations: A Guide for Executives* (Westport, CT: Quorum Books, 1989).

2. National Industrial Conference Board, *Trade Associations: Their Economic Significance and Legal Status* (New York: 1925), 289.

3. Walter Mitchell, Jr., *How to Use Your Trade Association* (New York: Prentice-Hall, 1951), xviii–xix.

4. American Society of Association Executives (ASAE), *Policies and Procedures in Association Management.* (Washington: 1987), 83–84.

5. ASAE, *Association Activities.* (Washington: 1985), 8, 23.

6. U. S. Chamber of Commerce, *1989 Survey of Local Chambers of Commerce* (Washington: 1989), 15.

7. Hudson Institute, *The Value of Associations to American Society.* (Washington: Foundation of ASAE, 1990.)

8. ASAE, *Policies and Procedures,* 84.

9. For more information on such services, see Mack, *Lobbying and Government Relations,* 11–28, 195–202. See also Lynn Hellebust, *State Legislative Sourcebook* (Topeka, KS: Government Research Service, annual editions).

10. *ASAE Coalition Directory, 4th edition* (Washington: American Society of Association Executives, 1989).

11. ASAE, *Policies and Procedures,* 85.

12. U. S. Chamber of Commerce, *1988 Survey of State Organizations* (Washington: 1989).

13. U. S. Chamber, *1989 Local Chamber Survey,* 15.

Part III

ASSOCIATION RESOURCES AND REGULATION

Part III

ASSOCIATION RESOURCES
AND REGULATION

6

Association Resources: Membership, Finance, and Planning

People are the common denominator of progress.
John Kenneth Galbraith

He who has his thumb on the purse has the power.
Otto von Bismarck

Trade associations, professional societies, and chambers of commerce share a family resemblance, at least at the mid-range of several statistical characteristics. Here is a statistical stereotype of each kind of business association:

- The average trade association has a membership of 315 companies, a budget slightly under $1 million, and a full-time staff of six with two part-time employees.
- The average professional organization has a membership of 3,000 individuals, a budget just over $1 million, and the same number of full-time and part-time staff employees as its trade association counterpart.
- The average chamber of commerce serves a community with a population of between 50,000 and 75,000. It has close to 800 members and an annual budget of about $275,000. There are five full-time and two part-time employees on staff.

In the aggregate, trade associations in America have over 10 million corporate members (with substantial overlaps, of course, because of multiple memberships). They employ the full-time equivalent of almost 54,000 people and have budgets totaling more than $4.4 billion.[1] Professional associations have a combined total of nearly 116 million members, the full-time equivalent of 89,000 staff employees, and budgets adding up to over $4.2 billion.[2]

Comparable calculations for chambers of commerce have never been made. Perhaps as many as one-fourth of the 4,700 local chambers in this country lack paid staff or a headquarters office. Rough estimates by the author indicate full-time chamber staff equivalents of some 20,000 employees, and aggregate chamber budgets of perhaps $1 billion.

Averages and aggregates are useful for approximate comparisons but often disguise vast variations: National and international trade associations and professional societies look quite different from state and local organizations. Chambers of commerce also vary substantially, and the size of their communities may not be a reliable indicator of their budgets and operations. State chambers also look different from local ones.

Even within each of these classes and sub-classes, there are large differences. Some business associations have budgets under $100,000 annually and no full-time staff. There are also associations with eight-digit budgets and staffs that number over a thousand. There are large local associations and small national ones.

Regardless of their differences, however, each association has resources that, taken together, determine its organizational vitality. Considerable information can be drawn upon to present a picture of the size, scope, and resources of America's business associations. Data on the operations of trade and professional associations derive from membership surveys of the American Society of Association Executives.[3] Data on state and local chamber operations come from surveys conducted by the U. S. Chamber of Commerce.[4]

Membership, finances, and the planning and budgeting process are analyzed in this chapter. Chapter 7 covers the quality of the voluntary or elected leadership, as well as association governance—board and committee structure and the policy-setting process. The role of the professional staff is discussed in chapter 8.

The heart of any business association, whether it be a chamber of commerce, professional society, or trade association, is its membership. The members, the revenues they provide (directly or indirectly), and the programs funded by those revenues are association resources whose management is critical to the organization's effectiveness and success.

MEMBERSHIP

The most basic strength of any association is its members, whose common needs and interests the organization exists to serve. Serving that commonality is what good associations have been all about. Organizational executives frequently derive much personal satisfaction from bringing members together to discuss and analyze a collective industry, community, or professional problem, and then helping those members to see beyond their own narrow concerns to develop a larger perception of the common welfare and even the public interest. The sense of synergy that can develop out of such situations—the feeling that the association *can* be greater than the sum of its parts, that it *can* move mountains—is a galvanizing experience.

More typical, though, are situations in which members meet to discuss their shared but individual problems. Particular matters and issues affect different members in different ways. They seek help from their association in dealing with the aggregate of those effects, which is subtly different from dealing with common effects. The sum of the parts is only the sum of the parts—nothing more.

It is important to realize that both attitudes are legitimate. There are individual member interests as well as common interests, and the association must tend to both as well as it can.

Marketing Strategy

Understanding this fact allows association staff and leaders to recognize that the membership is really a market for the association. Indeed, the membership may well be segmented, with different sub-sets having different needs that may have to be served in different ways.

Thus, the membership constitutes not only the association's fundamental resource and its ownership but also its clientele. Recognition of the members as the group's clients, as well as its owners, allows the association to develop market-oriented strategies to the construction and delivery of its programs and services. This approach is much more likely to enhance membership satisfaction and growth than one that treats the members as a passive lot who have an obligation to pay dues and come to association events.

Unfortunately, this latter attitude is more common among association staff and even elected leaders than might be wished. Not long ago, an association executive remarked, "I had two members who used to pay me a total of $10,000 in dues. Then they merged, and now I get only $7,000. Worse, a second member ran up such a big debt acquiring another company that it dropped out of the association to save money. Dammit, they owe me!"

Companies do not, of course, owe the association a blessed thing. There is no divine right to either members or dues. As with any business's customers, the support and patronage of members must be constantly earned and re-earned. That is accomplished by providing member services that meet not only their common needs, but also their individual ones. Because those individual needs differ, it is much harder to run an association this way. An association that is not operated under a philosophy of marketing to members, however, will find itself in difficulties, as cost-cutting in the business community produces retrenchments in association memberships.

Membership turnover in associations overall has increased very slightly in recent years, from 10 to 11 percent between 1982 and 1987. However, the membership of many individual groups is stable or shrinking while others are growing. Rival associations sometimes capture members at the expense of their competitors. Some members may choose to drop out of associations altogether, taking a free ride on their competitors who choose to stay in.

Membership Structure

As discussed in chapter 3, business associations are of four broad types: umbrella associations, trade associations, professional societies, and chambers of commerce, although many variations and additional specialized forms exist.

There are also various membership formats. Some organizations have chapters, for instance. These are local or state groups that are essentially components in a single, overall, legal structure. Typically, members' dues entitle them to belong to both the national group and its local chapters with a single payment. Sometimes, the dues are paid to a parent organization, which then funds and often controls the chapters. In this situation, members are likely to consider that their primary allegiance is to the national parent group. In other cases, the chapters receive the dues, passing a portion on to the national parent; member allegiance here is primarily local, and sometimes the "children" control the parent, politically if not legally. At a further level of complexity, in some organizations dues are paid to local chapters, which remit a portion to state chapters, which further remit a portion to the national parent; this system may also operate the other way around. Associations with chapters are more likely to consist of individual members rather than company memberships, but this is not invariably the case.

Organizations with chapters differ from federations, which are associations to which other associations pay dues and belong, although there may also be direct memberships from individuals or companies. There is normally no sharing of funds or controlling relationship in a federation.

The retail food industry provides an illustration of how national associations may relate to state and local groups in the same industry. Two national associations, the Food Marketing Institute (FMI) and the National Grocers Association (NGA) both have memberships comprised of retail and wholesale food companies. These same companies often belong to state or local food retail associations. NGA admits the state/local groups as members that pay it dues. FMI maintains close working relationships with the state and local groups but does not admit them as members. NGA is therefore a federation; FMI is not. Neither national association controls the state/local organizations, nor vice versa.

Some associations also have sections that each provide specialized services to a segment of the members. Section dues are often in addition to the basic dues paid the association.

In addition to the regular or primary membership category, many associations have special categories with different dues rates. The most common of these are suppliers of goods or services to the regular members. Almost two-thirds of trade associations accept supplier memberships (often called affiliate or associate members); less than one-third of professional societies do. Supplier members often pay higher dues than do the primary members, but have limited rights and privileges; they usually cannot hold office, for example. The justification for this apparent inequity is that the association is providing marketing access to potential customers (its own primary members) of the supplier group. The advantage for the association is the larger dues revenue base.

Most professional associations and some trade associations offer special memberships for interested students, educators, consumers, and so on, generally at a lower dues rate than regular memberships.

Dues

Associations levy dues by either a flat rate or a formula. The flat rate is used by over 80 percent of individual membership organizations and by a fourth of trade associations. Chambers of commerce and the majority of trade associations rely on percentages or more complex formulas related to sales or assets, units of production, numbers of employees, or other data. In some business associations, particularly chambers, dues can be negotiated down from scale. This is considered unprofessional, however, and most groups are trying to get away from the practice.

Among professional societies, dues can be less than $25 or over $500. The average is $162 and somewhat less for groups with international memberships. The range among trade associations is enormous. Dues for small members can be under $100, but can run into six digits for the largest corporate members of big national organizations. Averages are therefore meaningless. Chamber of commerce dues average about $160.

Membership dues, once virtually the sole revenue source for associations, have declined proportionally "to the point that it is rare for an association to claim less than 35 to 55 percent non-dues income."[5] Indeed, some associations are known to rely on non-dues revenues at even higher percentages. Median dues, as a percentage of total association income, declined from 53 percent in 1977 to 38 percent in 1988. In general, the larger the association, the smaller the dues percentage. Dues to professional societies provide a smaller share of total revenues than those paid trade associations.[6]

While dues are still the single largest revenue source for most associations, two factors account for their relative decline: Growth in expenses over and above what dues can support and membership resistance to dues increases.

Apart from inflation, a primary cause of increased association expenditures is member demand for additional or expanded services, not all of which can be supported by self-sustaining special charges. For example, government relations activities are a rapidly rising cost in most associations.

Dues resistance is considerable and growing. A 1982 ASAE survey reported that 66 percent of associations had increased their dues during the preceding three years by an average of 24 percent. The same question in 1987 revealed that the number of associations reporting a dues increase had fallen to 54 percent, for an average increase of 20 percent.[7]

Clearly, the worth of business associations to their members now has to be sold, or rather marketed, harder than ever, by demonstrating concrete value in terms of services, benefits, and specific results. The day is gone when members could be enlisted out of a sense of *noblesse oblige* or in conformity with what "everyone else" is doing. Associations now have to do market research to determine, by market segments, what their "customers" want and need. Then they must develop cost-benefit analyses of how best to provide it.

Almost all associations have some kind of program to ascertain their members' needs; nearly a third undertake a formal study at least once a year. The vast majority rely on committee members' views and membership mail surveys, but telephone surveys, personal interviews, and even focus groups are increasingly being used.

Whether to sign up new members or retain old ones, personal contact by a peer or staff member remains the most reliable membership sales technique. In associations with large numbers of members, however, that is rarely feasible. Telemarketing and direct mail are now widely used, with an ever-increasing sophistication in approach. A few organizations also retain professional fund-raising firms, with some success.

FINANCE

Many factors determine the vigor of business associations but their financial health, as in any organization, is critical. Associations are therefore becoming much more sophisticated in their financial management. For instance, the number using accrual accounting has climbed from just over a third in 1977 to more than three-fifths today, while those still on the cash method have dropped from 38 percent to less than 10 percent.[8] Nine out of ten associations are now formally audited, although almost a quarter still do not provide their members with annual financial reports or statements. Another 90 percent maintain liquid reserves, and about a third have investment policies. Accounting for expenditures by function or program is still less common than more traditional expensing (such as for personnel or postage).

Revenue Patterns

Average association income has risen over 5.5 times from 1972 to 1988. Since 1976, associations with budgets over $1 million have grown from less than one-fifth to more than half, 13.5 percent now have revenues over $5 million.

As noted above, associations are relying less on dues, but this income source remains far and away the largest. Conventions and expositions now account for over 15 percent of income, but the smaller the geographic base of the organization the less money it can make from conventions. Educational programs are the third largest revenue item (about 7 percent), more so for groups with individual members than for those representing companies. Associations derive 6.4 percent of income from periodical publications, more than half of it from advertising sales. Another 2.1 percent comes from non-periodical publications—for a combined 8.5 percent of total funding. Insurance and royalty income contributes 2.3 percent to total revenues.

Patterns of Expense

On average, executive and administrative costs consume about 30 percent of total association expenditures, followed by almost 12 percent for convention and exposition expenses. Publication costs (periodicals and non-periodicals) account for another 10.5 percent, while education and certification programs take 9 percent. Membership promotion costs almost as much as government relations—about 4.5 percent each—and a bit more than the 4 percent that goes for public relations. About 3.5 percent funds association governance and volunteer programs.

By more traditional expense accounting, salaries and sales commissions are the largest single line-item—30 percent. Adding in other personnel costs, such as benefits and payroll taxes, brings average total personnel expense to just below 36 percent. Meeting costs, the second largest expense item, are a bit over 10 percent. Other areas of expenditure are largely for various office costs.[9]

Financial Policies and Practices

Once hand-to-mouth organizations, there are several indications of the present financial health of business associations as a group. Long-term debt is minute—from 2.5 percent of total assets for small associations up to 4.5 percent for the largest ones. "This supports the conclusion," says ASAE "that associations may buy long-term assets and finance expansion with cash reserves instead of by borrowing funds. As tax-exempt organizations, associations receive no tax benefits from borrowed funds." [10]

The vast majority of associations seek to maintain substantial liquid reserves for expansion and to tide them over rough times. The median reserves goal is 40 percent of annual operating income; the median of funds actually salted away is 30 percent.

Moreover, fully a third of associations own their own office buildings. Larger associations are more likely than smaller ones to own both their own office space and their office equipment.

Nine out of ten associations rely on computers to support their activities in such areas as word processing, membership records, accounting, and convention registrations. Computers are somewhat less frequently used for periodical subscriptions, government relations, and order fulfillment. Association communications are making growing use of electronic mail and electronic bulletins. Three-fourths of associations maintain in-house computers; only one in twelve relies solely on outside service bureaus anymore.

A further indication of financial health is the existence of investment policies, since an organization that is perpetually broke hardly worries much about where to invest its money. The third of business associations that have such a policy are conservative in their approach; over half of them require that all funds be federally insured, and nearly 90 percent insist that at least some funds be so insured. Over two-thirds permit the C.E.O. to make the actual investments.

On the other hand, the staff chief is less trusted when it comes to signing checks. A counter-signature by a volunteer officer is required by 46 percent of all associations and by 69 percent of local groups, if checks exceed a certain amount. The average threshold for counter-signature is $5,000 for all organizations and $3,000 for state and local associations.

The growing proportion of non-dues income presents a constant problem for business associations, almost all of which are organized as tax-exempt organizations under Internal Revenue Service regulations. Under those rules, certain income classed as "unrelated" to the group's non-profit status is considered taxable. If unrelated income is too high, the association can lose its tax-exempt status, as some indeed have (see chapter 9). Revenue from publications advertising is the most common issue when the IRS comes to call, followed by questions related to income from insurance programs, trade shows, and the sale of mailing lists.

In general, the median percentage of total association income that is unrelated is about 10 percent. Almost two-thirds of the associations surveyed chose not to respond to this question, indicating the sensitivity of this issue.

Some organizations (about 15 percent) seek to avoid these problems by setting up taxable affiliates or subsidiaries through which activities that generate unrelated income for the association are operated. This protects the tax-exempt status of the parent. The creation of charitable foundations to fund certain programs and services is becoming even more popular among business associations: almost 30 percent had established foundations by 1988, up from 21 percent a decade earlier.[11]

PLANS, PROGRAMS, AND BUDGETS

Associations have traditionally developed single-year programs of work to guide their activities. Long-range and strategic planning is a relatively recent innovation. Budgeting has often been a separate process, in which expenses—for personnel, travel, overhead, printing, and so on—are only marginally linked to programming. While this process has worked well enough for associations that wish to know only how current outlays relate to current income, it does not really tie budgets to the programs and services they finance; nor does it connect revenue development to the costs of raising those revenues.

Program budgeting is a newer method increasingly adopted by well-managed associations. It assures that budgets are actually a means to implement programs and that both are vehicles to achieve the association's overall goals. The planning process, both short-term and long-range, involves linking finances and programs. Optimum planning is strategic, tying functions and dollars to fundamental association purposes and objectives. At the same time, the process enables the chief staff executive and, through that individual, the board of directors, to achieve personal performance accountability for each professional on the staff. The result for the membership is a better managed association that provides more value for the dues dollar.

Effective program budgeting can help solve a problem that many associations often encounter, that of excessive popularity of certain programs and services. This sounds like a "good problem" but it may present serious management issues. It is not at all uncommon for members, responding to their own needs, to urge the staff to broaden particular services or undertake new ones. There tends to be much less support for dropping an activity. Since association executives are almost always under budgetary pressures to restrain increases in staff and other expenses, they often experience difficulties in managing resources while satisfying the demands of the membership.

A number of associations try to solve this problem by engaging in a case-by-case, decision-making juggling act. A better approach is to make effective use of management tools such as long-term planning and program budgets, to determine priorities and allocate scarce staff resources accordingly, while still assuring the membership that priority needs will be satisfied.

Planning Elements

There are several phases in the planning process:

- Analysis of the association's current situation and member needs.
- Development of a new or revised overarching strategy.
- Negotiation of a mission statement for the association.
- Design of a long-term program and budget.
- Preparation of the short-term (one-year) program and budget.
- Development of performance accountability statements for individual staff members.

Situation Analysis. The planning process begins with an assessment of where the association currently is and how it got that way. This assessment analyzes the organization's strengths, weaknesses, and competitive situation relative to other groups that serve its membership.

A vital component is an evaluation of the external environment in which both the association and its constituency will have to operate. This includes a forecast of public and governmental opinion and emerging issues, and social and economic developments.

Since the purpose of the planning process is to assure that the association meets its members' current and future needs, a critical element involves a survey of the membership (or, in the case of large organizations, a statistically valid sample). A very workable approach is to send members a checklist of all the services that the association currently offers, plus all those it could develop in the future. The members are then asked to rate or rank the ones that are most valuable. Their responses then guide the remainder of the planning process. A parallel study should also be made of non-members to determine why they have not joined and what changes are required to make membership attractive to them.

The temptation to cut this process short by simply asking the opinion of the board of directors should be avoided. One association tallied the replies from the board separately from those of the general membership.

It found, to the board's chagrin, that the priorities of the rank-and-file members were quite different from those of the elected leadership.

Organizational Strategy. These inputs provide the basis for a new strategy for the association. Repositioning the association enables the organization to lead its members into the evolving environment in which it will have to operate, to satisfy their developing needs (and those of prospective members as well), and to challenge forcefully the services offered by competitive groups.

It is important throughout the entire process to distinguish between the needs of the organization as an entity and those of the industry, community, or profession that it represents: Although often confused with each other, they are very different. Dealing only with the situation of the association is at best a partial strategy.

An effective strategy is as specific as necessary to confront each of these needs. It is especially important to deal head-on with sensitive issues that pose potential problems both within the association and outside it. The strategy should be clear-cut, candid, and aggressive. Ducking touchy problems does not cause them to disappear: It merely postpones facing them—exactly the opposite of what a good strategy should accomplish.

Mission Statement. This brief document emerges from the foregoing analysis. It is a concise expression of why the association exists and what it wishes to achieve. It sets forth qualitatively the organization's fundamental priority objectives. In a sense, the mission statement is the charter of the association from which its programs flow.

Here is an example:

The Association of Median Processors is a trade association that exists to strengthen the economic and political environment for the median processing industry. It works to expand economic opportunities and markets for its members through programs to enhance quality standards; to collect and disseminate pertinent economic, regulatory, and other information; and to increase public and customer knowledge of the industry's products and services and their value to society. AMP also seeks to achieve a governmental climate favorable to the marketing of the industry's products and services, and to inform and assist its members in enhancing their professional skills in the light of advancing technical knowledge.

And another:

The Midworld Chamber of Commerce is an association of business enterprises in metropolitan Midworld that exists to advance economic opportunity for business firms, their employees, and their families, and to enrich the quality of life for the people of Midworld and Central County. The Chamber undertakes programs to attract new industry, expand marketing opportunities for existing employers, improve the educational and political climates, and strengthen public awareness of the Midworld area as a desirable location for conventions and tourism.

Mission statements of this sort provide a foundation and framework for the organization's long-term and current objectives and programs. They state the general purposes that programs are designed to implement. Budgets, in turn, facilitate program goals. Delivery of performance through personal accountability by staff (and, in some cases, by association members and leadership) is the means by which objectives are converted into achievements.

Long-Term Plans and Budgets. Each of the purposes expressed in the mission statement is the basis for one or more long-term programs, covering a three- to five-year period. Each program sets forth both a concrete objective and the specific steps or actions to be taken to achieve that objective. Each of those actions, in turn, has a target date for completion, with the phases or elements to be completed within each year of the program specified. The individual or department responsible for the program is specifically noted.

Some purposes may be achieved with a single program, such as a political action fund-raising campaign or the compilation of particular economic data. Others will require multiple programs: Standards development will involve a separate program for each standard; separate government relations programs must be developed for each legislative issue.

The aggregate of these programs, joined, perhaps, by an optional unifying statement, constitutes the association's long-term plan.

The long-term budget covers the same period as the long-term plan, specifying the dollars required to implement each individual program. The budget is expressed by function (such as "Conventions and Meetings," "Government Relations," "Economic Analysis," "Membership Sales and Promotion"), noting under each the pertinent programs and their associated costs and/or revenues. Revenue programs should also include the costs of raising those funds.

Short-Term Programs and Budgets. Both program plans and budgets for the immediate period are structured similarly to the long-term plans, but they lay out the specific details (by month or by quarter) required to organize the new year's activities and finances. The organization of these documents is functional, with departmental and/or individual accountability clearly specified.

Performance Accountability Statements. This is the element of the entire process that converts objectives into results. Individual staff members are now asked to frame quite specific personal performance goals with target dates (usually by quarters), the total of which will produce the program objective for that year. This is normally a negotiating process between the individual staff member and his/her superior.

Monthly or quarterly reports up the line, from the individual staffer to the C.E.O., and thence to the board of directors and pertinent committees, indicate progress against goals, noting completions and explaining variances from plan.

These concrete results become a major part of individual performance and salary evaluations for staff members. Obviously, this is not possible where accountability, even in part, lies with an elected leader or committee chairman, but diplomatic peer pressure may be a sufficient incentive or goad.

The Planning Process

The process of program budgeting and personal accountability works only if those with a stake in the association, particularly affected staff members, are involved in all phases of it. It is difficult to disclaim responsibility for program goals and budgets if the individual charged with their execution has been involved in their development from the very beginning. Conversely, that kind of personal involvement produces enthusiasm, pride, and a commitment to meeting program objectives.

Different associations use somewhat different approaches to the development of the planning and budgeting elements, but here is one model:

1. The situation analysis, data collection, and strategic and mission statements are developed by the board of directors, executive committee, or planning committee. (If another body does the drafting, ultimate approval by the full board of directors is essential. Indeed, the mission statement in particular is so critical to the association that some organizations may even ask the entire membership to approve it.) Extensive participation at every step by the C.E.O. and senior staff is equally necessary. Because so many vital interests are involved, associations often inject an element of neutral objectivity into the process by enlisting the aid of a knowledgeable consultant to act as process facilitator.

2. Association committees or task forces are asked to develop long-term programs within their functional areas, using the mission statement as the basis of their work. Detailed planning takes place within the staff, with staff drafts negotiated to completion with pertinent committees. Completed recommendations go to the C.E.O. and the board of directors for integration, further negotiations (if necessary), and final approval. Related cost/revenue elements are developed through the same process, generally being filtered through the finance committee for integration with the association's financial plan before the budgets and programs go to the board.

3. Detailed short-term program planning and budgeting result from the same process, with committees, board, and staff all playing critical roles. Details of particular programs are developed with heavy input from those staff members who have responsibility for carrying out the programs or their components.

4. Once the short-term programs have been approved, the C.E.O. begins the process of negotiating individual accountability statements with each department head and/or staff member.

5. Periodic reports from staff members keep all concerned abreast of progress, exceptions to plans, and remedial steps—and provide an on-going method of evaluating performance and assuring accountability.

This program budgeting process, or appropriate variations of it, can be utilized by any kind of association, regardless of scope or size. Adaptable to a wide range of situations, the process helps the association determine where it wants to go, plans the programs and actions needed to get it there, makes its budgeting process an integral part of its plans, and assures that all stakeholders, including staff, agree on every element and phase of the entire process.

DISTORTIONS OF RESOURCES

Even with the most capable staff, the most dedicated membership and leadership, and first-rate finances and planning, resource distortions can still work their way into association operations. These include problems, structural or political, that hamper the association in the efficient conduct of its mission. Not all distortions are recognized as such, which makes them all the more insidious. The following are among the more common resource distortions.

Imbalances of Power

A well-run association achieves a balance between dominance by the elected leadership on the one hand, and by the staff on the other. Some associations are dominated excessively by the voluntary leaders; others are staff-driven. Both extremes erect roadblocks to association effectiveness.

An illustration is a national association in which the top elected leader takes leave from his/her own business to serve full-time in the association offices, acting as the *de facto* chief executive of the organization. The group has a large professional staff headed by an executive director, but that individual lacks the authority to make major administrative decisions. Key staff positions, for example, are filled by the elected leader, not the executive director. Not surprisingly, turnover among executive directors has been quite high.

Underlying this situation is the assumption that experience in directing a business is a sufficient qualification to run a trade association for a year or two, a point with which most experts in association management would strongly disagree. An enterprise operated to make a profit for its owners is a very different kind of organization than a non-profit trade or professional association. This illustration is of a member-driven association that misuses its resources and fails to take the best advantage of both the continuity of professional association management and the talents of those elected by the members to set the tone and pace of the organization during their limited tenure in office. Associations that deny the chief staff executive hire-and-fire authority are always member-driven. They pay the price in terms of either weak staff executives or high turnover, and sometimes both.

A staff-driven association has its own sets of problems that may be equally bad. These are organizations in which most and sometimes all decisions, perhaps even policy questions, are decided in effect at the staff level. At best, the board of directors acts as a rubber stamp. Such organizations carry the concept of the member-as-customer to an extreme; here, the member has no significant voice in the association. These groups are often run as if they were commercial enterprises, and some actually are.

An extreme example is a relatively new national membership organization that is controlled by a direct marketing company. The association, nominally headed by a famous figurehead, has been very successful in selling memberships to a segment of the population susceptible to emotional appeals on a particular class of legislative issues. The association generates mailing lists through its legislative and membership activities and sells them to its parent company, which then utilizes them for a variety of commercial marketing purposes. Such situations are abusive and a gross distortion of the membership resource.

The focus of power in associations can be at any point along the spectrum between the two extremes. Staff does have a role to play in policy development, just as members do in policy execution. What is needed is a relationship that achieves a workable and effective balance between the resources of staff and membership.

Competition among Associations

Another resource distortion results from the competitive situations that exist among many associations. Sometimes, two or more trade associations serve major segments of the same membership base and compete for dues dollars.

A very important distinction must be made between *competing* associations and *opposing* ones: A state manufacturer's association may *oppose* the state AFL-CIO on certain issues, but it *competes* with the state chamber for prestige, image of effectiveness, and ultimately dues dollars. Note that there is no economic competition between the business and labor groups because they share no common membership base.

At the national level, such rivalries are commonplace, both within specific industries and among umbrella associations. The U.S. Chamber of Commerce, the National Association of Manufacturers, the National Federation of Independent Business, and smaller umbrella groups all engage in turf wars of varying degrees of severity. Competing associations, both trade and professional, are found in fields as diverse as financial planning and food retailing, among many others.

Unlike competition among companies, rivalry between associations is a weakening factor because it dilutes staff time and lessens effectiveness. It is a particular problem in government relations: The image of an industry in the eyes of legislators is hardly enhanced when they have to sort out the conflicting positions and priorities of interest groups with essentially similar constituencies. Such situations often leave the way clear for non-business groups to triumph when they otherwise would not.

Even when competitive associations advocate the same positions, they may follow different strategies to the same negative consequence. It is only when they act in unison that multiple groups have a reinforcing rather than a neutralizing effect. This does happen fairly frequently, but the company that belongs to more than one of these associations may then reasonably wonder why it needs to pay dues to several organizations that are doing the same thing.

The counter-argument that competing associations offer is that their memberships, and therefore their members' interests, may be similar but are not identical and that the differences merit special representation. This distinction is usually more perceived than genuine. As often as not, it justifies an institutional self-interest that can be quite expensive for the individual member that has to fund the differences.

Another aspect of trade association rivalry that is a particular problem for state groups is the prevalence of competing local associations in certain industries. In one of the largest states, there is not only a state association representing a particular distribution sector, but also two regional associations, one in the south and one in the north—and some large companies in that state also belong to a separate umbrella retailing group. In another state industry, there are four regional associations, each of which is stronger than the statewide organization which they often try to elbow aside. These situations of overlap and competition are wasteful and inefficient.

Dues Caps

In many trade associations that utilize formulas of some kind to calculate membership dues, the dues schedule has a ceiling above which members need not pay. The justification for dues caps is that they allegedly limit the leverage that the largest members can exert to pressure an association to adopt their points of view.

Dues caps distort association resources because they place a disproportionate burden on smaller members. Company X may be only half the size of Company Y, but a capped formula may result in both paying identical dues. The larger firm likes the unfair arrangement, of course, knowing that it usually has other ways of influencing association policy to its liking.

NOTES

1. Hudson Institute, *The Value of Associations to American Society* (Washington: Foundation of the American Society of Association Executives, 1990).

2. *Ibid.*

3. American Society of Association Executives (ASAE), *Policies and Procedures in Association Management* (Washington: 1987); ASAE, *Association Executive Compensation Study.* 6th ed. (Washington: 1988); and *Association Operating Ratio Report.* 8th ed. (Washington: 1989).

4. U.S. Chamber of Commerce, *1988 Survey of State Organizations* (Washington: 1988) and *1989 Survey of Local Chambers of Commerce* (Washington: 1989).

5. Wilford A. Butler, "Membership Development" in ASAE, *Principles of Association Management: A Professional's Handbook* (Washington: 1988), 124.

6. ASAE, *Association Operating Ratio Report.* 8th ed. (Washington: 1989).

7. ASAE, *Policies and Procedures.*

8. ASAE, *Ratios* and *Policies and Procedures.*

9. ASAE, *Ratios.*

10. *Ibid.*

11. ASAE, *Ratios* and *Policies and Procedures.*

7

Association Resources: Governance and Policy-making

It is not the practical workers but the idealists and planners that are difficult to find.

Sun Yat-sen

There go the people. I must follow them for I am their leader.

Alexandre Ledru-Rollin (1848)

The governing authority of business associations is vested in their boards of directors. These bodies determine policy, hire and fire the chief staff executive and sometimes other staff as well, and generally oversee all aspects of the administration of the association. The board also both shapes and reflects the philosophy and tenor of the association—its institutional personality and culture—which affect its approach to issues, problems, and administration.

Over 80 percent of associations also utilize an executive committee of the board, a smaller body usually consisting of at least the elected officers, which can act between meetings of the full board and often has other authority as well. Associations also commonly make use of a structure of specialized standing committees and/or task forces to help determine policy and participate in overseeing association administration. These bodies are the means by which the affairs of the association are directed, policy formulated, and the purposes of the organization carried out.

BOARDS OF DIRECTORS AND EXECUTIVE COMMITTEES

Members of the board of directors are generally proposed by a nominating committee and elected by the association's members at an annual business meeting that most state laws require. Election by mail ballot is an alternative and fairly common practice. In a minority of groups, boards of directors are self-perpetuating; current directors elect new ones. Some chamber of commerce boards include certain government officials as ex-officio members.

In a number of associations, directors can be nominated by petition or some other method. A majority of professional groups, some trade associations, and a substantial number of chambers (mostly small ones) choose their boards in contested elections, but single slates are the most prevalent technique in other business associations. Among those groups that conduct competitive elections, many actually have formal guidelines for the conduct of individual campaigns.

The average size of association boards is twenty-five, but some have fewer than ten members while others are known to have as many as fifty or more. Chamber of commerce boards are often larger, and larger chambers tend to have larger boards. A number have more than 100 members, and one state chamber has 172.

Terms of office of directors are typically two or three years and are usually staggered so that only a portion is elected in any given year: Directors are generally allowed to serve more than one term, sometimes with a limit, sometimes not. Boards of national and international associations typically meet two or three times a year. State and local boards meet more frequently, generally quarterly and often monthly.

The chief elected officer is always a member of that body, as often is his/her immediate predecessor, but they are not always voting members. In about a third of all associations, the chief staff executive is an *ex officio* member of the board with or without a vote. This occurs more often in trade associations than in chambers and professional societies.

Association executive committees average seven members, but are larger among state and local chambers. Membership almost always includes the current officers, often the past chairman, less often the incoming one; the staff chief frequently is also a member.[1]

Elected officers and directors are seldom compensated for their time and contributions by the organizations they lead. However, they are frequently reimbursed for expenses, more often by individual membership groups than by trade associations. The expenses of trade association and chamber of commerce voluntary leaders are commonly absorbed by the companies that employ them. The expenses of the chief elected officer are generally paid by the association to enable attendance at the annual convention, board meetings, and committee meetings. The association picks up the expenses for other officers and directors less frequently, and for committee chairmen and members only occasionally. A minority of associations pay spouse expenses, most often for the mate of the chief elected officer.[2]

How Boards and Executive Committees Function

Boards of directors and their executive committees exercise several functions: They adopt policy, not only on current issues and problems, but also on future plans and budgets. They usually determine dues schedules (unless this is reserved to the annual membership meeting) and sometimes service rates, and often play a major role in other kinds of fund-raising. They hire and supervise the C.E.O., generally oversee the staff and its execution of policy, and frequently assist in the implementing process.

The mix of these functions varies from organization to organization. In some, the board is all-powerful, and the executive committee is a ministerial or coordinating body. In others, the executive committee makes all the key decisions, which are then almost invariably ratified by the full board. Frequently, the executive committee approves the agenda for board meetings and tries to work out difficult issues in advance to minimize heated debate in the full board. In addition, the executive committee usually has authority to act on priority matters that may arise between board meetings.

Whether the primary governing body is the board or the executive committee, it engages in the following operations:

Policy. Recommendations on policy matters typically come to the governing body from committees, task forces, and staff. These may deal with positions on public policy issues and other external questions, as well as with internal policies. Particularly important among the latter are decisions on the association's mission statement, programs, and budgets, because they determine what the organization will do and how it will do it. Other internal policy issues include proposals to adopt new association services or drop old ones, change the dues schedule or other financial policies, and so forth.

Administration. The governing body also selects the chief staff officer (usually on recommendation from a search committee) and determines the individual's salary and benefits. In many organizations, these decisions are made for lower staff positions as well; in others, the C.E.O. makes the decisions regarding subordinates, perhaps after consultation with the chief elected officer or other leaders.

There is a direct relationship between the size of a governing body and its ability to function. Large boards of directors, with more than twenty members, are rarely more than rubber stamps for the executive committee. If the executive committee itself is of unwieldy size, an informal inner circle of some kind will usually be found, generally comprised of the chief elected officer and a few other leaders, some of whom may well be former officers and unelected elder statesmen. About a third of all associations institutionalize the role of these elders through a council of past chief elected officers.

Tribal Elders and Association Cultures

The importance of tribal elders to associations should not be underestimated. Almost every organization has them. Often but by no means always, they are past chairmen held in unusually lofty esteem: It is this high respect that allows them to retain power—sometimes great power.

One such figure was a major force in a professional organization for a great many years. He was almost always on the nominating committee and thus had great say in who the officers would be from year to year. He also exercised considerable influence on policy matters. On one occasion, his opinion was asked about a proposal that had been the subject of months of careful study by a blue-ribbon task force. He advised against the idea, which was thereupon dropped instantly, notwithstanding the extensive preparation it had received. (His opinion might not have been totally disinterested: The matter in question related to a reduction in the size of the board and hence the future power of both the executive committee and the association's elders.)

In a state trade association, the secretary plays a subtler but nonetheless powerful role. An outside attorney on retainer to the association for many years, he handles legal problems and takes minutes of both the board and executive committee meetings, rarely speaking except in answer to direct questions. His influence is exercised through the close personal relationships he has maintained over decades with three successive C.E.O.s and innumerable chief elected officers, as well as through his vast knowledge of where the association's bodies are buried. Highly respected, his advice is often sought and almost invariably taken.

Such elders play an important role in any association. They contribute to organizational continuity and institutional memory. They are a major instrument in the perpetuation of the association's culture and personality.

Institutions definitely have "personalities," just as individuals do. Institutional personalities frame the organization's philosophy, determining both the way the group operates and its outlook on the external environment.

Some organizations, for instance, take a fundamentally ideological approach to public policy issues; others are highly pragmatic. Some groups are loners, preferring to keep their distance from other organizations;

others are quite willing to cooperate with allies and coalitions. Some association boards give wide latitude on policy execution to the staff; others exercise close and detailed supervision.

Such characteristics tend to have long continuity, outlasting the tenure of individual board members and C.E.O.s. Their roots lie in the nature of the association, the characteristics of its membership, the ongoing influence of the elders, and the tendency of boards and nominating committees to choose new directors and officers who share their own values and attitudes.

It can be very difficult, therefore, for an association to alter its style of governance, even when necessitated by changing member values. One veteran association executive has identified three distinct governance styles: authoritarian/autocratic, consultative, and participative.[3]

Authoritarian/autocratic associations are dominated by a relatively small number of individuals who control the board, officerships, and chairmanships among themselves, seldom accepting newcomers to the in-group. Such associations can get away with cliquish governance for a while, if dues are not a major part of their revenue and if the association's activities are not terribly important to the general membership. "It is only when a crisis that demands widespread member action occurs that this group moves in the direction of the consultative association, unless it falls apart completely."[4]

Most contemporary associations are *consultative*. The elected leadership rotates, and new blood is added regularly. Services are significant to the members and adjust to their changing needs. Communications to the membership—electronic, printed, and personal—are frequent, and they help maintain interest and involvement. A broad committee network provides opportunities for member input before decisions are made on policy issues.

Participative associations are a much newer development. They make heavy use of market research and other devices to determine member needs before new services are launched. They actively seek to involve the membership in decisions on policy questions. At least one large national association determines its positions on issues by membership questionnaires and mail ballots instead of by board action.

Changes in social values are gradually pushing association cultures in participative directions. In principle, cultures that have difficulty accepting a high degree of member involvement may find it more agreeable when they see it as a good marketing strategy to increase member loyalty.

There is a hazard here, however. Computer technology and the ability of the staff to influence the results of membership questionnaires through the phrasing of questions can easily manipulate participative techniques to bring the association back full-circle to autocratic control by a small clique of voluntary leaders and top staff.

OFFICERS

Association officers usually serve for one year, although some organizations are moving to two-year terms. Many groups limit the number of continuous terms that officers may serve. Officers may be elected by the full membership or, following the corporate model, by the board of directors. In the case of trade associations, nominating committees usually select a single slate of officers that is almost always ratified. Many individual membership organizations, however, encourage competition for officerships and elections may be hotly contested.

Chief Elected Officer

Most groups use the title of president for their top volunteer officer, although a growing number of trade associations are trending toward the title of chairman of the board. Where the latter title is used, the chief staff official usually receives the title of president.

Regardless of what the principal elected officer is called, he/she has great authority, at least on paper. The office almost always holds the power to appoint all committees and their chairmen; it thereby can influence the policy recommendations that come to the board. Often, however, the top officer consults on these appointments with the C.E.O. and with other elected officers. Moreover, in practice many organizations find it difficult to recruit capable committee chairmen and members, so the appointive power may be reduced to an unfortunate scrounging for people to fill these posts.

The chief elected officer has great visibility with the membership, often spending his term traveling on speaking tours to local membership groups and other constituencies. Frequently, he or she is the association's public spokesman, perhaps sharing this function with the staff chief. The principal officer is generally the immediate supervisor of the C.E.O. and always presides at meetings of the full membership, the board of directors, and usually the executive committee; Occasionally another person, perhaps the immediate past holder of the post, chairs the latter body.

The individuals elected to this position generally have come up through the ranks, serving on important committees and then lesser offices. Many associations provide an office of chairman-elect, president-elect, or first vice president to groom the next top officer. In other organizations, there is a customary and orderly progression over time "through the chairs" from the lowest office up to the highest. Many groups seek to rotate the chief elected office among different regions, constituencies, or factions, to prevent the appearance of domination by any one segment of the association.[5]

Vice Presidents

Sometimes called vice chairmen, these positions may have great power or little. In some associations, the vice presidents represent particular geographic regions or membership segments. In others, each has responsibilities assigned under the by-laws. In still others, they are ex-officio committee chairmen. And in yet other groups, they have functions and responsibilities only if they receive assignments from the chief elected officer. A number of associations have a single vice president; others have a great many, some of whom may even be appointed.

Where chief staff executives carry the title of president, one or more of their principal subordinates may have the vice presidential title.

Other Offices

In smaller associations, the secretary and treasurer exercise the customary responsibilities of those offices—keeping organizational records and minutes of meetings, and tending to finances, respectively. In larger groups, the titles may be almost honorary. If there is a staff of any size, the secretary of the association does almost nothing. Sometimes, the general counsel also bears the title of secretary. In other associations, particularly very large ones, the secretary is a staff position with responsibilities for organizing board meetings and social functions, as well as for the overall care and feeding of individual directors.

The treasurer of larger associations may have little more to do than the secretary. The controller, a staff position, ministers to all the organization's financial affairs on a day-to-day basis. A typical treasurer may chair the association's finance committee (if there is one), meet with the outside auditors, and exercise whatever oversight is feasible, keeping his fingers crossed that nothing serious is getting by him. On the other hand, a treasurer who is knowledgeable about organizational finance can play a truly valuable role, advising the staff controller on technical issues, helping in the formulation of the budget, and particularly in persuading the board to adopt the proposed budget, which is frequently a ticklish issue in many associations.

A few organizations also elect an assistant secretary and assistant treasurer. These titles are generally empty and meaningless. They serve mainly to spread some officerships around for reasons of association politics, not governance.

COMMITTEE STRUCTURE AND PURPOSES

Associations seem absolutely to teem with committee meetings. They are so numerous that jokes about them are legion. In one, association executives debate whether their groups exist primarily to hold meetings or to churn out paper.

The average trade association has nine standing committees and four ad hoc committees. Professional societies and other individual membership groups have somewhat higher average numbers—fourteen standing committees and six ad hoc groups—reflecting both their larger memberships and the desire to involve more members in association policy-making and governance. The average number of members on association committees is nine. The smallest committees average four; the largest twenty.

Apart from the executive and nominating committees used by nearly all associations, the most prevalent committees among trade associations are those dealing with budget and finance, membership, government affairs, convention planning, education, long-range planning, and public relations. Professional groups use the same committees, but the mix differs somewhat: Education and long-range planning are more popular among these individual membership organizations.[6]

Committees are a valuable instrument for any organization too large to solve all its problems in one meeting of a single body. For business associations, though, they can also be costly to administer, and sometimes they seem as much a nuisance as a value. Meetings are expensive, for both the association and the members, and the benefits do not always seem to equate with the cost. In addition, associations find that committees can outlive their usefulness. Many groups are therefore drifting away from permanent or standing committees (occasionally also called councils), in favor of special, temporary, or ad hoc committees (more often called task forces or working groups).

Committees, whether permanent or temporary, exist in business associations to serve several important purposes. They provide a means to:

- Draw together specialists on particular problems or topics from among the membership. Some organizations have concerns that may range from science and technology to finance to marketing. Committees provide means to pull together experts from among the members to advise on such disparate matters.
- Get members more involved in the work of the association. Many individuals and companies prefer to remain relatively passive members of their associations. Others want to become involved in the association's direction and activities. These may become frustrated if an opportunity to do so is not available. Committees provide such opportunities.

- Involve key membership segments or interests. A trade association or chamber of commerce may make an effort, for example, to involve a substantial number of small member-companies on its committees so that these bodies are not dominated by large, active members. A professional group may take pains to assure that a minority interest within its membership is given an opportunity to express its particular viewpoint. Geographic balance is also a key factor taken into account by most associations in appointing committee members.

- Tap into membership opinion. The leadership of any organization, volunteer or staff, must always be concerned about staying in touch with members' views. Association leaders must always be alert lest they lead the parade down Fourth Street while most of the marchers are choosing to turn right on Main. Committees maintain two-way communications with the members on a variety of matters.

- Develop agreement on divisive issues. A broadly-based committee, reflecting all significant points of view within the association, provides a mechanism to work out a consensus on problems that are actually or potentially disruptive.

- Defer decisions on divisive issues. Sometimes, association issues are so heated that time is needed for cool heads to prevail. Naming a committee to study the problem at length is not so much the cynical ploy it may seem. Rather it is a useful device allowing ruffled tempers to calm and a moderate course of action to emerge.

- Motivate and stimulate the membership. An association may have an important need about which the membership is apathetic. Committees can develop and implement programs to raise member consciousness about a problem or issue, raise contributions to a political action committee or the association's foundation, raise support for controversial proposals such as the always touchy matter of a dues increase, or raise hell about a challenge or threat to the association that is being ignored.

- Assist in administration. Committees can aid and advise the board of directors on finance, budget, personnel benefits, communications, education, and a number of other areas in which both association policy and administration are involved. At the same time, they can also assist the staff in its implementation of board decisions.

- Train future leaders. The most frequently followed path to the top in associations is through committee membership and chairmanship, and eventually into the ranks of the officers. Committee service is a prime means by which associations both identify and train tomorrow's leaders.

- Provide peer interchange opportunities. Members have an opportunity to exchange information and expertise that can add an important dimension to a corporate executive's knowledge and skills. The members of association committees frequently gain not only from discussion of the agenda items but also from the opportunity to trade ideas, information, and experiences in the area of their specialty. For that reason, committee membership is frequently considered a valuable asset by both the individuals concerned and their companies.

Few organizations have developed satisfactory alternatives to committees to achieve these purposes. The trick is to assure committee effectiveness by careful selection of chairman and members, thoughtful preparation of meeting agendas and support materials, time-effective and orderly conduct of the meetings, and sound follow-up and execution of committee decisions or recommendations.[7]

In the future, however, associations may be able to employ new technologies (for example, teleconferencing and computer conferencing) to reduce somewhat the number of physical gatherings necessary to transact committee business.

ASSOCIATION POLICY-MAKING

Formal policy-making tends to follow similar procedures among business associations. Whether the question relates to public policy positions, budgeting decisions, authorization of a new program, or any other policy matter, proposals and recommendations work their way up to the executive committee and the board via two interrelated routes: staff and committees.

A proposal may originate on the staff; after research and other preparations, it will come to the attention of the most appropriate committee. Alternatively, a matter may have its origins among committee members, and the staff is asked to research its background and implications before the committee makes a decision. Either way, after an appropriate level of committee consideration and staff work, recommendations are made to the executive committee and/or board of directors, which makes the final policy decisions.

The meshing of staff work and committee consideration is important, because each group approaches the problem from a different perspective. The committee may say, "We can't live with that bill." The staff may respond, "The bill is definitely going to pass whether we like it or not, but there is an opportunity to modify it." Likewise, the staff may say, "This project could bring in a lot of new revenue," but the committee response may be, "The members won't pay extra to participate." This give-and-take strengthens the recommendations that the top policy body is ultimately asked to consider. It is rare for a recommendation to reach the board without the concurrence of both committee and staff. If there is a conflict, the committee view is more likely to prevail.

Once a policy question has been decided, implementation is left largely in staff hands. Even so, some measure of leadership involvement may still be in order, depending on the nature of the matter. A knowledgeable committee member may represent the association as an expert witness at legislative hearings. The chairman of the convention planning committee often has an important role in the convention itself. The members of a committee planning a special revenue project usually are charged personally with raising the money.

Practice, in other words, does not always abide by theory. Staff has a role to play in policy-making, and voluntary leadership has a role to play in implementation.

How to Win at Committee Meetings

Anyone who has ever attended even one committee meeting of any organization—is it conceivable that there is an adult in this country who has not?—quickly realizes that some people are notably successful in swaying the group to their point of view. We observe that these individuals are more articulate and often more forceful than most, but there is frequently more to it than that. They also share other characteristics that are not so readily apparent:

They are well prepared. Having done their homework on the agenda items to be covered, they understand the subject thoroughly. They can cite relevant and persuasive data and background information that others may lack. Knowledge truly is power. One does not gain such knowledge by skimming over meeting documents the evening before or on the flight in.

They know what result they want. Part of their effective preparation is deciding what outcome would be most favorable to their interests or those of their company and then leading the discussion in that direction. This frequently involves getting advance guidance from corporate policymakers and staff experts. To repeat the advice quoted in chapter 3, "Write the minutes *before* you go to the meeting."

They know how to lobby ahead of time. Working with association committee chairmen and staff to help shape the meeting agenda provides a valuable advantage to achieving a desirable decision. Advance orchestration with other committee members likely to share a similar interest in that decision also contributes to success.

They understand how to negotiate. If it is not possible to achieve the optimum decision, there may be several other results that are acceptable. Skill in bargaining and compromise can help assure that the outcome is reasonable and satisfactory, if not ideal. Stubborn insistence on "principle" generally produces resentment that, over the long run, hampers success in committee deliberations.

Informal Policy-making

Policy-making is a complex process—or rather set of processes. Not all policy-making necessarily involves formal decisions on new programs or public policy issues by the board of directors acting on equally formal recommendations by committees or staff. Much policy is made informally on a day-to-day basis:

> When a choice is made concerning the appointment of a committee chairman to provide leadership representation for a particular membership sector, that is a policy decision.
>
> When a West Coast site for a convention or board meeting is selected to recognize the growing importance of Sunbelt members, that is a policy decision.
>
> When a business association begins for the first time to implement an issues position through a coalition with non-business interests, that is a policy decision.
>
> When the staff concludes that it is time to let a program or committee quietly lapse, that is a policy decision.
>
> And when the chief staff executive consciously starts recruiting women and minorities to senior staff positions, that is a policy decision.

There are at least two significant points to be made here. The first is that policy questions generally involve deciding to do important things differently, or for the first time, or to stop doing them. The second is that is that not all policy decisions are made by the board of directors or the voluntary leaders; a great many are also made at the staff level, whether or not they are recognized as policy questions.

This only further underscores the importance of staff in the direction of business associations. Boards and other voluntary leadership bodies are the paramount policy groups in most associations, but the appropriate staff role is far from merely ministerial.

Indeed, a problem for many voluntary leaders flows from a conflict in attitudes concerning staff. On the one hand, boards of directors want the most capable staff management they can obtain and afford to manage the affairs of the organization. On the other, the more capable staff people are, the more likely they are to make administrative decisions on their own that not only implement policy but frequently make it. Walking this high wire is always a difficult problem for the staff. Understanding the nature of the staff's tightrope requires a degree of insight that an unfortunate number of voluntary leaders lack. This is one of the principal factors in association staff turnover.

Another policy dilemma for associations lies in the area of fundamental problem identification and long-term planning. One veteran association executive framed the issue in these words:

> In many organizations, the regular cycle of events—publication deadlines, annual meetings, educational seminars, budget preparation—dominate the staff's

time. . . . In professional societies, the CEO frequently spends his time on regular administrative tasks or on "firefighting." The officers often have tunnel vision and are primarily interested in their term of office. Because leadership and policy responsibilities are divided in most associations between the volunteer leadership and the senior staff, basic issues of some organizations sometimes go unaddressed.[8]

This is a real problem for all kinds of business associations. The long-term planning process outlined in chapter 6 is the best way to attack it. That process can work, however, only when the management staff and the elected voluntary leadership each have both the will and the ability to see past today's crises and tomorrow's budget, in order to grasp the conditions that could fundamentally affect future policy decisions and perhaps the nature of the association itself.

NOTES

1. American Society of Association Executives (ASAE), *Policies and Procedures in Association Management* (Washington: 1987); U.S. Chamber of Commerce, *1989 Survey of Local Chambers of Commerce* (Washington: 1989); and U.S. Chamber of Commerce, *1988 Survey of State Organizations* (Washington: 1988).

2. ASAE, *Policies and Procedures.*

3. Samuel B. Shapiro, "Volunteers Involvement in the Future," chapter 9 of Foundation of the ASAE, *Future Perspectives* (Washington: 1985).

4. *Ibid.*, 105.

5. Useful guidelines for the selection of new directors and chief elected officers will be found in Bernard J. Imming, "Governance: Elected Leaders," chapter 2 of ASAE, *Principles of Association Management* (Washington: 1988).

6. ASAE, *Policies and Procedures.*

7. See also Bernard J. Imming, "Committees and Their Work," chapter 3 of ASAE, *Principles of Association Management.*

8. Henry Ernstthal, "Changing Public Policy," chapter 13 of Foundation of ASAE, *Future Perspectives.*

8

Association Resources: The Staff

The president . . . is leader, educator, wielder of power, pump; he is also office-holder, caretaker, inheritor, consensus seeker, persuader, bottleneck. But he is mostly a mediator.

Clark Kerr

The men and women who direct the staffs of business associations must be masters of many arts. Their days are filled with the concerns and problems of managing everything that the association does and the details of how it does it: educational and economic services, government and public relations, membership, meeting management, publications, personnel and financial matters, routine administration, and crisis management. No two days are ever the same, any more than any two associations are, but the following fictitious case illustrates the kinds of problems that associations and the executives who manage them must deal with on a "typical" day.

A DAY IN THE LIFE OF AN ASSOCIATION EXECUTIVE

Ralph Philips was at his desk at the offices of the Institute of the American Cryoptics Industry at 7:45 am, as usual. As IACI's executive vice president, he had a full day ahead.

He unloaded the reports and reading matter he had taken home the night before into his out-box, a route slip clipped to each item to indicate referral to a staff member, filing, or other disposition.

Then he reviewed the two parts of the day's calendar. One column listed his appointments: 8:30, weekly staff meeting; 9:30, budget review with his controller; 10:00, meeting on plans for the annual convention; lunch with an official of the National Bureau of Standards; 3:00, a conference call with his board chairman and the editor of a trade paper; 6:00, a political fund-raiser for a congressman; and 8:00, dinner with a board member and their wives.

The second part of the calendar noted what he wanted to accomplish that day: nail down the speakers and entertainment program for the annual convention; make a decision on a new education director for the association; review the article list for the next issue of the association magazine; discuss legislative strategy with the government-affairs vice president on a tax bill and an International Trade Commission proceeding; and start on a speech he had agreed to give the following month at a business school seminar.

He reviewed his notes for the staff meeting. Then he spent the half-hour before it started going over his interview notes and the resumes in the file for the education staff opening.

At 8:15, the chairman of the IACI's membership committee was on the telephone. "Ralph, I saw Tom Barton at a party last evening and had a chance to talk with him about bringing his company into IACI. I think I've finally got him talked around, but he needs a favor. He wants to see Senator Brown personally about a problem, but he hasn't been able to get to first base with the Senator's staff. Do you suppose there's anything you could do?" "I wouldn't be surprised if we could help," Philips replied, "but let me look into it. That's really great news, Howard. We've been trying to get Barton's company into the association for three years. You're a super salesman!"

They rang off, and Philips went for another cup of coffee on his way into the conference room. He greeted his staff members as they arrived, inquiring particularly about the magazine editor's wife who had had an operation earlier in the week.

The staff meeting went smoothly as developments of the current week and plans for the next were reviewed. Philips announced the news about the new member. Bill Francora of government relations thought there would be little problem in getting the appointment with Senator Brown, whom they had recently helped on a problem that one of his constituents had been having with an IACI member-company. Francora also said that the hotel in Denver, where they had planned to hold the fall regional legislative conference, was raising its rates over their budget. Muriel Jackson, the convention director, said that the Milton hotel chain had been after her for more IACI business. She offered to see if she could arrange a package deal for the whole series of regional legislative conferences. After discussion of some routine personnel matters—one of the secretaries was going on maternity leave, the receptionist was complaining about the air conditioning again—the meeting adjourned.

Wendy Matsui, the controller, walked back with Philips to his office to discuss the budget for next year. The revenue side looked slightly better than the current year, she said. Dues income seemed likely to be flat, but magazine advertising was rising nicely, and hopes were high that the new convention marketing program would boost both registrations and trade show exhibits. Additional revenues seemed promising from a planned upgrade of the educational program, though principally in future years.

Expenses were projecting a greater increase than income, however. The additional position on Francora's staff for state government relations, the possibility of high relocation costs depending on the choice for education director, and announced price hikes in the staff health plan were all boosting personnel costs. Together with other miscellaneous increases, the first draft of the expense budget projected a 14 percent rise in expenditures against an 8 percent revenue jump. In addition, the capital budget would be up because of the new computer and work stations that had been ordered to replace their old PCs. Matsui promised to come up with a list of possible cost cuts for Philips to prioritize.

She left, passing Muriel Jackson on her way in for the convention plan review. The immediate need was to finalize the list of speakers and entertainment in order to book them for IACI's Chicago convention. A former cabinet member, a new best-selling author, last year's winner of the Nobel Prize for physics, two senators, and a network news anchor were all possibilities for the three general session opening spots. They picked three first choices and turned to the entertainers. "The booking agency says we can get the Thunderbirds for the Wednesday banquet for $10,000 less than Peter Paul Puma because they'll be in town for another group the night before," Jackson said. "Take 'em," Philips told her. "I hate rock groups, but $10,000 is $10,000. Speaking of which, Wendy just poured a little gloom on my desk, so see where else you can shave costs, will you?" Jackson left a draft of the convention workshop schedule with him for later discussion.

After she left, his secretary brought in five message slips for calls from members that had come in that morning. He returned them, sending notes to staffers to handle the problems they had raised. As he prepared to head for his lunch with the standards official, the man called to say that he had just been summoned to a meeting with the bureau director and would have to cancel—not an unusual occurrence with people in government. They rescheduled for the following week. Philips ordered in a sandwich, feeling as though he had just received a gift of time.

He pulled out the resume file again and reviewed his notes on the candidate interviews. The credentials of the two top candidates were about equal on paper, but he felt that one would bring more enthusiasm and ideas than the other. The trouble was that the one he liked best would have to be relocated from the West Coast, while the other was local. He weighed the matter, then decided to offer the job to the Californian. It was the right choice, he felt sure, but Wendy would kill him.

He spent the next few hours working on the legislative matters and his speech, taking a relatively mild barrage of telephone calls as he worked. The creative juices were finally starting to flow when the intercom announced that the conference call was coming in. Sighing, he hit the save button on his terminal and picked up the telephone once again.

He greeted George Anthor, his new board chairman for this year, and Randy Briley, a trade reporter who was doing a profile on IACI and Anthor's plans for his year in office. The interview lasted half an hour. Then Anthor and Philips talked for a few minutes more after Briley rang off. Philips told Anthor about his choice for education director and brought him up to date on a few other matters.

Looking at his watch after the call, he decided that he had better sit down with Francora about the tax bill and the ITC hearing. They discussed strategy at length, until Muriel Jackson burst in: "Did you hear about the Graystone Hotel? There was a huge fire this morning, and they're canceling all bookings, including our convention."

"Have you got your hotel back-up list?" Philips asked. "Good. You take half and I'll take half. Let's see if we can get space elsewhere. It will really louse up the travel discounts we got for the members if we have to change cities. Bill, we'll finish this in the cab on the way to the reception."

Philips and Jackson spent the rest of the afternoon calling hotels in Chicago to try to rebook the convention. It would be another three days before Jackson got alternative space for IACI, and it would cost 5 percent more than they had budgeted.

Philips and Francora arrived at the political fund-raiser twenty minutes late, but had time to talk briefly with the congressional guest of honor and with a couple of administration officials who stopped by.

Afterward, Philips stopped off at the office to call Anthor and the convention committee chairman about the convention hotel problem, packed the unread articles list and a few other items into his briefcase, and walked to the restaurant for dinner with board member Pat Schuster and their wives. Philips' wife, Harriet, had gotten there ahead of him and was entertaining the Schusters when he arrived. The dinner passed pleasantly enough, and they finally arrived home at 11 pm.

Philips spent the next half-hour in a hot bath, reading the articles list for the next magazine issue. Then he went to bed for the six hours of sleep that was generally all he could manage on week nights.

Commentary. Philips' day covers a fairly typical range of concerns: He deals with a membership solicitation opportunity, engaging in favors-trading both to enlist the new member and to solve a problem for him. He handles personnel, administrative, and budgetary problems, finding, as most association executives do, that there is never quite enough money to do what ought to be done.

In planning the association's annual convention, he concerns himself with its substantive content and logistics as well as with the need to give the members a good time and provide other incentives to increase attendance. He relates to top officials and lawmakers to help satisfy the association's government relations and political needs, but finds his schedule at the mercy of theirs.

He is in constant contact with his members, contending with their individual problems as well as the association's and also socializing with them to maintain and strengthen personal relationships. He is responsible for the organization's management, but abides by the "no surprises" principle and keeps his VIPs informed of important developments. He tries to be well-organized, but also must contend with the unexpected when it occurs.

His job, in sum, embodies all that the association does to carry out its mission and to maintain itself.

ROLES OF THE STAFF

"An army marches on its stomach," said Napoleon. In the same sense, business associations travel logistically on their staffs. Under the authority of the board of directors, the staff runs the organization, raises the revenues, solicits memberships, and carries out the organization's policies and programs.

The point is sometimes made that the distinction between staff and elected leadership is often not that clear-cut: Staff also helps make policy, and leaders also help carry it out. Nonetheless, the effectiveness of the staff determines the effectiveness of the organization as a whole.

Although this section treats associations with full-time staffs, it should be noted that some trade and professional groups are operated by commercial firms that specialize in association management. These firms service multiple associations and provide the full range of staff support that each group requires, from financial and meeting management to lobbying. Most of the client associations are small, without the resources to afford a full-time staff. A few, however, are large but have very limited programs. There are, for example, at least three different large associations of IBM users, which provide only a periodic educational conference for their corporate members and lack the other programs to justify a full-time staff. Each is therefore managed on behalf of its members by a firm specializing in this service.[1]

The vast majority of associations, however, have their own full-time, professional staffs. All have executive directors (by whatever title), with varying amounts of authority, responsibility, and compensation. Nearly all have other management and professional staff personnel, from one to hundreds.

Chief Executive Officer

This is the one position found in every organization with a full-time staff. The title differs from association to association: In some groups, the C.E.O is called executive vice president or executive director. Increasingly, the title of president is being adopted, especially in trade associations where the C.E.O is the group's principal public spokesman. The titles of secretary, executive secretary, or managing director are largely antiquated but are still found occasionally. One U.S.-based international association recently brought in a new C.E.O. with the title of director-general, a title more common in Europe than in the United States. In some associations, the staff chief may also be formally designated as the chief executive, operating, or administrative officer.

Whatever the title arrangements may be, the C.E.O. (as we will term the position here) is the focus of the association. He or she is ultimately responsible for membership maintenance and growth, the organization's financial health, and the execution and implementation of all the association's policies, programs, and services.

Association C.E.O.s must be expert managers—knowledgeable about all aspects of the association's activities, proficient in crisis management, and skilled in the motivation and direction of both volunteers and staff subordinates. They must be able to maintain good personal relationships with the membership, other constituencies (external and internal), and particularly the rotating elected leadership. They must have strong leadership and communications skills, but also be able to lead without always being personally on center stage. Yet, if the situation requires it, they must be comfortable in the limelight.

It is not an easy job. Clark Kerr's statement about the leadership roles played by the heads of large academic institutions, quoted above, describes equally well the tasks of association executives.

The staff chief is frequently an ex-officio member of the board of directors and of the executive committee as well. Designation of the chief executive as the official spokesman for the association is increasing in trade associations and chambers, although this role is still widely shared with the top elected officer. More and more large associations are selecting individuals who have had prominent government experience or who are otherwise well-known for their established contacts both in government and with the press. In some cases, this individual is chosen with little concern for his or her managerial ability; internal management then becomes the responsibility of the deputy C.E.O.

The larger the group, the greater the need for an executive who can manage organizational complexity and delegate responsibilities to subordinates. The smaller the organization, the more of a hands-on generalist the C.E.O. must be. In practice, most associations need a staff chief who represents a balance between a one-man band and a management virtuoso; the balance point, however, is different for every association.

Responsibilities. Whether the chief executive is a generalist or heads a vast staff, he/she is directly or ultimately accountable to the board of directors for a wide array of responsibilities. These include:

- *Administration:* Personnel management; finance and budget; data processing; and office administration.

- *Membership:* Marketing programs to retain and expand the membership, including associate members and other special categories.

- *Policy and program implementation:* Government relations; public relations; legal matters, education; convention and other meetings; economic analysis; technical research and standards; and other member services and functions.

- *Information:* Monitoring external, industry, and other developments; communicating that information via conferences, publications, and electronic media.

- *Planning:* Short-term program planning and marketing, as well as long-range planning.

This last activity is perhaps the most important function of the C.E.O. and, at the same time, the one given the least attention. The demands on association executives—for maintenance of the organization and for delivery of current programs and services—are so great that it becomes exceedingly difficult to focus on the long-term changes affecting the future of the association and its membership. Yet, assuring the future of the organization is a prime responsibility of any chief executive, regardless of the group's nature and purpose. (See chapter 13.)

Staff Organization. Structuring these functions in the most effective and efficient manner, particularly in the area of management control, seems to be a difficult problem for many associations. Business associations have always emulated the structure and job titles of the U.S. corporations that they represent (directly or indirectly) and that have long been considered the models of effective organization. At the same time, association executives must manage a large and varied range of activities with a relatively small number of personnel.

Association C.E.O.s have commonly dealt with this issue through multiple tiers of management. The workable span of direct supervision is widely considered to be six to ten subordinates. Many mid-sized associations, however, have a staff structure of four tiers, or even more.

As one association C.E.O. has noted, "Associations often have more layers of management for their size than any other type of organization. Two of the major reasons for this may be the willingness of associations to grant expanded titles more rapidly than pay increases and the fact that even relatively small associations may need a variety of specialists in order to serve their members."[2] As associations face increasing revenue crunches, organizational charts will need to be tightened up in ways that do minimum damage to the delivery of priority association services.

Association staffs are most commonly structured by a combination of function and process: Government relations people are in one department, publications or communications in another, administration in a third, convention and meeting arrangements in a fourth, and so on. There are variations, however.

A common approach is decentralization. Some decentralize certain process responsibilities, whereby each department issues its own publications, organizes its own meetings, and so forth. This gives considerable latitude and autonomy to staff units and departments, but undoubtedly boosts the number of employees. Many national and international associations (about one in six) have regional offices. A number of these are geographically decentralized with the regional offices responsible for all programs and services for members in their jurisdictions.

An association may also be decentralized even though its staff is based at a single location. Some associations with multiple sub-interests within the membership focus most, or even all, programs and services for a particular membership sector within a staff group dedicated exclusively to its needs. The small business members of many larger associations frequently benefit from this approach. The political benefits of special treatment for sensitive constituencies are believed to outweigh the higher costs. Some very large trade associations consist of several self-supporting divisions with a policy coordinating staff at the top; each of these divisions is a virtual industry association by itself.

These decentralized forms work well when objectives other than cost-effectiveness need to be served. However, associations confronted with reduced revenues may find that they must convert to more centralized forms, particularly as corporate mergers reduce the number of members to be served. Centralization can also facilitate the development of comprehensive marketing programs.

In smaller associations, staff organization is structured with far less formality and complexity. So many functions have to be performed by relatively few people that some individuals may have several supervisors, depending on which hat they are wearing that day. Many of these groups, nonetheless, tend to maintain a staff size needed only at peak times, such as convention periods. An alternative suggested by one expert "is to develop a strong cadre of managers who have the ability to supervise a changing number of part-time workers and consultants, rather than staffing up for peak periods or emergencies."[3]

Compensation. C.E.O. compensation is very much a function of association size and scope, but also reflects the characteristics of the membership. Trade associations in some industries pay their association executives more than others do, manufacturing being the most generous and construction the least. On the average, the staff chiefs of professional societies are paid about 80 percent as much as their trade association counterparts. Perhaps predictably, C.E.O.s of individual membership groups in financial fields are the best paid, on average, while those in social welfare are paid the least.

The general rule for any comparable group of associations, however, is that the larger the staff and budget, the more the C.E.O. is paid.

The median salary (including bonuses) for all association chief executives in 1988 was $75,900, a 7 percent increase over 1987; for the deputy staff chief, $54,000. Once again, medians disguise a broad compensation range. For associations with budgets of $200,000 or less, the median C.E.O. pay was under $36,000. For groups with budgets over $10 million, the median was $160,000. National and international associations pay better than state groups, with local association executives the least well paid (by a ratio of 8:5:4, respectively).

The highest paying associations are located in the metropolitan areas of Washington, New York, Chicago, Houston, and Atlanta—cities with concentrations of national organizations. The least well-paying groups are in the metropolitan areas of Portland, Nashville, Phoenix, Des Moines, and Harrisburg; these are all primarily state association headquarters communities.

On the average, state chamber of commerce C.E.O.s are better paid than state association chiefs, by a ratio of about two to one. The state chamber range is from $50,000 to $165,000, with an average pay of $86,000.

Among the largest local chambers, median pay is $125,000, with a high of $180,000 and a low of $66,000. Among the smallest, the median is $14,000, with a high of $23,000 and a low of $6,500! The overall average is about $35,000, a bit less than local association executives.

Authority. Normally, the board of directors (or other designated leadership body) determines the budget for the organization. Within that budget, the C.E.O. of any organization should have authority to hire and fire staff, and to determine salaries for individual positions. It is surprising, however, how often association chief executives lack that authority. Almost half the time, individual salaries are determined by a leadership body, not by the C.E.O. About a quarter of all associations deny the staff chief ultimate hire-and-fire authority—hardly an indication of a well-run organization.

Experienced association executives nail this issue down during their hiring negotiations. Yet even when a new executive's authority seems to be firmly set, problems can arise. One executive, shortly after taking the helm of her association, decided that a member of the staff would have to be replaced. Shortly after giving notice to the staffer, she received a call from a powerful member of the board who pressured her strongly to retain the individual. Knowing that her authority and ability to function were being severely tested, she held firm in her decision to discharge the staffer. Her board backed her up, but she was never able thereafter to establish a good relationship with that board member. Despite the potential problems with the staffer's political sponsor, the C.E.O. who allows such situations to continue is inviting permanent trouble.

It is not at all uncommon in loosely managed associations for mid-level staff personnel to develop a protected relationship with an important patron. After all, personal friendships often arise when people work closely together. It is when the patron on the board and the staff protege carry friendship to the point of interference with management prerogatives that problems arise.

Sometimes, though, a weak C.E.O. invites problems. An illustration of how this can happen is provided by a non-profit organization that was directed by an individual highly respected for his professional expertise but with little management ability. The group, which he had founded, grew rapidly as a result of the innovative programs he developed and the esteem in which he was held in the field.

After a few years, the organization became over-extended and financial and personnel problems developed. Growing fearful for his job, the C.E.O. began to allow board members to meddle in internal matters, which some of them did repeatedly. Several staff members took advantage of the situation, going around the C.E.O. to lobby board members directly on their personal concerns and complaints, and to advance their personal interests. As the situation worsened, the personal relationships between board members and their staff proteges went well beyond mere friendship in at least two instances.

The group's finances also continued to decline. These problems were resolved only when the organization was placed in voluntary bankruptcy and went out of existence. The demise of a valuable institution was a consequence for which the C.E.O., some of his subordinates, and the board of directors all shared in the blame. Granted that this was an extreme situation, it nonetheless indicates what can happen when staff executives fail to manage their organizations, personnel, and board relationships properly.

Background and Tenure. Most association staff chiefs come to their posts with association experience, either in their present association or from another one. About one in five comes from a position in government or education. Similarly, only a fifth have had direct experience in private industry.

Association C.E.O.s have occupied their positions for an average of six to nine years. Long tenure is unusual; only 16 percent have held their posts for fifteen years or more. These are difficult jobs, because they are intensely political and very dependent on personal relationships and the goodwill of boards of directors. While some C.E.O.s are discharged for poor management, most of the departures are for essentially political reasons: Boards and elected leaders rotate, and executives may not have as good a relationship with the new group of leaders as they did with those who hired them. Some associations simply tire of old faces and styles, and choose from time to time to bring in new ones. In one large national association, in which the chief staff employee shares executive responsibilities with the chief elected officer, the top staff post is virtually a revolving door.

Very few association executives have formal employment contracts, and outplacement service is unusual. Severance arrangements vary wildly. In an industry with a number of state associations, three C.E.O.s left in a single summer. One highly regarded individual who had been with his association for ten years departed with three-weeks pay. The second got none, and yet, the third received salary for seven months after he left.

Whether severance is voluntary or involuntary, annual employee turnover is high on association staffs—about 20 to 25 percent on the average. Various causes account for this situation, some general to associations and some particular to each individual group. It is not a healthy pattern.

The chief staff executive of a well-managed association must have both the authority and the will to recruit and retain a competent staff, compensating its employees (in hard dollars and benefits as well as intangibles) to maximize staff tenure and organizational continuity.

Other Management Staff Positions

Despite the diversity of associations, there is considerable uniformity in their professional staff positions. Almost all have managers responsible for administration, finance, membership, meetings, publications, government relations, and so on, although associations often combine several functions in one individual. Small associations will have only a few of the positions described below, while the largest groups may have dozens or even hundreds of additional employees. Those listed include the positions found most often. They also describe the staff functions that associations must carry out in one way or another.

Titles for similar or even identical positions differ from organization to organization. Those used here are at the director level. In many associations some or all of these individuals may be managers, and in others vice presidents.

Average 1988 total compensation is indicated for each position: Salaries actually range widely, according to variables similar to those described for C.E.O.s In general, salaries in professional societies and chambers of commerce are lower than those in trade associations of comparable size.[4]

Director of Administration. Also called *Business Manager* in some groups. Manages office, personnel, and support services. May also be responsible for finance, if there is no separate controller. Average compensation: $40,500.

Communications/Publications Director. Responsible for association publications, such as magazines, newsletters, or newspapers, and perhaps for non-periodical publications. Average compensation: $38,000.

Controller. Manages all association financial matters, including records and reports. May supervise data processing activities, and analyze systems and procedures. Average compensation: $39,300.

Conventions and Meetings Director. Responsible for all logistics of association conventions, conferences, and other meetings, including on-site arrangements, and often programming and/or promotion. Average compensation: $36,200.

Education Director. Manages educational programs of the association, whether for members or the public. Average compensation: $40,800.

Government Relations Director. Manages legislative and regulatory relations programs, maintaining contacts with appropriate officials. Analyzes and reports on issues. May also be called *Public Affairs Director,* with or without public relations responsibilities. Average compensation: $54,700 and rising rapidly (13 percent up from the 1987 level), indicating increasing association priority for this activity.

Public Relations Director. Responsible for publicity, promotion, and media relationships. May share responsibilities with *Communications/Publications Director* in some associations or be the same individual in others. May also be called *Public Affairs Director,* with or without government relations responsibilities. Average compensation: $41,500.

Membership Director. Manages programs to maintain current members and bring in new ones. Average compensation: $34,300.

Member Services Director. Administers service programs for members and develops new services as needed. Average compensation: $38,300.

Marketing Director. Manages association's marketing programs, including market research and other services to expand industry markets. Average compensation: $42,200. Separate positions include *Advertising Director,* who has charge of advertising placement and programs in nonassociation publications (average compensation: $39,400) and *Advertising Sales Director,* who is responsible for sales in the association's own publications (average compensation: $37,200).

Technical Director. Likely to be a specialist in a relevant technical field in the association's industry or profession. Responsible for association technical programs. Average compensation: $52,300. A related but separate position is Research Director, who is responsible for technical research (average compensation: $51,100). A still different post is *Information Director,* who administers the association's library and technical information services (average compensation: $39,600).

Chief Staff Attorney. This is a staff position, not to be confused with outside lawyers. Responsible for staff legal matters. May or may not be association *General Counsel.* May or may not also act as *Government Relations Director.* Average compensation: $63,700.

Other association staff positions may include:

· Chapter relations director

· Chief economist (new position for many groups)

· Consumer affairs director (declining in use)

· Field staff director

· Foundation director

· Human resources (or personnel) director

· Regional office manager ⎫
· Washington office director ⎭ for associations based elsewhere

Chambers of commerce have many of these same staff positions, along with directors or managers in such areas as:

· Economic development

· Community development

· Convention and visitor programs

· Transportation programs

· Retail/downtown services

· Small business

· Agricultural affairs

· International affairs

Personnel Policies

The amount of paid vacation, sick leave, and holidays that associations grant their employees annually is fairly standard—about nine or ten days a year in each category. About two-thirds of associations have retirement programs, most of them funded entirely by the organization. The large number that do not provide a pension program may be one of the causes of high staff turnover. On the other hand, one association in eight has an Individual Retirement Account (IRA) program, and one in six offers a "401-k" plan, a tax-deductible contributory retirement program.

Benefits for management employees are fairly broad, though far from uniform: 80 percent of associations provide paid life and over 90 percent paid health insurance; more than 40 percent offer paid dental insurance, while two-thirds pay for accidental death insurance and over 60 percent offer paid disability income insurance. Chief staff executives may also receive additional benefits, ranging from cars and club memberships to financial planning and tax services. These are provided for other management employees far less frequently.

As a general rule, the larger the association, the more likely it is to offer employees a broad program of benefits. Much the same pattern occurs among state and local chambers of commerce.

THE CHALLENGES AND SATISFACTIONS OF ASSOCIATION WORK

Association members often ask staff personnel why they have chosen that line of work. After all, the salaries and benefits are hardly lavish. There may be considerable job security with some associations but little in others, especially if changes at the top produce upheavals below. While many organizations are well-managed, others can be intensely political. Pressures may be great and hours long, particularly in such peak periods as the time preceding and during major meetings or when important issues are reaching climactic stages.

Association management as a profession offers a variety of offsetting satisfactions, however. For one thing, association work provides numerous opportunities to bring people and groups together in an effort to solve common problems. Staff people often play a mediating role and achieve considerable personal leverage in such problem-solving. Association management resembles public service in that it offers opportunities to make a significant impact in such areas as government relations, education, and standards development, among many others. There is considerable pleasure in seeing the results of one's efforts reflected in the shape of a public law or some other product of association activity.

More than in most other businesses, association management can provide opportunities to learn and apply a wide range of skills and management techniques in a fairly short space of time. The kinds of problems that the men and women on association staffs work on are frequently broader than the concerns of many corporate managers. These advantages frequently appeal to young people, including those who find the field useful preparation for a later career in business, but also those who believe they might not find as much latitude in a business setting. They also profit from the personal visibility and wide range of personal contacts that association personnel can develop.

Moreover, association service often provides considerable interaction with very senior corporate ex∩cutives and government policymakers. It is stimulating to assist and advise such people on major matters.

Some of these benefits are evident in an amusing experience that an employee of a large association once had. As the principal staff person for a significant policy area, he was in frequent contact with an important member, a top executive of a major corporation, who chaired a committee of the association and served on its board of directors. One day, the staffer got an idea for an association project that would have substantial impact on its policy concerns. He discussed it with the committee chairman.

The VIP liked the idea immediately and urged the staff member to propose it to the association's C.E.O., the executive vice president. "I told him it would have more impact if the proposal came from him," the staffer recalls.

"All right, draft it for me, and I'll send it to him on my letterhead," was the committee chairman's response.

A week later, the staff member got a call from his boss: "I just got a letter from Mr. X, with a proposal for a new project. Do you know anything about it?"

"Yes sir," the employee responded. "We've discussed it, and I think it's a fine idea."

"So do I," his boss said. "Write me up a reply I can send him, will you?"

For several weeks thereafter, the staffer continued to write letters back and forth to himself, as the correspondence between the association's executive vice president and the committee chairman worked out the project details. The project was subsequently approved by the board and proved quite successful.

Such are the peculiar pleasures of association work.

NOTES

1. An interesting collection of articles appears in: American Society of Association Executives (ASAE) and Institute of Association Management Companies, *Selecting among Association Management Options* (Washington: 1987).

2. Lee VanBremen, "Staff Organization", chapter 4 of ASAE, *Principles of Association Management* (Washington: 1988).

3. Ibid.

4. For further details, see ASAE, *Association Executive, Compensation Study,* and U.S. Chamber of Commerce, *Surveys of State and Local Organizations* (Washington: 1988, 1989).

9

The Law of Associations

Extreme law is often extreme injustice.

Terence

Ignorance of the law excuses no man.

John Selden

Business associations are subject to a wide range of federal and state statutes, regulation, and case law. These cover antitrust and trade regulation, taxation, lobbying and political activities, and specific association economic services. Laws also govern the organization of associations.

This chapter broadly addresses the principal legal concerns to which all those involved in associations—executives, leaders, and members—need to be keenly sensitive. It should be noted that this discussion is not intended to offer legal advice nor is it a substitute for various comprehensive works on association law authored by legal experts in the field.[1]

ANTITRUST LAW

As noted in chapter 2, the history of business associations, both in the United States and abroad, teems with illustrations of the proclivity of business groups to allocate markets, control production, and regulate prices through agreements among competitors. This is no recent development, as Adam Smith pointed out in his famous observation about business conspiracies and price fixing over two centuries ago.

Laws and Enforcement

In the United States, a series of federal laws, enacted over a fifty-year period beginning in 1887, prohibited such activities. These laws included:

> *The Interstate Commerce Act* (1887), which commenced federal regulation of the transportation and communications industries.
>
> *The Sherman Antitrust Act* (1890), which banned monopolies and combinations in restraint of interstate commerce.
>
> *The Clayton Antitrust Act* (1914), which forbade discriminatory pricing and related arrangements.
>
> *The Federal Trade Commission Act* (1914), which outlawed unfair or deceptive acts, practices, and methods of competition.
>
> *The Robinson-Patman Act* (1936), which tightened the prohibitions against price discrimination and related trade allowances.

These statutes have been progressively strengthened over the years by case law—court decisions in individual cases interpreting legislative acts—and through state antitrust laws.

At the federal level, antitrust enforcement is shared by the Federal Trade Commission and the Antitrust Division of the Department of Justice. State attorneys general typically enforce their jurisdictions' own antitrust laws. Federal criminal penalties for violations are severe: Individuals may be fined up to $100,000 and jailed for as much as three years. Corporations and associations can receive fines to a maximum of $1 million. Civil suits by those injured as a result of antitrust violations can result in awards of up to three times the actual damages. Although enforcement of the antitrust laws can be rigorous or spotty, depending on the philosophy of the administration in power at any given time, the law has sharp teeth in powerful jaws.

Areas of General Association Exposure

It is mainly the economic programs and functions of business associations that contribute to antitrust problems. To the extent that they fall under constitutionally protected freedom of speech, lobbying and other political activities are immune from antitrust concerns. The courts have held that constitutional guarantees take precedence over antitrust requirements, which are merely statutory. Thus, association members are free to adopt joint legislative positions or courses of political action without fear of antitrust prosecution because of their concerted actions.

This protection is not likely to apply to most association economic services. By definition, business associations are voluntary organizations of individuals or companies that are in competition with each other. These competitors come together at official association functions and receive a stream of information affecting their businesses from the organization's programs and services. Thus there is always a risk of actions that could run afoul of the antitrust laws.

Generally speaking, therefore, business associations should be wary of any activity that could appear to restrain competition, give advantages to one group of competitors over another, boycott suppliers or customers, control production or markets, or provide information in ways that could look like attempts to fix prices or to regulate trade and commerce. Note that it is not only actions like these that are illegal, but also conspiracies to commit such actions. Because competitors routinely gather under association auspices for formal and informal discussions, business organizations, like Caesar's wife, must avoid even the appearance of possible wrong-doing.

Business associations are vulnerable to the antitrust laws, both for the actions of the organization itself and for those committed by its members under association auspices. Moreover, an important 1982 Supreme Court decision held an association liable for the acts of members and junior staff personnel, even though the group's leadership had neither approved the actions nor even known of them.[2]

Special care must be taken at association meetings of any kind to be sure that no improper discussions take place.[3] For that reason, it is important that an attorney be present at many official meetings of the organization and, depending on the nature of the group, perhaps at all its gatherings. Even if a lawyer is not in attendance, both members and staff should be vigilant, lest even innocent discussions edge too close to the line. Most association executives can recall incidents when staff personnel acted to end a discussion, or even a meeting, when comments moved toward dangerous waters.

This is not to say that associations or their members should be paralyzed in fear of possible antitrust prosecution. With some notable exceptions, it is not so much what associations do as how they do it that can raise antitrust concerns. They need to be sensitive to potential problem areas and to get competent legal advice about which approaches are safe and which may be risky.

Many companies have adopted antitrust compliance programs. The adoption and publication of a similar program is a prudent course of action that many business associations have chosen to take. Antitrust compliance statements commonly include not only a clear statement of the policy that all those involved in the organization—staff, voluntary leaders, and members—abide by the antitrust laws, but also enumerate specifically banned actions in those areas that may be particularly sensitive for the association. These certainly include a prohibition of any discussion or treatment of pricing if there is any risk whatever that it could be construed as directly or indirectly promoting price-fixing.

Furthermore, the publication of a compliance statement is not sufficient by itself. A program of continuing education and consciousness raising for everyone affiliated with the organization is a vital supplement to the antitrust compliance policy.

Areas of Specific Association Exposure

Listed below are some significant areas of association involvement about which antitrust concerns could arise.

Membership. Membership in the association should be broadly attractive to all those who fall within the stated parameters of the association. An association of Wyoming retail furniture salespeople must normally be open to all individuals in the state who sell furniture to consumers. It need not accept members from Colorado unless they also work in Wyoming, nor those who sell clothing or computers. It might have to take in salespeople of, say, household appliances, if the effect of membership restriction would be to give a competitive advantage to some salespersons over others. The same would be true if the association chose to admit those who sell for furniture manufacturers as associate members or in some other classification.

The general rule is that associations cannot *unreasonably* deny or restrict membership to those who compete with the organization's members and who meet reasonable association requirements. The association should seek to foster competition, not restrain it in any way.

Many associations divide their membership into sections or classes, depending on interests and other characteristics. The same general rules of reasonableness apply to such section memberships.

Since almost every association seeks the largest possible membership in order to broaden its base and its dues revenues, these requirements seldom present real difficulties in practice. At the same time, associations are voluntary organizations. While membership must be open to all who qualify, the organization cannot compel membership nor try to penalize those who choose not to join.

Services to Non-Members. Association services must be available on request to non-members as well as to members, but reasonably higher fees or charges are legitimate so long as they do not have the effect of compelling membership. Non-members who wish to purchase association publications, for example, can be charged more than the members pay. As a practical matter, most associations use such price differentials as an inducement to membership, marketing the attractiveness of their services, publications, and meetings to highlight the benefits of membership.

If a service offered by the organization—such as a trade show, a group purchasing program, or the findings of an important research study—would give a competitive advantage to those who obtained it, non-members cannot be barred from access. Such a ban would not only have antitrust implications but could also result in the loss of tax-exempt status.

Codes of Conduct. Many trade and professional associations have adopted codes of ethical behavior, professional conduct, fair business practices, industry self-regulation, and so forth. Well over half of associations have some kind of code, and two-thirds of these codes include an enforcement mechanism.[4] Such programs are considered legitimate even if they contain sanctions against violations, provided that the effects of the code or program are not anti-competitive and are carried out under fair and stated procedures. For instance, a professional society's code can bar false and misleading advertising, but cannot bar practitioners' advertising in general. A few associations, notably stock exchanges and other groups in the securities industry, have stringent codes and disciplinary measures that have been granted by law under the supervision of a government agency; they can therefore take actions not normally available to other business associations.

Statistical Surveys and Programs. A great many associations conduct surveys and studies within their industries, professions, or communities to compile economic data of interest to their members—for example, costs, production, sales, wages and salaries, personnel and other policies. Frequently, the results of such studies are used as benchmarks against which individual companies or professionals can measure their own performance. These services are considered wholly legitimate, provided that they are not intended or operated as anti-competitive devices.

The surveys are intended to collect and disseminate economically useful information that would not have anti-competitive effects. Participation in them must be voluntary. The confidentiality of individual submissions is imperative. For that reason, some associations retain an accounting or management consulting firm to receive and compile the data. It is safer to seek historical data rather than future or projected information, avoiding the subject of pricing altogether if at all possible. The study results should not be presented or discussed in a way that might appear to urge competitors to take a common course of action.

Distribution of statistical compilations can be restricted to only those who contributed data, but if the results are made available to non-participants, then they must also be available to non-members of the association.

Many associations also provide their members with statistics compiled and published by federal, state, or local governments. These are in the public domain, of course, and available to anyone.

Research Projects. Research conducted by associations to ascertain members' policies and practices in particular fields resemble the statistical programs discussed above and are subject to much the same guidelines.

However, many business groups also sponsor or undertake joint research projects to develop technical standards, for instance, or to examine such common concerns as pollution, product or workplace safety, raw material or energy utilization, and so forth. Sometimes the association uses its own research facilities or commissions an academic or other third-party institution. Often members agree to pool research results of projects they have conducted internally.

Government agencies have published guidelines regarding the antitrust implications of joint research.[5] Public policy generally condones and promotes joint research if the effects are not anti-competitive. Some restrictions apply with respect to patents and licensing, however. In addition, Congress has granted broader antitrust exemptions for cooperative research and development among companies and by associations to promote national security and the international competitiveness of American industry.

Standardization, Simplification, and Certification. Association programs to develop voluntary standards for products and services are widespread. So are simplification programs that seek to reduce the proliferation of products or services. Provided that these programs are not used to control prices, restrict competition, or deceive customers, they have few antitrust implications. They should be operated under stated and fair procedures, and compliance must be voluntary. Associations may also engage in programs that certify products or services based on established standards, provided they are fair, objective, and avoid anti-competitive elements.

Group Purchasing and Sales. Many associations sponsor cooperative programs to take advantage of volume discounts for the purchase of goods and services. Access to these services must be broadly available to both members and non-members that compete with each other; legal bars to price discrimination apply.

The same requirements apply to group selling programs. These activities must avoid market allocation or price-fixing. Some special antitrust exemptions, however, may benefit associations promoting exports to other countries under the Webb-Pomerene Act of 1918 or the Export Trading Company Act of 1982.

This is by no means an exhaustive survey of association activities that are subject to antitrust considerations. Professional and trade associations often engage in programs to certify the competency credentials of individual practitioners or to accredit institutions. Local chambers sometimes provide joint credit reporting services. These and other services of business associations must be carried out in ways that do not restrict competition, promote boycotts, or otherwise transgress the purposes of the antitrust laws.

As this brief summary indicates, the law of antitrust and trade regulation is exceedingly complex. The safest rule on all these matters is, if in doubt (and even if not), consult a knowledgeable and competent attorney before acting.

TAX LAW AND REGULATION

Business associations generally fall into one of three classes, according to their income tax status:

Associations eligible for tax-exempt status as "business leagues" under Section 501(c) (6) of the Internal Revenue Code. Two-thirds of trade associations and just under half of professional groups fall into this class.[6] Association executives often refer to "c-6 organizations" as a shorthand description for groups organized as business leagues, an archaic term used today only in discussions of tax status.

Scientific, charitable, educational, and other such organizations, which are not only tax-exempt but which may also receive tax-deductible contributions under Section 501 (c) (3) of the code. About a third of professional societies and a fifth of trade associations are so classified.[7] In addition, many associations have organized foundations or similar "c-3" affiliated bodies to fund activities under more favorable tax treatment than the parent association would enjoy.

Associations that are not tax-exempt and that must pay taxes on their income, just as any other business enterprise must do. Only 4 percent of associations are in this category. Another 8 percent or so are in various other tax classes. About a fifth of trade and professional associations have organized for-profit subsidiaries whose income is taxable.[8]

Business Leagues

To qualify as "business leagues," associations must meet several requirements: They must be not-for-profit organizations, whose members have a common business interest that the association exists to promote and serve, through activities devoted to the improvement of at least one line of business.

The line-of-business requirement has been construed to mean that the association's services must be available to both members and non-members, but this rule may not be iron-clad. The non-profit requirement forbids any private benefit to members from association income. For instance, there can be no payment of anything resembling dividends or dues rebates. It also means that the group's income must be related to its principal purposes in order to be tax-exempt.

This latter requirement is particularly tricky for almost every business association. Income unrelated to the principal purposes is considered taxable. Moreover, the association can lose its tax exemption altogether if the activities generating unrelated income become a principal source of the group's revenue. There have been cases in which tax-exempt status was denied because more than half of the organization's income was from unrelated sources. This is not, however, a safe guide on which to rely.

Unrelated income is revenue from regularly conducted business activities not connected with the association's primary purposes. Which income sources are related or unrelated will obviously depend on each association's particular purposes and operations, but there are some general categories:

Cooperative Selling and Purchasing. Income from these activities is commonly regarded as unrelated, unless the activities are incidental or quite minor.

Credit Programs. Credit reporting or collection services operated by associations are generally viewed as unrelated activities.

Insurance Programs. If the association derives substantial income from group insurance programs, the income is probably taxable.

Labor Relations. Programs serving the industry are usually tax-exempt activities, but those benefiting only particular members are not.

Lobbying and Political Activities. Direct lobbying on issues that affect the membership is completely tax-exempt, as are the costs of legislative and political communications to members. Grass-roots lobbying to stimulate members to contact their legislators on particular issues is a gray area. While the association itself may not be directly affected, members are not allowed to deduct the portion of dues that finances grass-roots lobbying if it is a substantial activity of the association.

Political contributions are not tax-deductible. In any event, associations are not permitted to make political contributions in federal elections if the associations are incorporated (as virtually all are). Different rules apply in some state elections, however.

Publications. If revenue from advertising and circulation (for example, subscriptions) in a periodical or other regularly issued publication exceeds production costs, the net is normally considered unrelated income. Note that there are very complex ramifications to this apparently simple rule.

Advertising placed by the association to promote the industry or profession as a whole is probably related. If individual members are named or otherwise benefit, however, it is probably unrelated.

Real Estate. Many associations often choose to own their own buildings rather than lease office space. If the building is used to house the group's primary functions, its tax status is not likely to be questioned. If, however, the bulk of the space is rented out or otherwise used to produce income, the income could be considered unrelated and capital gains taxes could be levied when the building is eventually sold. There could be additional complications if the organization borrowed to finance all or part of the purchase price for income-producing property.

Research, Testing, and Certification. If these services are available to the entire industry or profession, they are generally tax-exempt, but not if they are restricted to the association's members only.

Trade Shows. Expositions conducted as part of the association's convention to promote interest in the industry's products or services are considered related activities. Income from them is normally tax-exempt, as is income from the convention itself.

Charitable and Educational Organizations

Associations organized under Section 501(c) (3) have a more favorable tax status than "c-6" business leagues. They may solicit and receive tax-deductible contributions, sometimes benefit from lower postal rates, and be exempt in some states from the real estate and sales taxes that "c-6" groups usually must pay. However, "c-3" organizations must meet more stringent requirements than "c-6" business leagues. They must be organized for public benefit and not the private interests of their members. Unrelated income must be only a minor revenue source. Lobbying activities must be insignificant, and political activity is forbidden. Transgressions of these requirements can result in a change of tax status from "c-3" to "c-6," or even the complete loss of tax exemption.

Many "c-6" associations have established affiliated foundations with "c-3" tax status. A fifth of trade associations and twice that number of professional associations have done so. Education and research are the most common purposes of such foundations, which must make their services available to the public, not just the association's members.[9]

Taxable Associations and Subsidiaries

A small percentage of business associations have lost tax-exempt status or may never have had it in the first place. In most cases, this situation exists because the income of these groups was obtained primarily from unrelated activities. One tax-paying association, for example, derives most of its revenues from advertising in a monthly publication, and less than 5 percent from membership dues.

To protect their tax-exempt status, almost one-fifth of trade and professional associations have established for-profit subsidiary corporations. These engage in income-producing activities that would probably be considered unrelated if they were carried out by the non-profit parent. Insurance, publishing, and data processing are typical functions of these subsidiaries.

The financial benefit to the parent association from its subsidiary's profits can come through several avenues. Frequently, a portion of the association's overhead can be allocated to the subsidiary. The subsidiary can also pay a management or other fee for time and services provided by the parent's staff personnel. Dividends or royalties may also be paid in some cases. In several instances, the for-profit company has been completely spun off from the association, while continuing to provide services to the group's members and perhaps other clients.[10]

LAWS GOVERNING LOBBYING AND POLITICAL ACTIVITIES

Since lobbying and government relations are the most important functions that business associations perform (as discussed in chapter 5), it is important to be familiar with the laws governing these activities. Pertinent laws also concern the political involvement of associations.

The most important point about lobbying is that there are no restrictions on the right of any organization to communicate with federal or state legislators or any other group of policymakers to express opinions on any public issue. The right to lobby is protected as freedom of speech under the United States Constitution and hence takes precedence over any statute or regulation.

The law makes a distinction, however, between the right to lobby and the tax treatment of the funds used to do so. As noted above, for instance, 501(c) (3) organizations may not use a substantial portion of their tax-exempt income for lobbying. There are also some restrictions on the use of public money (such as from government contracts and grants) for lobbying purposes.

The laws regulating lobbying do not limit that activity but do require record-keeping and the public disclosure of certain information related to lobbying activities.

Federal law in this area applies only to lobbying members of Congress and to presidential and congressional elections. A wide range of state and local laws governs lobbying and political action within their jurisdictions.

Lobbying Requirements

Laws governing direct lobbying cover two areas—registration and reporting. Many differences exist between federal and state treatment of these matters.

Federal Regulation. Although Congress enacted a comprehensive lobbying law, very little of it was left after a 1954 Supreme Court decision; the remainder is feeble. Direct lobbying is narrowly defined as contacts with members of Congress concerning legislative issues. Contacts with legislative staff and the entire executive branch, testimony at hearings, and grass-roots lobbying all fall outside the purview of the law.

Associations and other organizations are required to register if direct lobbying is their "principal purpose." Many groups argue that their principal purposes lie elsewhere—member information and education, the spectrum of economic services, and so forth. Relatively few of these actually register. Umbrella organizations and other associations that engage in extensive lobbying generally do register, as should any group that might feel embarrassed if asked publicly why it has not. If in doubt, the safe course is registration. The burdens associated with registration are hardly onerous.

Individual lobbyists who meet the "principal purpose" requirement are required to register if they receive compensation to lobby, either as employees or as retained lobbyists.

Associations and their employees who register are required to file periodic financial reports on their activities with certain officials of Congress. These offices are merely receptacles for such reports, which are rarely if ever audited.

Quite another matter, however, are the federal laws governing lobbying by foreign agents (that is, lobbyists for foreign governments), former executive branch officials, and organizations with federal grants or contracts. These laws are more stringent and enforced, often with considerable publicity. Former Reagan White House aides Michael Deaver and Lyn Nofziger were convicted of transgressing the restrictions against lobbying by previous members of the executive branch. (Nofziger's conviction was overturned on appeal because of the law's vagueness, a decision that may discourage future prosecutions.)

So-called "ethics legislation" to broaden certain federal lobbying requirements, among other matters, has been endorsed by President Bush and important members of Congress. It may be enacted in the early 1990s.

State Regulation. Each state has its own lobbying registration and reporting requirements, no two of them quite alike. In addition, many local governments have their own systems of regulating lobbying.

Every state requires organizations and compensated individuals who plan to lobby legislators on particular matters to register with a state official or agency. Thirty states also require registration by lobbyists planning to contact executive and regulatory agencies. Many require an authorization statement from business associations and other lobbying organizations before they will accept the registration of the individual lobbyists working for them or on their behalf.

Forty-five states require periodic lobbying reports of widely varying scope and complexity. Some ask for only very sketchy information on lobbying activities. Others demand information on compensation, expenses, identification of legislators and officials lobbied and on which issues, details of entertainment, grass-roots lobbying, and the like.[11]

Regulation of Political Activity

Tax considerations aside, business associations can engage in a variety of activities to affect the political process. They may encourage political activity on the part of their members and endorse candidates for elective office under certain conditions. They may, however, be restricted in their ability to provide financial support for those candidates.

The comments in this section relate to "c-6" and tax-paying associations. For the reasons discussed above, "c-3" organizations are barred from any political involvement.

Political Communications. Business associations may urge their members to play an active role in the political process and may undertake training programs to help their members develop and hone political skills.

The Federal Election Campaign Act allows associations with individual members (mainly professional groups) and other non-corporate members to endorse candidates for federal office, to urge their members to vote for those candidates, and to provide a variety of services on their behalf. Speeches by endorsed candidates at association meetings are permitted, although with some limitations; for instance, similar opportunities must be available on request to opposing candidates. Associations with corporate members can engage in similar activities, provided that the communications are limited to executives of those associations and not the work force as a whole. Both categories can engage in non-partisan communications, like "get-out-and-vote" campaigns.

State laws concerning political activity often differ from federal law. State laws cover all elections for state and local offices within their jurisdictions; some local governments have their own election laws. All vary widely.

Political Finance. Corporations are prohibited from contributing to political candidates or committees in federal elections. Since virtually all business associations are incorporated, this bars direct financial support. About half the states allow direct corporate contributions (with some limits or restrictions) to state and local political committees and candidates.

Until recently, political expenditures by associations and other business groups that are completely independent of the activities of candidates and political committees were considered expressions of free speech that could not be regulated. An example is the National Rifle Association's independent campaigns against legislators who favor gun control. In a 1990 decision, however, the U.S. Supreme Court said that the federal and state governments have power to regulate direct political expenditures by corporations, including incorporated business associations.

Business associations have other means to funnel political contributions to favored candidates. The most important of these are political action committees (PACs), which are organizations established to collect voluntary contributions from individuals and distribute them to preferred candidates and political party organizations. (See chapter 5.)

Like corporations and other kinds of organizations, associations can sponsor PACs as separate groups and can fund their administrative and solicitation costs. Solicitation is subject to much the same rules as those applying to political communications. Association PACs organized under federal law can solicit only from the members of the association and, with their permission, once a year from executives and shareholders of member companies. State PACs operate under different, and often less restrictive, rules.

Business associations may also make contributions of cash or in-kind goods and services to political organizations in the states where corporate contributions are legal. This so-called "soft money" frees up other campaign funds for purposes to which associations cannot directly contribute. It should be noted that Congress is considering legislation restricting soft money.

Such approaches must be carefully devised and operated to stay within pertinent federal and state laws. This is a rapidly evolving area of government regulation. It is important to stay abreast of current requirements.[12]

OTHER LEGAL CONCERNS

The main subjects discussed in this chapter are the most important ones particularly affecting business associations. State and federal laws also regulate many other aspects of association administration and operations. Some of these include:

· *Establishment of associations:* selection of the organization's name and acronym, incorporation, statement of purpose, bylaws, and policies and procedures.

- *Copyright and libel laws:* of particular concerns for association publications.
- *Product liability:* area of possible exposure for associations with testing and certification programs.
- *Insurance law:* the vast spectrum of federal and state laws affecting association group insurance activities.
- *Labor relations:* federal and state law affecting associations that engage in collective bargaining or other labor relations services for their members.
- *Contract law:* agreements concerning meeting facilities and speakers, trade show exhibitors, real estate and equipment leases, purchasing, staff executive employment, and so forth.
- *Employee relations:* employee rights in such areas as discrimination, termination, wages and hours, worker's compensation, occupational safety, as well as pensions and other regulated personnel benefits.
- *Liability of officers and directors:* exposure of association voluntary leaders for decisions or actions that could make them personally vulnerable to criminal or civil litigation.

Comprehensive works on association law listed in the bibliography treat such subjects in considerable detail.

NOTES

1. A very useful and understandable summary of association law will be found in Jerald A. Jacobs, *Association Law Handbook,* 2nd ed. (Washington: Bureau of National Affairs, 1986). This compendium is a principal source for much of the material in this chapter. Other works that delve into the subject in varying degrees of detail and complexity appear in the bibliography.

2. American Society of Mechanical Engineers v. Hydrolevel Corporation 456 U.S. 556 (1982). See Jacobs, *Association Law,* chapter 53, for a discussion of this case.

3. Jacobs, *Association Law,* 215–18, contains a valuable summary of discussion topics that are legally hazardous as well as those that are usually safe.

4. American Society of Association Executives (ASAE), *Policies and Procedures in Association Management.* (Washington: 1987.)

5. See Jacobs, *Association Law,* chapter 54.

6. ASAE, *Policies and Procedures.*

7. *Ibid.*

8. *Ibid.*

9. *Ibid.*

10. *Ibid.*

11. For additional information on federal and state lobbying requirements, see Charles S. Mack, *Lobbying and Government Relations: A Guide for Executives* (Westport, CT: Quorum Books, 1989), 195–202.

12. For additional information, see ibid., chapters 10 and 11. See also Jacobs, *Association Law,* chapters 31–39.

Part IV

BUSINESS ASSOCIATIONS
AT WORK

10

National Associations

A form of government that is not the result of a long sequence of shared experiences, efforts, and endeavors can never take root.

Napoleon Bonaparte

If the end be clearly comprehended within any of the specified powers, and if the measure have an obvious relation to that end, and is not forbidden by any particular provision of the Constitution, it may safely be deemed to come within the compass of the national authority.

Alexander Hamilton

As a group, national associations are the strongest of all American business organizations. They have the biggest budgets, the largest staffs, and the most significant issues. The government officials with whom they deal are typically more sophisticated and have more resources available than their state and local counterparts. For these reasons, national associations have tended to be more glamorous, often attracting more senior and more talented executives to their staffs, their committees, and their boards of directors than state and local associations have been able to do.

Statistical comparisons tell part of the story:

- One-third of all associations have annual budgets in excess of $1 million; half of the national associations do.
- The staff size of national organizations is 50 percent larger than the staffs of all associations as a group.

• The average memberships of national groups are more than twice the size of those of associations as a whole.[1]

Some of these figures may change over time, as state and local issues assume greater importance, but they will never change completely. If only because national associations have a broader revenue base, they are always likely to be stronger than associations that are more limited geographically.

This chapter deals with three kinds of national business organizations: the comprehensive umbrella groups; the more narrowly focused trade associations that represent individual industries, lines of business, or other specific business interests; and the professional associations composed of individual members.

THE UMBRELLA ASSOCIATIONS

In chapter 1, we described umbrella associations as organizations of business enterprises that encompass all industries, or at least comprehensive sectors of industries. They are sometimes called "horizontal" associations or "peak" organizations. *Broad* umbrella groups accept members without regard to their lines of business, although some may have other limiting criteria. *Restricted* umbrella groups accept only certain lines of business and exclude others.

The broad national umbrella organizations are the American Business Conference (ABC), the Business Council, the Business Roundtable (BRT), the National Federation of Independent Business (NFIB), and the U.S. Chamber of Commerce. The principal restricted umbrella organization is the National Association of Manufacturers (NAM), which is largely limited to producers; distributors are ineligible for membership. The umbrella group for retailers and retail associations is the National Retail Federation (NRF), a much smaller organization than the NAM. NRF was formed in 1990 by the merger of two retail associations. Not all such groups have endured. The Transportation Association of America, an intermodal restricted umbrella organization established in 1935, was dissolved in 1983 because of irreconcilable differences among its members.

Although they carry out various economic functions, umbrella associations emphasize public affairs and government relations. They are important to individual companies because they concentrate on issues that affect multiple industries. Few single-industry trade associations have the individual resources or ability to influence the sweeping tax, environmental, labor, or personnel issues that affect large segments of the business community. The large umbrella groups generally have the capability to do so on their own. In addition, they can often coordinate the activities of a number of smaller business organizations.

While each of the umbrella organizations has a special focus that may be important to individual companies, the most significant and comprehensive of these associations is the Chamber of Commerce of the United States.

Profile: The U.S. Chamber of Commerce

Not all umbrella groups are large, but the U.S. Chamber is huge. It is probably the largest business association in the United States and very likely the world.

The Chamber was founded in 1912 at the suggestion of President William Howard Taft for the purpose of providing a unifying voice for businesses of every size in every industry. Today it is a federation of both business associations and individual companies. Its membership includes 2,800 state and local chambers of commerce (and American chambers of commerce in many countries abroad), plus 1,200 trade and professional associations.[2]

There are also 180,000 direct members, from the largest corporations to small "mom-and-pop" operations. Because the Chamber is often accused of representing only "big business," it should be noted that three-fourths of its members employ fewer than twenty people; three out of five members have fewer than ten employees. Sixty percent of the Chamber's dues revenue comes from firms with under twenty employees.

The Chamber is sensitive about the question of how significant a voice small business has. For that reason, a Small Business Council has been established with the rather unusual power to challenge, before the board of directors, the policy recommendations of any committee that the council feels reflect small business interests inadequately. The Chamber maintains that the council has prevailed on every occasion when it has made such an appeal.

Although businesses with over a hundred employees provide only 16 percent of the dues revenue, the Chamber's larger members predominate in terms of participation and governance. Companies represented on the board of directors include the likes of Xerox, 3M, Chrysler, J.C. Penney, Merrill Lynch, Marriott, BellSouth, and Reynolds Metals. There cannot be many "Fortune 500" companies (and their counterparts among retailers, financial, and service companies) that have not been represented in the Chamber's policy-making structure at one time or another. However, executives of a number of mid-sized and regional firms also sit on the board. Most of the directors are the chief executives of their companies, but the very largest firms are sometimes represented by senior officers below the C.E.O. level. In addition, the interests of trade associations and state and local chambers of commerce are represented by specific directors.

Board members are frequently politically active. A number have held, or gone on to, major governmental positions. A past board chairman, Allan Shivers, was governor of Texas. Another, Winton M. Blount, became postmaster general in the Nixon Administration.

What distinguishes the Chamber from other umbrella organizations is not only its sheer size but also the diversity of its membership and the ways in which it mobilizes that diversity to achieve its legislative objectives. It may not have as many small business members as the NFIB, nor be able to summon the personal involvement of C.E.O.s to the same extent as the BRT but no other business organization has the Chamber's comprehensive sweep.

The Chamber is widely regarded as a bastion—perhaps *the* bastion—of American business conservatism, a charge to which it would happily plead guilty. For all its philosophical intransigence on key issues, however, the U.S. Chamber has often urged its members to support voluntary programs to deal with social and economic problems that have prompted legislative proposals it opposes. It has also long supported an active and varied program for education, which probably sells few memberships to small businesses concerned mainly with taxes and labor costs.

One of the Chamber's chief assets has been its continuity of strong staff leadership. Richard L. Lesher has served as the Chamber's president and chief staff executive since 1975. He succeeded the veteran Arch Booth who, for some three decades, had overseen much of the Chamber's earlier growth. Lesher made few changes in the staff Booth had built; in fact, he contributed to its continuity by a significant upgrade in compensation. Lesher has made his mark through substantial innovations. For example, under his leadership, the Chamber became a leading proponent of "supply-side" economic policies. He also developed the Chamber's electronic communications capability.

The Chamber's strengths and resources are so vast that it is worth examining them in some detail.

Finances. In 1988, the Chamber had revenues of $67.2 million (not counting those of its subsidiaries described below), a 6 percent increase over 1987. About 70 percent of its income comes from dues and contributions, 16 percent from advertising revenues, about 3 percent from investments, and 10 percent from publication sales, meeting fees, and so on.

Its fund balance is nearly $12 million. The Chamber has been expanding another asset—its building (which it owns), a Washington landmark on Lafayette Square facing the White House.

One-third of its expense budget supports membership sales and marketing, including an aggressive telemarketing program that has helped to build and retain its large membership. Another third finances its electronic and print communications. Direct lobbying, plus economic and public policy support functions, account for a bit over 8 percent, while services for state and local chambers and trade associations consume 7 percent. Administrative costs amount to 18 percent.

Policies and Programs. As in most associations, the Chamber's policy-formulation process is carried out through a structure of committees, councils, and task forces. These groups examine issues and recommend positions to the board of directors. The Chamber limits its purview to issues that are national in scope and that affect more than one industry. In addition to the tax, labor, and employee benefits issues to which the Chamber has always given great attention, it also concerns itself with issues ranging from acid rain to economic policy to white-collar crime. Its 1989 issues list contains ninety-nine topics of legislative concern. Although not all of these are equally critical, this is still an enormous span of domestic interests, to which must be added the Chamber's heavy involvement in international economic and business affairs.

Policy implementation is a staff function carried out through several different program areas. All operate, directly or indirectly, in support of its government relations mission:

• **Legislative and Issue Specialists.** The Chamber has a distinctive staff organizational structure that appears to separate its issue experts from its legislative personnel. The distinction is more organizational than real.

Some eighty-five issue specialists staff the Chamber's committees, research the issues, develop legislative strategies, coordinate coalitions, testify at hearings, lobby congressional committees and regulatory agencies, and generally manage the implementation of the Chamber's issues positions in all their aspects. A separate group of lobbyists provides supplemental liaison with Congress, monitors day-to-day developments, and coordinates with the cadre of Washington corporate representatives who are frequently enlisted in particular legislative campaigns. National trade associations are also involved (through still another staff department) if the issue is one that affects particular industries.

Chamber staff personnel play a coordinating role in bringing various business elements together through ad hoc issue coalitions. These usually involve Washington corporate representatives and trade association executives, sometimes other umbrella groups like the NAM, NFIB and the BRT, and occasionally non-business interest groups. On rare issues, organizations like the League of Women Voters and even the AFL-CIO (the Chamber's favorite antagonist) have come together with the Chamber and other business organizations when they shared common ground. A recent list of issue coalitions in which the Chamber is involved tallied ninety of them, in such areas as construction, energy, international business, transportation, and labor and taxation, among others.

• **Grass-Roots.** The Chamber's ability to reach business people in every congressional district is one of its greatest strengths. Through both its direct and its organizational members, the Chamber coordinates a network of 3,000 congressional action committees—groups of business people who pay special attention to the issues and frequently write their senators and representatives about them, based on a regular flow of legislative information and issue alerts.

Local and state chambers of commerce are a bulwark of this network, supplemented by the work of trade associations with their own "back home" members. This is why the Chamber lavishes so much tender loving care on its organizational members. Counseling them in their management problems, helping their staff executives to improve their professional credentials (and sometimes get better jobs), the Chamber asks little in return, save that they faithfully attend to their legislative devotions whenever they hear its calls to prayer.

The Chamber's principal media in keeping its grassroots system informed and motivated on legislative developments include a special newsletter, a monthly newspaper, and various action alerts when major bills reach critical stages. On high-visibility issues, the result can be an outpouring of mail and telephone messages to members of Congress from their business constituents, exhorting them to support, oppose, or amend particular bills.

The difficulty for the Chamber lies in maintaining a high pitch of member enthusiasm and action on all its issues. Even narrowly focused trade associations with only a handful of concerns find it difficult to keep their members constantly fired up. It is an impossible dilemma for an organization that covers a hundred issues a year. Some members complain that the Chamber's pleas for grass-roots action are incessant. "If I responded to all their appeals for action, I'd never have time to do anything else," one businessman carped.

Yet, when the system works, it can be devastating. A former Chamber staff member once instigated a communication to members on a then hot issue. The language of the action appeal was factual, if somewhat inflammatory, and succeeded in motivating a vast number of small business people to write their congressmen to oppose the bill. The staffer remembers well the protests from members of Congress about the mailbags being dumped in their offices daily—and the House vote, when the bill was resoundingly defeated. The experience taught a lesson in the power of grass-roots lobbying that the ex-staffer has never forgotten.

• **Communications.** Business people who join the U.S. Chamber need never again feel lonely. They will be invited to meetings, find a magazine and perhaps a tabloid in their mailboxes each month, and be barraged by a seemingly unending gush of legislative information bulletins and memos. In addition, television brings the Chamber into their homes, offices, and even hotel rooms every day. All of it carries the Chamber's pro-business message, often preached with the zeal of electronic evangelists.

The Chamber's principal publication is *Nation's Business,* a magazine sent to all members. It is also sold to subscribers and on newsstands. With a circulation of 850,000, *Nation's Business* competes for advertising linage and readership with *Fortune, Business Week,* and similar publications. A tabloid newspaper, *The Business Advocate,* focuses less on the management topics covered by the magazine and more on economic and public policy issues.

The Chamber's electronic communications system, *BizNet,* produces a morning program of business news carried to cable stations around the country by ESPN. BizNet also produces a debate program on business issues that is syndicated to 150 stations. In addition, the Chamber uses its BizNet facilities for satellite video-conferences with both domestic and international participants.

Affiliates. The Chamber has four subsidiary organizations that support its activities in special areas:

- *The National Chamber Litigation Center* is a public policy law firm that extends the Chamber's representation of business interests into the courtroom. It has initiated or intervened in roughly 200 cases in which a basic business issue was involved (mostly on labor relations and environmental cases). It claims to have been on the winning side 60 percent of the time. Created in 1977, the center has a professional staff of three, operating on a budget in excess of $300,000.

- *The National Chamber Alliance for Politics* is a modest PAC that spent about $10,000 in 1988. NCAP does not make direct contributions to candidates, but provides support and services to those endorsed by the Chamber.

- *The National Chamber Foundation* undertakes business and economic research studies and publishes the *Journal of Economic Growth.* It focuses on both current problems and emerging trends. The foundation operates on a $2.5 million annual budget.

- *The Center for International Private Enterprise,* federally funded ($2.5 million in 1988) through the National Endowment for Democracy, provides financing and support for democratic, business-oriented development in less-developed countries.

The U.S. Chamber enjoys the benefits of its vast size, resources, and diverse membership. It also suffers from them: The state and local chambers, which are the heart of its grass-roots efforts, gain from the services and counsel they receive from Washington, but have been known to say that they sometimes get a little more guidance than they need. Its trade association members happily utilize its issue research, coalitions, and legislative coordination, but often feel like mice in bed with an elephant. Large corporate members, a prime influence on policy, are happy to have small businesses provide the bulk of the funding and grass-roots support. The small members think the Chamber is into too many issues but accept the situation, so long as the Chamber fights tax and minimum wage increases and helps keep the unions off their backs. The membership as a whole thinks the staff really runs the organization, while the staff wishes good members would become more personally involved.

These tensions are normal in associations. The Chamber has so many because it has so many different elements. Given these varied elements and tensions, the remarkable thing about the Chamber's performance, as Samuel Johnson said about the dog that walked on its hind legs, is not that it does it so well but that it manages to do it at all.

Its very size and visibility make the U.S. Chamber a favorite target of criticism from its rivals, competitors, and antagonists. Some of that may well be deserved. It is a tribute to its structure and its staff, however, that it achieves so many of its objectives and continues to thrive. It fills an important niche in the ecology of American business organizations.

Other National Umbrella Organizations

National Association of Manufacturers. Historically, the NAM has been the Chamber's principal rival for business leadership on national public policy issues. The NAM lacks the breadth of the Chamber's membership—it does not admit companies in distributive, financial, or service businesses—and it is substantially smaller; it has fewer than 200 employees, compared to 1,200 for the Chamber. Its annual budget is about $12 million, less than a fifth of the Chamber's. A group closely affiliated with the NAM is the National Industrial Council, a federation of national and state manufacturers associations that functions something like the Chamber's Association Department.

Because of the substantial overlap in membership between the Chamber and the NAM, these two business umbrella organizations made a serious attempt to merge in 1976. The purpose was to reduce cost duplications and have a single voice in Washington, ending embarrassing situations in which the two groups took conflicting public policy positions. Difficulty in merging two boards of directors (the NAM's is considerably larger than the Chamber's) was the principal reason given for the failure of the merger. In addition, many NAM staff members feared, no doubt correctly, that the consolidation would be less a true merger than an acquisition by the Chamber, in which many NAM staffers would lose out. NAM staff employees were highly vocal and probably decisive in killing the merger. Since 1976, the Chamber has continued to grow, while the NAM's membership has fallen—due at least partly to corporate mergers and to the general decline of the manufacturing sector.

Sheer size and breadth produce liabilities as well as advantages. A principal reason for the proliferation of business associations is the desire of their members for a consensus of views on problems and issues, if not complete unanimity. No membership organization feels comfortable taking positions that are opposed by a significant internal minority. Relatively homogeneous associations can reach consensus much more easily than heterogeneous groups.

The Chamber—anything but homogeneous—has frequently been accused of taking positions at the lowest common denominator of members' views and then being inflexible about negotiating. Despite its relatively greater homogeneity, however, the NAM has even more frequently faced charges of conservative rigidity. This situation seems not to have been appreciably altered by the fact its recent chief executives have been alumni of the liberal Democratic Johnson and Carter administrations.

Business Roundtable. Top executives of the nation's largest corporations have worried that both the Chamber and the NAM are too ideological in their positions and too rigid in their legislative strategies. These concerns contributed to the formation of the Business Roundtable. Underlying the operation of the BRT are the beliefs that direct personal lobbying by corporate chief executives of the largest companies has more legislative impact than the efforts of association staffs and that C.E.O.s have the latitude for greater flexibility in legislative negotiations.

The Roundtable is unusual in that it has a very small headquarters staff. Its issues research and legislative coordination are conducted largely by corporate staff personnel employed by the 200 companies whose chief executives comprise the BRT's membership.

Direct lobbying is the Roundtable's forte. It has little capability to mount grass-roots legislative campaigns.

The Business Council. A group with a membership similar to the BRT's, the Business Council exists primarily as a forum for top corporate executives and senior government officials. It is not a lobbying organization as such.

National Federation of Independent Business. Ironically, the suspicion of corporate dominance of the Chamber and the belief that the Chamber was insufficiently vigorous in championing small business led to the rapid development of the NFIB. Established in 1943, it has undergone much growth since the late 1970s through aggressive membership marketing efforts. These rely on personal sales calls to recruit members, an effective but very expensive strategy that reportedly consumes about four-fifths of its $40 million-plus budget. The Chamber, in comparison, uses telemarketing for membership recruitment and retention, a technique in which it was a pioneer among business associations. As a result, the

NFIB is the only one among the national umbrella groups whose size continues to increase substantially. It currently includes about 500,000 owners of small business. The NFIB and the Chamber are widely considered the most effective of the umbrella associations in stimulating massive grass-roots business communications on legislative issues, especially on the tax and labor matters which both groups stress.

The NFIB has an unusual policy structure. As discussed in chapter 7, almost all associations set policy through a process that involves committees and boards of directors. The NFIB, however, gets its policy "mandate" through frequent, direct polls of its membership. The strength of this approach is that it is participatory governance at its best. The weakness is that there is no latitude for negotiation among membership segments, nor for nuance in issue positions. Moreover, the ability to frame the poll questions is the ability to shape the answers, a reality that the opinion research industry discovered decades ago.

American Business Conference. Still another umbrella group is the American Business Conference, created in 1980 to represent about a hundred mid-size, high-growth companies interested primarily in regulatory reform and tax incentives to promote investment.

The Effectiveness Issue

The question of whether the American business community is served well by this proliferation of umbrella associations is a real one. Even in a nation of several million employers, there are only so many memberships to go around, so the umbrella groups spend considerable staff time and money competing for dues dollars. They also engage in turf battles, seeking legislative prestige points and publicity as *the* leader of U. S. business, as well as more members, at each other's expense.

A senior staff executive with one of these associations sees two larger problems, however: Disagreement on issue positions and disagreement on legislative strategy. The first happens rarely but is disastrous when it occurs. Business interests were badly hurt by the 1982 tax bill, for instance, because the major umbrella organizations took conflicting positions on its provisions. Divisions over strategy are much more common. Although strategy disagreements are less ruinous, they still seriously chip away at potential successes. The late Bryce Harlow—arguably the most respected business lobbyist of his day—was fond of pointing out that the combined strength of business organizations is so great that they almost never lose when they are firmly united in positions and strategy on public policy issues. The converse is also true. Irving Shapiro, DuPont's former board chairman and a founder of the BRT, once noted that the business community tends not to be heard when it speaks with several voices. That happens more often than the members of the umbrella groups might wish.

Certainly, the sheer number of business lobbyists representing these different groups has an undeniable impact when they all troop into congressional offices seriatim to advocate the same position on a major issue. Yet, if the combined resources of the Chamber and its competing umbrella groups could be *permanently* united in the interest of the American business community as a whole, disagreements over legislative positions and strategy questions would disappear, duplicative costs would be saved, and, if Bryce Harlow was right, business would be nearly invincible on its big issues.

It can be argued, of course, that the lowest common denominator might drop even further, were the U. S. business community represented by a single organization. That, however, is a point in support of more effective policy-making, not an argument against unified advocacy for American business.

NATIONAL TRADE ASSOCIATIONS

The associations that represent particular industries are a very different species from the national umbrella organizations. Their memberships are smaller and much more homogeneous. While each of their members has its particular interest, they can usually find common ground on the issues that affect them. Indeed, one reason for the proliferation of national trade associations is that membership segments sometimes split off to defend their own interests when that common ground cannot be reached often enough.

Because their constituencies are so much narrower, the number of issues with which each association is concerned is much smaller. This enables their staffs to develop a high degree of expertise on those issues. A good measure of that expertise is the frequency with which people in government call for information on which many associations are considered uniquely authoritative.

At the same time, trade associations often engage in a broader range of activities than the umbrella groups. The large horizontal associations focus almost exclusively on public policy agendas. The vertical trade associations, in addition to their government relations activities, are frequently deeply involved in providing the economic services discussed in chapter 4.

Membership recruitment and retention are also of a different dimension for trade associations. Their constituencies are relatively confined and precise; membership is usually marketed on a retail basis, rather than through the mass marketing techniques used by groups like the U. S. Chamber and the NFIB. The size of trade associations does not always reflect the number of members. Large, concentrated industries like automobile manufacturing may be represented by trade associations with few members but substantial budgets.

Like the organisms that comprise a biological species, national trade associations share many common traits, yet the range of individual differences is considerable. The two associations profiled below typify many of these similarities and differences. One is a small group of relatively low-technology manufacturers, who sell directly to other industrial processors but must keep a close eye on the consumer market. The other is a large organization of high-technology manufacturers heavily involved in international trade and technical standards. Both are headquartered in Washington, D.C., and are active in influencing public policy, though in very different ways.

Profile: The Glass Packaging Institute

The Glass Packaging Institute (GPI) is a small association with an aggressive program and staff, but one considerably reduced in size from its earlier years. The shrinkage of the association reflects the decline and consolidation that has beset the industry it represents.

GPI's current primary members are down to about a dozen American, Canadian, and Mexican manufacturers of glass containers for food, beverages, health products, cosmetics, and household and industrial chemicals. There are also associate members who supply the primary members with ingredients, chemicals, and equipment for glass manufacture.

An affiliated group, the Closure Manufacturer Association (CMA), is comprised of companies that make caps and lids for glass containers. Several glass manufacturers are also in the closure business and belong to both associations. CMA has its own board of directors but is administered by the GPI staff.

Glass has been used for containers since its invention in ancient times. Its enduring use over the millennia attests to its relative strength, transparency, and low cost, the ease with which it can be cleaned and sterilized, and its high chemical stability and neutrality. In modern times, however, glass has faced severe competition from plastic and aluminum containers, both of which, though more costly, are lighter than glass and virtually unbreakable. Plastic containers are also nearly as transparent as glass, an important characteristic for many consumer products.

Glass reached its production peak around 1980, when the number of containers shipped to U. S. customers neared a third of a billion gross, according to U. S. Census Bureau surveys of manufacturers. By 1985, shipment volumes had fallen nearly 16 percent, with the biggest sales drop among glass's largest customers—beer brewers, soft drink bottlers, and food manufacturers—as all three customer groups accelerated shifts into aluminum or plastic packaging. The sales decrease in these three marketing categories over the five-year period very nearly equaled total 1985 sales to all other glass container customers combined. Glass shipments made a partial recovery in 1986 but then began sliding down again. The sales decline has cut the industry's former profitability deeply. In fact, a large number of glass manufacturers have gone out of business or been acquired by competitors.

The principal cause of this loss of business has been increased consumer preference for the lighter, less breakable container materials. This trend was seriously aggravated by the beverage container deposit laws enacted in several states. If consumers and retailers had to handle each beverage container twice, once at the sale and again at the return, the heavier, more fragile material was clearly at a severe competitive disadvantage to plastic and aluminum. GPI's highest priority has become the vigorous promotion of recycling programs as its alternative to bottle laws, while also fostering new consumer applications for glass.

Structure and Funding. GPI was founded in 1945 as the Glass Container Manufacturers Institute. The present name was adopted in 1976. The current primary membership is now eleven as the industry continues to consolidate. Even with mergers, however, its members represent over 90 percent of total industry sales.

The headquarters staff has eleven members, seven of whom are professional personnel. These include the institute's president, Lewis D. Andrews, Jr., vice presidents for operations and public affairs, a recycling director, a federal/technical director, a manager of closure activities, and support personnel. In addition, there are eight directors of recycling programs around the country, some of whom are employees and some independent contractors.[3]

The board of trustees consists of one representative from each of the domestic manufacturers, plus three additional members representing respectively the foreign manufacturers, the associate members, and the closure companies. The board is the chief policy body, approving programs, budgets, and current and long-term strategies.

Direct association revenues were $1.4 million in 1988, of which dues from container and closure manufacturers and from associate members represented about half. Dues revenues are assessed as a flat percentage of net dollar sales. Other principal revenue sources include interest income and allocations for staff time and overhead levied against its two affiliates—CMA and a special trust called the Industry Union Glass Container Promotion Program.

This $6.5 million program, which the GPI staff administers, is supported jointly by the industry and its labor unions and is financed by contributions of ten cents per man-hour. The trust provides financial support for the recycling programs that both the manufacturers and their unions consider critical to the industry's future and the jobs of its employees. It has a somewhat different membership from GPI and a separate board of directors.

GPI has a structure of committees, subcommittees, and task forces that focus not only on recycling, but also on technical problems relating to environmental issues, the development of voluntary industry standards and specifications, and the promotion of basic research. There is an on-going cooperative research effort with energy suppliers to develop environmentally cleaner and more energy-efficient glass melting and processing techniques.

Public Affairs Programs. The promotion of recycling, along with opposition to the spread of deposit legislation, is far and away the glass container industry's most important cause. Recycling gives glass a competitive advantage over plastic packaging, because recycling technology for glass (like aluminum) is well advanced while that for plastics is still in its early infancy. Moreover, all the beverage packaging industries see recycling as the answer to the state container deposit laws, from which the non-glass manufacturers have benefited at the expense of glass but which none likes. GPI sponsors glass recycling operations in twenty-three states and the District of Columbia. It devotes major efforts to expanding these and similar campaigns, particularly community curbside pick-up and recycling programs for all container materials.

Virtually everything GPI does involves outreach through government relations and public affairs. It lobbies on behalf of recycling through staff and member contacts with customer industries and with legislators and environmental officials at every level of government. GPI also commissioned a guide for local governments, *Comprehensive Curbside Recycling: Collection Costs and How to Control Them,* that it has distributed wisely in both print and video form.

GPI, like other business organizations that cannot achieve their objectives on their own, makes much use of coalitions with others that share its views and aims on particular issues. It promotes recycling through alliance with environmental groups and simultaneously cooperates with food, beverage, and other container industry associations to oppose deposit laws. These are important areas of coalition activity.

The industry has also undertaken a national advertising campaign to sell the virtues of glass recyclability. Communications with trade publications and local and national media are a significant element in the institute's public relations activities. GPI engages in programs to build acceptance of glass packaging among consumers and thereby with its industrial customers. For example, as part of its program to broaden uses for glass containers, GPI has undertaken publicity projects to boost consumer acceptance of glass-packaged foods for use in microwave ovens.

This is a vigorous program for a small national trade association that is trying to revive an industry fallen on hard times. Whether or not GPI succeeds, its programs illustrate the diversity of tools that even a small organization can aggressively utilize in pursuit of its objectives and its members' vital interests.

Profile: Computer and Business Equipment Manufacturers Association

If GPI represents a modern industry whose roots date back to prehistoric times, the technology of CBEMA's members is at the leading edge today and the wave of tomorrow. CBEMA (pronounced "see-beema") is the acronym for the Computer and Business Equipment Manufacturers Association, a national trade group for a $500 billion industry whose revenues are expected to more than double over the next decade.[4]

The information technology companies that CBEMA represents fall into two major industries: computer and business equipment, on the one hand, and telecommunications, on the other. Computer and business equipment (which also includes software services, and manifold business forms) now generates more revenue than telecommunications and is also growing faster. Despite some recent flattening of computer sales, the information technology industry is expected to account for 10.5 percent of U. S. gross national product in the year 2000, up from 8.9 percent in 1989.

This is gigantic growth for an industry whose first computer was introduced only four decades ago. Its technology is developing so rapidly that prototypes of optical computers, which use photons of light instead of electrons to transmit data, have already been developed. Still further dazzling innovations, such as holographic visual displays, are expected by the end of the century.

The association that represents this dynamic industry is older than many of its leading members. CBEMA was established in 1916 as the National Association of Office Appliance Manufacturers. Several name changes followed (to the Office Equipment Manufacturers Institute and later, the Business Equipment Manufacturers Association); the present name was adopted in 1972.[5]

CBEMA's thirty members represent about half of the industry's sales volume. They include such U. S. corporate names as IBM, AT&T, Kodak, and Xerox. They also include U. S. subsidiaries of Japanese corporations, such as Matsushita and Hitachi, and of European companies, such as Philips and Bull.

The association's mission statement and goals focus on four main areas of activity: public policy advocacy, executive education, international activities, and domestic and international standards. CBEMA also has a comprehensive statistical publications program.

As a trade association based in the United States, CBEMA's major focus is domestic. Because its industry is heavily multinational in operations and marketing, however, international linkages are a substantial part of CBEMA's work. The industry's government relations activities are coordinated on a global basis through the International Information Industry Congress (IIIC), a worldwide federation of CBEMA and its counterpart associations in Australia, New Zealand, Japan, Canada, Brazil, Denmark, West Germany, France, Ireland, Great Britain, Italy, and Sweden.

CBEMA is far from the only association in the U. S. information technology industry. About forty trade and professional associations directly serve the industry, and several compete to some extent with CBEMA. CBEMA focuses strictly on the interests of manufacturers. Some of the other groups, like the National Computer Graphics Association, the Information Industry Association, and the Computer Law Association, have a narrower focus than CBEMA. Others are broader, such as the Electronic Industries Association and the American Electronics Association. These groups often work in coalition on their shared public policy concerns.

Finance and Structure. CBEMA carries out its programs with a budget of about $4 million. Member dues provide over 80 percent of the association's revenues. The remainder comes from its standards programs, meeting registration fees, interest, publication sales, and other sources. Personnel costs are the largest single expense item. Dues are calculated on a sliding scale based on each member's gross revenues. Minimum dues are $5,000; maximum are $800,000. The average is $93,000.

CBEMA reports the amounts of direct support it spends on its programs. Exclusive of overhead, administration, and self-supporting fees (like meeting registrations), the association spends about 30 percent of its program support on domestic government relations, 15 percent on international issues, 36 percent on its standards activities, 1 percent on management education, 9 percent on statistical compilations, and 9 percent on press and media communications.

The association's staff of thirty-four is headed by its president, retired general John L. Pickitt. Other key staff positions include an executive vice president, vice presidents for domestic and international issues, and directors or managers responsible for government procurement, proprietary rights, telecommunications, industry programs and statistics, standards program and secretariat, communications (public relations), education and member services, and administration.

CBEMA's board of directors, consisting of one representative from each member company, is its governing body. A ten-member executive committee acts on the board's behalf when necessary. Several operating committees exercise responsibilities that are reserved to the board of directors in many other associations. The association's plans and programs committee develops the annual program and oversees the development of industry policy positions. The long-range planning committee is concerned with the organization's mission statement, five-year plans, and overall association goals. Still another committee reviews staff performance and determines compensation ranges. In addition, CBEMA has a large number of committees and subcommittees that focus on domestic and international issues; others address industry services.

Government Relations. At the federal level, the association concentrates on subjects such as antitrust changes to allow joint manufacturing ventures; chlorofluorocarbon phaseout schedules; computer virus legislation; various employee benefit measures, government procurement policies; tax treatment of research-and-development costs and other tax matters; and copyright protection for computer programs and other intellectual property issues. The association lobbies on such issues with members of Congress and their staffs, officials of executive departments and agencies, and, through coalitions, with other business associations and individual companies. At the state level, CBEMA has lobbied legislators and regulatory officials on such issues as computer warranties, video display terminal restrictions, and proposed uniform software laws.

The association's international government relations activities are devoted largely to shaping congressional legislation, as well as the trade and negotiating policies of U. S. departments and agencies, especially the International Trade Commission and the Office of the U. S. Trade Representative. But CBEMA has also been active, directly and indirectly through IIIC, in the European Economic Community, in GATT (the General agreement on Tariffs and Trade), and in other forums for international trade negotiations. Its concerns have included various export and import control issues and procedures to reduce trade restrictions on industry products and components

In its government relations activities, CBEMA acts as direct lobbyist, source of authoritative industry data, and coordinator of its members' own legislative activities. It participates substantially in both domestic and international coalitions and alliances. The association does not sponsor a political action committee.

Other Programs. CBEMA has an extensive program to support the development, promotion, and harmonization of domestic and international standards affecting the information technology industry. Its interests range from environmental, health, and safety standards to technical issues related to worldwide computer compatibility (so that products and systems can interconnect and communicate with each other). CBEMA acts as the U. S. secretariat on information-processing systems for the American National Standards Institute, the U. S. umbrella organization for voluntary standards development. The association also staffs a U. S. technical advisory group for the International Standards Organization.

Management education for CBEMA's members takes place through four councils that provide opportunities for information exchange on common operations. These councils deal with human resources, equipment servicing, taxation, and transportation logistics.

The association's statistical program maintains databases on U. S. and global industry shipments, revenues, international trade, consumption, employment, research and development, and related topics. These compilations are released to the industry and the public in both monthly and annual publications.

CBEMA's public relations efforts have concentrated on increasing its visibility in the press on its public policy activities. It has also developed publications and visual materials for consumers and workers on the use of video display terminals.

CBEMA is basically a conservative, multi-service association that pursues its objectives through the prestige and expertise of its members. It also benefits from its own reputation as an authoritative and comprehensive source of industry data and coordination. Particularly notable are the extensive international and standards activities that complement its domestic services on behalf of an industry that grows as a global technological and economic force.

INDIVIDUAL MEMBERSHIP ASSOCIATIONS

While the members of most business associations are companies, some business-related organizations have memberships comprised of individuals. Such groups have quite a different orientation from trade associations. Rather than representing specific industries or lines of business as trade associations do, individual membership groups usually consist of practitioners in distinctive occupations or professions. Many of these associations are in academic, scientific, or medical disciplines, but some serve professionals in fields in or allied to business, such as lawyers, accountants, computer specialists, industrial security experts, association executives, and the like.

Individual membership organizations share many characteristics with trade associations, but there are some important differences. As a group, individual membership associations place more stress on professional education and training than do trade associations, and less on government relations, but these are far from universal traits. Often but not always, the groups that do have public policy concerns communicate their issue positions to lawmakers rather formally, refraining from intense direct and grass-roots lobbying.

Professional organizations often create sections based on distinct specialties or fields of interest. They frequently develop chapters of members located in particular geographic areas. Both kinds of sub-organizations are likely to have their own educational and related programs, coordinated with but separate from those of the parent association. Usually, but again not invariably, membership in the parent association is a prerequisite to section or chapter membership, and an additional dues surcharge is sometimes levied.

Because they are comprised of individuals rather than enterprises, professional/occupational organizations typically have substantially larger memberships than trade associations—an average of almost 17,000, compared to 1,080 for industry organizations. Dues, however, are generally much lower. The average is $182, compared to $855 for associations with corporate memberships.[6] Individual membership groups usually assess dues at a flat rate rather than as a sales percentage or other formulae commonly utilized by trade associations.

The potential membership base for individual membership groups is generally large, and membership recruitment is always a high-priority activity. Peer contacts (through membership committees at both the parent and chapter level), direct mail, and sometimes telemarketing are common techniques for membership sales and renewal. Some groups also contract with professional solicitation firms for membership marketing.

Individual membership organizations usually have much greater numerical attendance at their principal meetings than trade associations do because the memberships are so much larger, even though the percentage attending is typically only half that of trade groups.

Many professional organizations have a venerable history. Some American groups date back to the eighteenth century. There are even older societies in Europe. Others were formed more recently—sometimes because a new profession developed, other times because a specialized interest split off from an existing organization. The group profiled below is in the latter category. Although a relatively new association, it nonetheless typifies the programs and problems of more established individual membership organizations.

Profile: American Corporate Counsel Association

The mother church of the legal profession, the American Bar Association, is a vast organization of over 300,000 members that represents more than half of the practicing attorneys in the United States. The ABA has a $50 million budget and a staff of almost 600. It has many sections and committees that represent the range of specialties and interests within the profession; some are virtually mini-associations in their own right.

Most lawyers are in private practice, while the rest are employed by governments and non-profit organizations of different kinds, as well as by corporations. Most corporate legal work has traditionally been farmed out to private law firms. That is where the best practitioners are to be found—or at least so the traditional wisdom in the profession has held.

In the 1970s, however, many companies responded to escalating outside legal costs by expanding their legal staffs. They brought much work inside that had traditionally been performed by retained outside law firms. As a result, both the size and the quality of corporate law departments grew substantially. Many in-house attorneys roiled professional waters by demanding greater accountability from the law firms that they continued to use, requiring budgets, itemized bills, detailed statements of expenses, and so on. This new group tended to more aggressive than their older, more established corporate colleagues and called for increased representation for corporate lawyers within the ABA.

The American Corporate Counsel Association (ACCA):

grew out of a meeting in December, 1981, in Dallas, attended by about 40 corporate general counsel. The group discussed the growing influence of the corporate bar and how the interests of the corporate bar differed in many respects from those of the private practice bar. The American Bar Association was not willing to establish a separate section for inside lawyers, although at the Dallas meeting, the ABA executive director met with the group and promised that the ABA would be more responsive to the needs of corporate counsel. In spite of these assurances, the founding group moved ahead.[7]

ACCA was formally established in 1982. Articles of incorporation were adopted, a board of directors was established, and an executive director was hired. Less than a year after the Dallas meeting, ACCA was up and in business.[8]

Even large associations take a dim view of new organizations formed from among their members. "Splinter groups," association executives sometimes call them, and it is not a term of endearment. ABA therefore sought to counter the formation of ACCA by expanding opportunities for in-house corporate attorneys within some of its sections and committees.

Nor was the new organization unanimously welcomed by corporate lawyers. Many of the old guard viewed ACCA as divisive and believed that corporate attorneys should work for greater acceptance within the ABA, instead of setting up a "renegade bar association." Some pre-existing local corporate counsel associations affiliated with ACCA as chapters, but others still have not.

Nonetheless, ACCA thrived and grew. It now has 7,700 members and thirty-four affiliated local chapters. It has been working to minimize tensions with the ABA by cooperating on specific projects and by trying to avoid duplication of effort. ACCA exists to promote the common interests of its members, contribute to their continuing education, advance the standards of corporate law practice, and encourage increased understanding of the role of corporate attorneys.

Public Policy Issues. The association has taken positions on a variety of issues of concern to its members. ACCA avoids extensive direct lobbying but does express its views to both Congress and the states. It has intervened with the courts in a number of cases. It also lobbies bar associations on pertinent issues, although it prefers the more lawyer-like term "advocacy."

It concentrates on eliminating bar association restrictions on the ability of corporate attorneys to practice law on behalf of their companies and to provide active legal counsel to them. It has also taken positions on legislation affecting antitrust law, securities regulation, and product liability.

Some of the association's recent issues have included:

- Adoption of uniform standards of bar admissions;
- Equal treatment of corporate counsel and outside attorneys;
- Salary increases for federal judges;
- Opposition to state legislation that might permit discharged corporate attorneys to violate employer confidences;
- Support for federal legislation clarifying standards relating to interlocking corporate boards of directors;
- Antitrust changes relating to litigation settlements;
- Public disclosure requirements in corporate merger negotiations; and
- Opposition to limitations in federal courts on certain cases involving state laws.

On occasion, ACCA has asked its chapters and individual members to contact their legislators on particular issues but, like many other professional organizations, it has no active grass-roots lobbying program.

Membership. ACCA had 7,700 members at the end of 1989—a remarkable number for a professional association less than a decade old. Only attorneys practicing in the law departments of corporations (and other private-sector organizations) are eligible to join. Dues are $120 for the first member from a company and $100 each for subsequent members. A portion of the dues payment is rebated to the member's local chapter.

ACCA has been adding about 1,500 new members a year, but recently retained a marketing consultant to accelerate its membership growth to a new goal of 2,400 annually. Membership solicitation costs have been averaging about $70,000 per year, primarily for direct mail. Its membership retention rate of 85 to 90 percent is typical of individual membership groups.

Services to members include the association's public policy activities, publications, meetings and programs, and a resume clearinghouse for corporate attorneys and companies with legal department openings.

Structure. ACCA is governed by a thirty-eight-member board of directors whose members can serve two three-year terms. The board is self-perpetuating, since the existing board elects new directors. A fairly unusual provision allows directors unable to attend board meetings to send alternates. An executive committee of twelve has the customary authority to make decisions between board meetings.

Every association with chapters debates whether they should have board representation; ACCA is no different. There is no formal number of seats reserved for the chapters, but many directors are past chapter presidents, offering a kind of informal representation utilized by many chaptered organizations.

A board-level policy committee studies issues and recommends positions on them to the board. This committee confers frequently by telephone conference calls as well as in meetings and has been one of the most active ACCA committees. Other committees concern themselves with chapter relations, membership, and education.

Chapters. ACCA has an aggressive program to increase the number of chapters. It currently has thirty-four. These are subordinate to the parent, share the association's nonprofit tax status, and are financed by a dues rebate of $20 per member.

ACCA provides the chapters with services that include an organizational manual, directories of chapter officers and committees, rosters of members for each chapter, mailing lists of current members and prospects, and program suggestions. Meetings of chapter presidents are held twice a year. The association updates the general membership on chapter developments through a special bulletin, plus news items in its quarterly magazine and annual report. Chapters may adopt their own positions on public issues if they coordinate with the parent and if those positions are consistent with the parent's policies.

Staff and Budget. ACCA currently operates on a budget of about $1.1 million. Dues make up just under two-thirds of its revenues. Other major income sources are meetings and educational seminars, plus publication and advertising sales. On the expense side, personnel and other administrative costs consume about 70 percent, meeting costs 18 percent, and chapter rebates 11 percent.

Nancy Nord, an attorney, was ACCA's executive director from its founding through 1990. Other staff positions include a director of programs and publications, a publications coordinator, a membership director and assistant, a chapter liaison, a program director for the association's foundation, and four administrative and support personnel—for a total staff of eleven.

Affiliate. The American Corporate Counsel Institute (ACCI) is the association's educational foundation, a "c-3" organization. One of its important programs promotes free legal representation for the needy and for various charitable groups. Through another institute project, a computerized database has been developed to access texts of testimony by expert witnesses against corporations in suits involving toxic substances; this is a valuable research tool. ACCI has also undertaken research projects on legal management practices, ethical problems, and the corporate use of arbitration and mediation as alternative dispute settlement processes.

Education. In cooperation with the Duke University business school, ACCA has sponsored week-long seminars for the corporate legal profession. The "Executive Program for Corporate Counsel" is intended to broaden general management skills. A second seminar, "Managing the Corporate Legal Department," provides further management development for corporate lawyers who are likely to move into managerial roles within their companies.

Publications and Meetings. The association publishes a quarterly journal, *ACCA Docket,* that contains news about the organization, articles about corporate law practice and issues (contributed by both members and non-members), and advertising. Other periodicals include bulletins for chapter officers and committee chairmen.

ACCA also publishes a variety of print, audio, and video materials. Books and pamphlets include a survey of the current bar admissions system, a study of malpractice exposure and insurance, a model code of business conduct, a layman's manual on the legal responsibility of corporate managers, a guide to the protection of privileged information, a directory of legal counsel in foreign countries, and a professional standards manual. Some of these have been developed by members' companies and are made available by ACCA to other members on an exclusive basis. Video and audio tapes have dealt with problems of legal ethics, strategic planning for law departments, and orientation for new corporate attorneys.

In addition to its publications, ACCA holds an annual membership meeting, a new mid-year meeting, and various educational seminars on relevant topics.

ACCA could well be considered a prototype for new professional associations planning rapid growth through vigorous membership marketing and highly innovative programs. It remains to be seen whether its leadership and management can unify all of its potential constituency under the ACCA banner. Its very existence, however, stands as a signal warning to established organizations that neglect motivated interest groups within their own membership.

The associations portrayed in this chapter illustrate the breadth and scope of national business associations—umbrella, trade, and professional. For all their differences, they have much in common. For all that they have in common, these profiles only begin to suggest the diversity that characterizes national business groups. All are important to their members precisely because they are *national* organizations—and as such the dominant species within the genus of business associations.

NOTES

1. American Society of Association Executives (ASAE), *Policies and Procedures in Association Management* (Washington: 1987).
2. Information from publications, reports, and documents supplied by the U. S. Chamber of Commerce, and communications with staff members and other knowledgeable individuals.
3. Information from publications, reports, and documents supplied by the Glass Packaging Institute, and communications with staff members and other knowledgeable individuals.
4. Computer and Business Equipment Manufacturers Association, *The Information Technology Industry Data Book, 1960–2000* (Washington: 1990).
5. Information from publications, reports, and documents supplied by the Computer and Business Equipment Manufacturers Association, and communications with staff members and other knowledgeable individuals.
6. ASAE, *Policies and Procedures*.
7. Letter to the author from Nancy Nord, executive director of American Corporate Councel Association, dated November 30, 1989.
8. Information from publications, reports, and documents supplied by the American Corporate Counsel Association, and communications with staff members and other knowledgeable individuals.

11

International Associations

International life normally has in it strong competitive elements. Just as there is no uncomplicated personal relationship between individuals, so, I think, there is no international relationship between sovereign states which is without its elements of antagonism, its competitive elements.

George F. Kennan

Industries and professions that cross national borders have become increasingly common and have produced a growth of international memberships in business associations. Many businesses in other countries find it useful to join U. S. associations. Over 60 percent of national associations, 18 percent of state associations, and 8 percent of local associations report members based outside the United States.[1] Undoubtedly, many American businesses operating abroad participate successfully in trade and other associations in those countries.

The globalization of business and professional activity has spurred a considerable increase in international associations. Some that choose to describe themselves as international are really only national associations with a handful of members in Canada or Mexico, but many are genuinely international. These are of two types.

First, the majority of international associations are probably continental in scope.[2] In the Western Hemisphere, these associations have members throughout North America and, in some cases, perhaps Latin America as well. Across the Atlantic, the number of continental business associations that exist to interact with the European Economic Community

(EEC) and other European institutions is growing apace, often as federations or confederations of national organizations. The second category consists of business associations whose memberships cross both national and continental boundaries; these may actually span the globe.

Characteristics and Distinctive Problems

International associations closely resemble national organizations. Professional societies make up a somewhat larger percentage of international groups than of national associations, while trade associations are somewhat fewer.[3] At the same time, international trade associations tend to have more members than national trade groups, while international professional groups tend to have fewer. Staff size and budgets are about the same.

Perhaps the most notable distinction is that international associations are less likely to be involved in government relations than are national groups. This is an important clue to the nature of international associations. Because public policy objectives can be implemented only where there are governments, business associations operating internationally must play an essentially coordinating role, working either through their national affiliates or with inter-governmental organizations.

An example is the International Information Industry Congress (IIIC), a federation of thirteen national associations on four continents representing the computer and business equipment industry. Common positions are developed and coordinated through IIIC, which can lobby directly for them only with such bodies as the EEC and GATT (the General Agreement on Tariffs and Trade, an inter-governmental negotiating forum). Lobbying for changes in national policies must be carried out by IIIC's member associations.

Some 28 percent of trade associations report participation in federations of related organizations around the world,[4] a number that testifies to the globalization of business and industry. Many cross-border associations begin life with an international membership. Others start as national organizations and later evolve into international status.[5] Either way, international organizations have problems that other U. S. associations do not face.

Assessing and collecting funds in different currencies. Fluctuations in currency values can make the payment of dues and other fees economically complex and a touchy matter among members. Some associations establish dues and fees in a single official currency, typically the U. S. dollar, on the assumption that imbalances will even out over time; this they may or may not do. Other groups publish their rates in multiple currencies, based on currency values at the time. This appears to be the fairest solution, provided that the rates are updated with some frequency.

Managing language problems. International associations have to decide whether publications should be issued in more than one language. They must also manage the complexities of simultaneous translation at association meetings. Some international associations, particularly scientific groups, have a single official language in which all publications and meetings are conducted. This is the easiest solution logistically if all the members are fluent in that language.

The answer is not that simple, however, for many other international associations, especially business groups. Even if its membership is predominantly in the Western Hemisphere, the organization may need language capabilities in French, Spanish, and Portuguese, as well as English. The problem is even more complex if there is a substantial membership in Europe and Asia.

These problems can be political as well as logistical, if members outside the United States see the organization as focused on a single country rather than globally. More than one international association member has echoed the opinion of the European business executive who criticized his association for viewing its headquarters location as "the navel of the universe."

Delivering services fairly to all members. International associations may provide services to their host country membership that they cannot render to their members in other countries. Government relations is the most common example of this type of problem. Such an organization must find ways to demonstrate to its members abroad that they do not have second-class status.

One common solution is differential dues schedules. Over a third of international associations, especially trade associations, have a separate dues schedule for their overseas members.[6] Lower dues to these members do more than reflect an inability to provide the full range of services offered to domestic members. They also serve as a promotional device to stimulate international membership.

The fairness problem likewise appears in the association's conference and communications programs. Meeting sites must be selected with an eye to their geographic accessibility for members coming from a number of points, as well as the political implications within the association of particular conference or convention locations. International associations are much more likely to hold meetings outside the headquarters country than are national organizations. International groups based in the United States often have foreign meetings in Canada or Europe. Groups headquartered outside the United States frequently meet in North America, Europe, or the Mexico/Caribbean region, but Australia is also a popular location.

The organization must be sure that its publications are received as promptly by its overseas members as domestically, no small problem even using premium-rate airmail. A number of associations are experimenting with electronic communications media to ease this problem.

The rapid spread of fax machines provides a virtually instantaneous medium of communications to any member having comparable equipment. Telex machines, on which so many international businesses and associations have relied, may become obsolete as a result. Association communications via electronic mail (e-mail) and bulletins are entirely feasible for any organization whose members have as little as a personal computer with modem, let alone more complex gear. (E-mail refers to computerized messages sent to identified recipients. Electronic bulletin boards consist of notices or information displayed whenever participants log on to the system.) About a fifth of associations of all kinds now utilize their computers for e-mail and half that number for electronic bulletin boards. Both those numbers are higher for international associations.[7]

As an interesting experiment in global communications, a three-week international conference on the Chernobyl nuclear power disaster was held in the fall of 1986 entirely by e-mail. As reported by staff personnel of the American Nuclear Society, the conference "was accessible to anyone with a personal computer and modem or other communications computer. Any number of people worldwide could send messages for all other conference members on-line to read simultaneously; or the messages could be stored until a conference member signed on. The conference host computer was open continuously so persons in all time zones could participate at their convenience."[8] There are substantial implications for associations arising from this communications innovation.

Managing relations with overseas affiliates. More often than not, international associations must maintain relationships with national or continental associations serving similar memberships. Good relationships with these groups are important because they serve the common constituency. Moreover, because the local affiliates are closer to the membership, they are generally in a strong position either to help or harm the international group among the shared members.

Lines of communication can be maintained through informal contacts between the international organization and the national associations. There may also be more formal ties:

• The international association may be a federation to which continental or national associations belong.

• The international group may organize chapters or sections in the countries where it has active corporate or individual members. Over a third of international associations have chapters in other lands.[9]

Whatever the formal or informal relationship, considerable effort is frequently invested by international associations to coordinate activities and communications with the local affiliates and to avoid competitive situations with them. When the international group plans a major meeting in a country, it may coordinate arrangements with the local organization or use the affiliate as its arrangements agent. Educational and other programs are frequently coordinated with national or continental affiliates, often with speakers from or provided by the international organization.

Even though international associations are rarely able to lobby national governments outside their host countries, there are other government-relations services they can provide. For one thing, they can lobby international organizations of governments—whether those be regional groupings like the EEC and the Organization of American States, global structures like the United Nations and its own affiliated organizations, or GATT and other trade negotiating structures. International associations can also provide mechanisms for the coordination of national lobbying policies, as the IIIC does for the information technology industry and as the International Advertising Association (profiled below) does in the area of commercial free speech.

Finally, their communications media are a means to keep their entire membership posted on pertinent developments in particular countries or in inter-governmental organizations.

Profile: The International Advertising Association

The advertising industry teems with associations. There are over fifty national associations in the field, plus hundreds of state and local organizations. Outside the United States, there are innumerable advertising associations in countries all over the world, a few of them international in scope. These groups represent different kinds of advertisers, advertising media, advertising agencies and other kinds of marketing companies.

There is, however, only one organization that represents all three advertising interests on a global scale—the International Advertising Association (IAA). The IAA's members include nearly a hundred major corporate advertisers, advertising media companies and advertising agencies; national or continental advertising associations from every part of the globe; and 2,600 individual members in 74 countries with one or more chapters in thirty-seven of them.[10] It has chapters in Hungary and China, and members in the Soviet Union, and several Eastern European countries, as well as throughout Western Europe, the Western Hemisphere, the Middle East, Africa, and the Asia/Pacific region.

For all that breadth, IAA has been a small association that depends heavily on an active cadre of volunteer leaders. Its current budget is under $900,000, and it has a staff of half a dozen. However it has embarked on a global growth plan to double its revenue by 1993 and substantially increase its staff and services. New professional leadership has been brought in recently.

There is a natural tension among the three sectors of advertising, but also a strong sense of interdependence. The advertisers are the central focus. They buy advertising to market their products or services; they thereby provide the funds that support the media and agencies. Advertisers include giant multinational corporations, small neighborhood merchants, and every enterprise in between that utilizes marketing communications to sell its wares.

No advertising exists without the companies that purchase it, but neither can it exist any without the print, electronic, and other media in which it appears. Advertising media range well beyond newspapers, magazines, television, and radio. They also include neon and other signage, books, motion pictures, catalogs, direct mail, sales promotions, and a host of other techniques, as ordinary as billboards and posters and as exotic as skywriting and dirigibles.

Advertising agencies provide the technical expertise and creative skill that translate the advertiser's needs into an attractive and persuasive message placed in one or more media. The agencies are therefore a bridge between the other two sectors.

These advertising sectors all have their own needs and interests that frequently lead them to form their own separate trade associations at every level—locally, nationally, and internationally. But all three sectors also need each other. They have therefore formed other associations in common wherever they have shared needs or problems.

IAA was founded in New York in 1938 as the Export Advertising Association to serve the international needs common to all three sectors. Originally oriented to the needs of advertising to promote foreign trade, its membership remained primarily in the United States until the 1950s. When the group's name was changed to its present one in 1953, four-fifths of its members were Americans. By 1990, nine out of every ten members were from countries outside the United States.

Organizationally, IAA is a hybrid. It is a trade association with corporate members of various sizes in all three sectors of the industry. It is a federation of thirty-one other associations around the world. And it is an individual membership organization to which about 2,600 advertising professionals belong.

IAA's primary mission is the advancement of freedom of commercial speech and consumer choice around the world, and opposition to "unwarranted restrictions" on advertising by governments. It encourages the adoption of self-regulatory codes and processes. It also supports education and works to "demonstrate the economic and social values of advertising and marketing through research, publications, and public service."[11]

Membership. The association has three classes of membership:

Individual members, who pay $150 per year (plus local chapter dues). These are employees in the three advertising sectors.

Organizational members, which are advertising and other industry associations that pay $350 per year. There are thirty-three such members.

Corporate members, which are advertisers, agencies, and media companies that currently pay $5,000 in annual dues. This is the category targeted for strongest future growth. IAA's strategic plan projects an increase to 150 such members by 1993 from the current level of 94.

Staff and Budget. IAA's staff underwent a major reorganization after the former executive director, Mary W. Covington, left to take a European assignment. An international advertising executive, Norman Vale, an American citizen, was recruited to head the staff with the title of director general. Richard M. Corner, a British subject, was promoted to executive director reporting to Vale. The support staff includes communications, editorial, membership, and information systems specialists.

The 1989 $900,000 budget funded staff salaries, office overhead, and other general and administrative expenses (70 percent), plus various programs (30 percent), of which publications form the largest component.

An ambitious program to upgrade the association has been initiated. IAA describes its parameters thus:

The new strategic plan focuses on the repositioning of the IAA as a world class organization.

To achieve this and to increase global impact and recognition, the full-time leadership of the World Secretariat has been strengthened by the newly created position of Director-General.

A full review of all programs and activities is underway and a worldwide public awareness campaign has been launched.

Regular contacts with all categories of members will be increased and an electronic communications and information system is being introduced for the membership network.

Much greater attention will be paid to the IAA's regional representation under the leadership of the vice president/area directors. These elected officers, working with their regional committees, will also have specific responsibility for membership recruitment and retention and for chapter development.[12]

Governance. IAA has a large and complex—perhaps cumbersome— leadership structure. Until recently, the board of directors has sixty-three members of whom ten represent the chapters. Officers include a world president and senior vice president, five vice presidents/area directors who represent different geographic regions, and appointed vice presidents who have specific program responsibilities. An executive committee acts for the association between the annual board meetings. The World Council, consisting of 120 members, includes at least one delegate from every country and elects the officers and board members at its biannual meetings.

The board and committee structure has been revamped, to focus more closely on public policy issues and implementation. Board and executive committee members are now expected to become personally involved in government and public relations.

Chapters. IAA's national chapters play an essential role in the association's programs. Individual IAA members are automatically members of their local chapters if any exist in their countries. New chapters are considered for admission if they have at least fifteen members. Each of its far-flung chapters is staffed by voluntary leaders, except those in the United States, Great Britain, and Japan which have at least part-time paid staff. The association's elected leadership and staff travel widely to attend chapter meetings and carry the IAA message. IAA provides organizational manuals and publications to assist the chapters and holds workshops for chapter presidents from time to time.

By necessity, the chapters operate with considerable autonomy. There is thus always the danger that an individual chapter may take positions or actions inconsistent with IAA policies. This is particularly a risk in chapters with long-time, entrenched leaders who have occasionally been known to act more from self-interest than in the interest of the organization.

Government Relations and Public Affairs. IAA's charge to protect commercial free speech requires extensive monitoring of advertising issues and advocacy of its point of view wherever challenges arise. Among the issues with which the association concerns itself are taxes on advertising, advertising regulation and self-regulation, and restrictions on marketing communications generally, as well as for specific products like tobacco and alcoholic beverages, among others.

The association engages in some direct lobbying, primarily with intergovernmental organizations with which it has official status. These include UNESCO (the United Nations Educational, Scientific, and Cultural Organization), ECOSOC (the United Nations' Economic and Social Council), and WIPO (the World Intellectual Property Organization). In the main, however, IAA's government-relations activities must be carried out through its national chapters, organizational members, and key sister associations. What the association provides through its headquarters staff in New York is leadership, strategy, information, research, policy guidance, and overall coordination.

Because of increasing legislative activity and the multiplicity of national and international governmental bodies in Europe, where over 45 percent of IAA's membership is located and where many of its non-European members also have a strong interest, the association has arranged to have the European Advertising Tripartite, an association based in Brussels, provide IAA with public affairs representation in Europe.

IAA views both industry self-regulation and better public understanding of the importance of advertising as essential to its opposition to excessive governmental controls. The association plans to enhance its external public relations and to provide better information and educational programs for the membership to strengthen these government-relations support activities.

Meetings and Publications. An association as thinly staffed as IAA has had to utilize its chapters for national and regional meetings to a very great extent. The association does, however, hold its own three- or four-day world congress every two years in different cities around the globe: Sydney in 1988, Hamburg in 1990, Barcelona in 1992, and Acapulco in 1994. Some 1,300 to 2,000 advertising executives attend these congresses, which focus on current issues, trends, and prospects for the advertising industry—globally, regionally, and nationally. The association and its chapters also co-sponsor meetings on special subjects important to its members, such as a conference on "Communicating with the European Consumer in the 1990s," held in London in 1989. IAA expects to centralize more of its meeting and conference management in coming years.

Publications, vital to any association's membership communications, have been a problem for IAA. A new newsletter covering chapter news and public issues has been developed; utilizing a desktop publishing facility, to replace its former magazine.

The association has published a number of impressive monographs and survey reports on advertising issues. These include, for instance, multi-national surveys on government regulation and industry self-regulation, advertising trade and investment barriers, and the use of premiums and other sales promotions. Other studies have dealt with worldwide advertising expenditures, children's advertising, the role of sponsorship, advertising taxation, and the like. Many of these reports are prepared for IAA by academic consultants. A comprehensive membership directory is also published annually.

IAA actively promotes the use of public service advertising and, in conjunction with an arm of the United Nations and The New York Festivals, sponsors a competition for the best such advertisements around the world. The association also plans to expand its educational programs for young advertising professionals. These programs, run by accredited academic institutions in eighteen countries, offer certificates and diplomas in international advertising.

Relations with Other Organizations. Apart from its relations with national advertising organizations, IAA has overlapping concerns with other international associations. The International Chamber of Commerce, through its Marketing, Advertising and Distribution Committee, focuses on self-regulation of marketing and advertising. The World Federation of Advertisers, based in Brussels, primarily stresses government relations.

Some frictions have arisen from time to time among the three organizations. They recently adopted a joint statement pledging mutual cooperation in objectives, programs, and meetings, as well as the avoidance of duplication. It remains to be seen how well this statement will work in practice.

IAA's new management is also working out arrangements to cooperate on policy implementation and pool resources with other associations—the European Advertising Tripartite, as noted above, and the American Advertising Federation in the United States.

In sum, IAA is an organization in transition. It has been led by a capable staff, which has had to do more than revenues would permit, and by a corps of active volunteers, which has not always been fully mobilized to move effectively and in concert. Yet, it has produced substantial accomplishments and has had an effect well beyond what might be expected of an association of its size. If its new management and long-range plans succeed, IAA will be positioned for still greater growth and achievement. It is an organization poised for a remarkable future in a global business environment where it—and business associations like it—will have a vast role to play.

International business associations are likely to assume increasing importance to their members in the coming years as a result of economic globalization. A small but growing number of national associations based in the United States are establishing offices in major capitals abroad for purposes of public policy monitoring and lobbying; they also provide liaison with members' branch offices there. Some of these organizations may evolve into international groups.

The ability to carry out supranational government relations will almost certainly take on increasing importance. A number of associations now seek to influence the policy-coordinating activities of various inter-governmental organizations such as GATT and Codex Alimentarius, as well as those affiliated with the United Nations (such as the Food and Agriculture Organization and the International Labor Organization). Currently, however, only the European Economic Community has the authority actually to adopt policies with the force of law within its member states.

Arenas for direct supranational lobbying may increase in the future. As financial markets link to span the globe, for example, pressures to regulate them by supranational mechanisms can be expected. Parallel demands for regulation may well arise in other fields of multinational corporate activity. The evolution of associations with the ability to lobby governments on a worldwide basis would inevitably follow.

Managing corporate memberships in international business associations presents problems for companies not unlike those faced by the associations themselves: language difficulties, scope and adequacy of services, and so forth. The growing importance of these groups will make effective participation a critical concern for companies with global or regional interests in the 1990s and beyond.

NOTES

1. American Society of Association Executives (ASAE), *Policies and Procedures in Association Management* (Washington: 1987).

2. Continental associations are sometimes also called "regional." To avoid confusion, the latter term is used in this book to describe multi-state domestic organizations.

3. ASAE, *Policies and Procedures*.

4. *Ibid.*

5. An interesting case study of how the International Association of Refrigerated Warehouses developed from an originally domestic trade association is J. William Hudson, "Achieving International Status," in ASAE, *Association International Activity* (Washington: American Society of Association Executives, 1988).

6. ASAE, *Policies and Procedures*.

7. *Ibid.*

8. Octave J. Du Temple and Lois Webster, "Electronic Communications," in ASAE, *Association International Activity*.

9. ASAE, *Policies and Procedures*.

10. Information from publications, reports, and documents supplied by the International Advertising Association; interviews with staff members.

11. International Advertising Association, "Mission Statement" (New York: 1989).

12. Letter to the author from Richard M. Corner, executive director of the International Advertising Association, dated May 16, 1990.

12

State and Local Associations

There has been a cyclicality in the relative role of state governments, with the swing variable in this cyclical pattern being political ideology. In conservative periods, the role of state governments has been enhanced, whereas in liberal or progovernment periods, the role of the national government has grown. In liberal periods, those who favor increased governmental activity often find that it is efficient to lobby for their interests at one place, the center. In conservative periods, the proponents of increased governmental activity have fewer opportunities; they have to try to get changes adopted wherever they can.

Richard P. Nathan

Although state and local business associations engage in a variety of activities, just as national and international groups do, their public affairs and government-relations programs are the most important reasons for companies to join them. Indeed, such associations are the principal means of conducting government relations for most companies concerned with state legislative and regulatory activities. This includes even those companies that employ on-staff government liaison personnel or that retain independent lobbyists.

The importance of these associations is underscored by the steady growth of state legislative activity in recent years. Overshadowed by the federal colossus during the New Deal and three wars, many state governments gained a renewed spirit of activism and innovation beginning in the late 1960s. In part, this was stimulated by revenue sharing—a program of grants from Washington that enabled state governments to partake in the largesse funded by the federal income tax. The rise of consumer and environmental issues, which provided opportunities for state activity apart from the federal government's own involvement, also contributed. Clearly, a more recent factor is the shrinking of federal programs that resulted both from fiscal difficulties and the philosophical shift of the 1980s.

A number of organizations active in enhancing the role of state government strongly encouraged reforms to increase the professionalism of the legislatures and to enlarge their staffs. This, in turn, eventually led to longer legislative sessions, more safe seats, fragmentation of leadership, and increased careerism among legislators who now frequently view their political offices as full-time vocations. A large number of activists and innovators have won election to the legislatures and, more recently, to governorships and other statewide offices.

Public demand for services has remained high, but state and local governments have begun to suffer revenue problems. Revenue sharing disappeared in the 1980s, a casualty of chronic federal budget deficits, and other forms of federal aid have steadily waned.

Massachusetts, described as a fiscal "miracle" during the 1988 presidential campaign of Governor Michael Dukakis, teetered on the brink of financial chaos one year later and imposed massive tax increases on both business and individuals. The government of Westchester County, New York, a large, affluent suburban area, threatened substantial employee layoffs *after* winning local property tax increases in the range of 17 to 40 percent.

Undiminished voter demand for services, coupled with these financial pressures, has led elected state and local leaders to become innovative and frequently, as they like to say, entrepreneurial.[1] Their innovations have included experiments in privatization of some services. They have also demanded that business provide costly services that government had either previously supplied or now proposed to require for the first time, including mandatory parental leave and employee benefits.

To defend itself against the new demands, business has gradually increased its use of state government relations professionals[2] while continuing to utilize ad hoc independent lobbyists. Most companies, however, still lack state lobbying specialists. In a few cases, these companies rely on their national associations to provide state government relations services. For the most part, however, American business relies on state and sometimes local associations to handle legislative problems and often regulatory ones as well.

In many industries, these associations help assure the economic well-being of their members even more than their national counterparts do.

This is obviously true of those industries that are heavily regulated by state governments, such as banking, insurance, and utilities. It is also true of many other companies, even those that have fewer resources of their own in state capitals than in Washington.

CHARACTERISTICS OF STATE ASSOCIATIONS

State and local associations differ from national organizations in a number of important respects. They are usually small, financially strapped, and often dominated by their more active members. It is the rare industry whose state associations have the internal strength of their national counterpart.

The number of state associations in the United States is about equal to the combined total of groups with national and international memberships. Slightly less than one out of five associations is a local group. Although the vast majority of state associations serve a single state, there are some regional organizations with members in two or more states, at least one of which is usually small.

An indication of the growing importance of state associations is the decision by a public affairs publisher to issue a new directory of these groups, supplementing the listing of national groups that it has compiled for many years.[3]

State associations often labor under stringent conditions. Dues are frequently much lower than those of national organizations and, since the state groups also have a smaller membership base, revenue is almost always a major problem. Corporate mergers are putting increased revenue pressures on all associations—state and national—forcing them to seek out non-dues revenues. Management time thus becomes diluted and diverted from programs, including government relations. The executive who has to organize trade shows, sell insurance or advertising, or undertake other kinds of fund-raising has that much less time to lobby. One large state association (profiled below) raises over 90 percent of its income from non-dues sources.

Total revenues of state associations are usually substantially smaller than those of national groups. So are salaries. The top staff executives of state trade associations are paid about two-thirds of what their national counterparts earn.

State association staffs are also typically smaller, by about half. Few associations have as many as half a dozen staff members—and many operate with only one or two professionals plus a secretary. It is the rare association that has a staff of more than twenty, and these are usually found only in the largest states. Even among state umbrella groups, only a handful are this large.

SOME COMPARISONS OF NATIONAL AND STATE ASSOCIATIONS[4]

	National	State
Median pay to top staff executive	$84,000	$57,000
Median staff size	9	5
Association revenue	Half OVER $1,000,000	Half UNDER $500,000
Average dues	$8,966	$2,812
At least one staffer dedicated solely to government relations	33%	38%
Registered lobbyist on staff	25%	65%
Have government affairs committee	44%	71%
Have PAC	19%	55%

The largest state groups often resemble national associations more than they do their smaller brethren. These large groups can afford considerable specialization and sophistication. The smaller the group, the more its staff must operate as "jacks-of-all-trades."

STATE GOVERNMENT RELATIONS

State associations as a group give greater stress to government relations than do national organizations. Slightly more of them, proportionately, have one or more staff members whose time is exclusively devoted to government relations. Many more of them by far have registered lobbyists on staff, although registration may be partly a result of state lobbying requirements, which are generally much tighter than the federal law. State associations are almost three times more likely than national groups to have political action committees; this disparity is only partly due to the fact that many states permit corporate political contributions. Compared to national and international associations, they are also more than half again as likely to have a government affairs committee.

State groups have important political advantages over national associations. They are able to develop close personal relationships both with their members and with elected officials, giving them a degree of grassroots political strength that national organizations often envy.

Not many national association executives, for example, can claim a personal friendship with the President of the United States, but many state association executives have relationships with their governors that go back for years. They may have dealt with them when they were state legislators or local officials, maintaining the friendships as political careers progressed. Such relationships are also common with other top state officials, whether elected or appointed.

State association executives are also likelier to have a proportionately broader network of relationships in the state legislature than national association executives do with members of Congress. National groups tend to focus on the members of a few congressional committees, plus Senate and House leaders. State association staffers, by contrast, often have strong relationships throughout the legislature, an asset likely to grow as legislative careerism and incumbent re-election increase.

State associations often have more members in any one legislative district than national groups have in a given congressional district. Therefore, they can exert greater grass-roots legislative influence. An experienced state executive is likely to know which association member is personally acquainted with a particular legislator, so calls to the membership for grass-roots communications on issues are more informal, personal, and effective than the canned "all-points-bulletin" on which national associations often rely.

For that reason, some national groups cultivate good relationships with state associations, both in their own industry and in allied but separate industries. The Grocery Manufacturers of America, for instance, has long relied on state food and general retailing associations for grass-roots help on certain national issues—as, of course, have the national food retailing associations.

Another government relations dimension in some states, notably California, is the prevalence of referenda and initiatives. These processes resemble elections, and few individual state associations have the financial resources to wage effective public campaigns against ballot measures, much less to initiate them. Coalitions of business groups can be assembled and funded on the broadest ballot issues, but state associations may be all but helpless to deal with a popular measure that strikes narrowly at a single industry. If the state or the issue is important enough, help can sometimes be obtained from national companies or a well-financed national association, but such aid is far from universal.

Another dimension of state government relations that has no parallel at the federal level is the number of lobbying opportunities that exist among the various state government organizations. Governors, legislators, and other categories of state policymakers all have their own separate national and sometimes regional associations, through which they coordinate information and developments. These also provide opportunities for business groups to lobby en masse. A related policy organization develops proposals for uniform state laws. An important new group, the Council of Northeastern Governors (CONEG), is developing uniform policies, especially on environmental issues, for the New England and Middle Atlantic states. These are critical arenas in which state associations need to become more active. Many of their larger member-companies already are.

STATE UMBRELLA ASSOCIATIONS

The ability of individual companies to participate effectively in a state association depends heavily on the nature of their business and operations in that state, as does their ability for effective direct lobbying. If a company has its headquarters or other major operation in a state, it has the potential to be a significant force in the relevant state associations. If it lacks operations there, however, its potential influence is less, but it can still do much to fulfill that potential. Even today, after decades of issues affecting out-of-state companies, many firms operating in multi-state markets still give short shrift to the need to develop a local champion, in case of crisis.

Companies that do seek out an organizational advocate often look no further than a state umbrella group, usually either a state chamber of commerce or a state manufacturers association. While these groups offer a range of services, state government relations is generally the paramount function.

Chambers of commerce are umbrella associations in specific geographic areas whose members typically span the full range of business enterprise: manufacturing, wholesale and retail distribution, banking and finance, utilities, transportation, services, and so on. Members commonly range from large corporations to small businesses, often including individual professionals and entrepreneurs.

Chambers are autonomous organizations, each with its own revenues, programs, and governing structure. Local chambers are often dues-paying members of the state chamber; both groups usually belong to the U. S. Chamber. The relationship to the larger organization is that of members in a federated structure, not controlled chapters.

Like most trade and professional groups, chambers of commerce are typically organized as ''c-6'' non-profit associations. Some have tax-paying subsidiary service companies through which taxable income is channeled. Some also have established charitable and educational foundations (''c-3'' entities) for various purposes.

Local chambers usually stress economic services, although many, especially larger ones, engage in varying degrees of government relations. State chambers, on the other hand, place a higher priority on government relations. However, umbrella groups focus on broad business issues, not on those affecting specific industries. Membership in a state or local chamber is therefore no substitute for active participation in an appropriate state or local trade association.

The chamber of commerce profiled below, considered one of the most effective of the state umbrella groups, illustrates how these groups operate.

Profile: Michigan State Chamber of Commerce

Measured in terms of number of members, the Michigan State Chamber of Commerce is the largest state chamber in the United States, although several other such organizations have larger budgets. Although it is only thirty years old, the Michigan chamber is widely regarded as one of the elite within the chamber movement.

The organization sets forth its purposes in these words:

The Michigan State Chamber of Commerce was established in November of 1959, to represent employer interests by working to promote conditions favorable to economic development in Michigan.

On behalf of Michigan's job providers we:

· Analyze and distribute information on laws and regulations of interest to employers.
· Make our members' views on laws and regulations known to state and local government officials.
· Further the training and education of our members through a wide variety of conferences, seminars and publications.
· Function in the public interest by encouraging our members to maintain and observe ethical business practices and standards of conduct.
· Encourage our members to be actively involved in the legislative and political process.
· Litigate issues of importance to job providers.[5]

Structure. The Michigan chamber has about 7,000 members, considerably more than any other state business umbrella organization. By contrast, the umbrella groups of the nation's two largest states, the California Chamber of Commerce and the Business Council of New York—the latter, an amalgam of the old state chamber and state manufacturers association—have about 3,500 members each. The Michigan chamber's membership includes some of the largest corporations in America, including the automotive giants headquartered in the state. Four members out of every five, however, employ fewer than a hundred people.

State chambers often have huge boards of directors, and the number on Michigan's, eighty-eight, is far from the largest. Directors are elected for two-year terms and must rotate off after three terms. About a fifth of the board is elected at large; the remainder is elected to represent eight geographic districts. One member represents the 255 local chambers in the state, about two-thirds of which are state chamber members. Sixty-five trade and professional associations in the state also belong to the Michigan chamber, but they do not have board membership.

An executive committee, with the usual responsibilities, is comprised of the officers—chairman, immediate past chairman, eight vice chairmen, treasurer, and the president, who is the chief staff officer. There is also a secretary, but that is a staff position, not an elected office. Officers serve one-year terms and may be reelected as long as they are directors; the chairman, however, is limited to two terms.

Policy-making follows typical business association practice. Recommendations on issue positions and other matters come from committees and staff to the board or the executive committee for adoption.

Staff. The staff of thirty-six is headed by the state chamber's president and chief executive officer, James Barrett, who is the designated official spokesman for the organization. The headquarters are located near the state capitol in Lansing. Three vice presidents head specific staff departments.

The first vice president, for government relations, supervises two lobbyists, one for tax and regulatory issues, the other for environmental and natural resource issues. The second vice president directs political affairs, doubles as general counsel, and oversees the chamber's foundation. A political finance director and a manager of small business programs and local chamber networking report to him. (It is unusual among business associations for political activities to be separated organizationally from the government relations function; the distinction here indicates the Michigan chamber's emphasis on the political area.) The third vice president oversees membership sales and services, the for-profit service subsidiary, and advertising for the chamber's magazine.

Also reporting to the president are a communications director and an assistant who manages administrative functions.

Finance. The Michigan chamber operates on a budget of $2.8 million, over 90 percent of which comes from membership dues. Dues are assessed basically by number of employees, but there are some variations in this formula for financial and other businesses. Annual dues payments range from a low of $195 to a high of $35,000. Advertising and project revenue comprise most of the remaining income. The largest expense item, staff salaries, consumes 43 percent of outlays. The remainder covers miscellaneous general and administrative costs.

Government Relations. Like other umbrella organizations, the Michigan chamber emphasizes issues with a broad impact on business, such as taxes, labor, product liability, and environmental problems. It has a traditionally conservative preference for private sector economic development and thus generally opposes increases in taxes and government spending.

The chamber urges that employee benefits be left to the marketplace and not mandated by government. It opposes the expansion of the state's sales tax to services. It supports an extensive revision of the unemployment insurance program to reduce the burden on business. It backs changes to reduce the cost of product liability litigation. It argues for better enforcement of existing state environmental laws (in preference to new ones) and opposes efforts to toughen those laws above federal standards. It has, however, also supported bond issues to fund environmental and recreation projects; it also seeks a restructuring of Michigan's budget to provide more money for education.

To implement such positions, the chamber uses a full range of tactics to influence Michigan's governmental and political processes:

• The chamber engages in direct staff lobbying to persuade state policymakers to its point of view on the issues. Three full-time lobbyists, plus its president and general counsel, lobby extensively to make the organization's influence felt and convincing. The chamber is immensely proud of a 1987 survey of the effectiveness of interest groups and individual lobbyists. The survey queried legislators, legislative staff, executive and regulatory officials, the press, and lobbying groups themselves. The state chamber was rated the most influential organization in the state, and four members of its staff were ranked among the ten most effective individual interest group lobbyists.

• The chamber reinforces its direct lobbying with extensive grass-roots legislative communications. A staff member works full-time at mobilizing members, especially small business owners, to develop and utilize relationships with individual legislators on the group's priority issues. He also works with the state's local chambers of commerce to stimulate legislative communications from them and their own members.

• The state chamber also leverages its own influence through coalitions of trade associations, local chambers, and individual companies. One such coalition stimulated a major grass-roots letter-writing campaign against a compulsory, employer-funded health care proposal, delaying the legislation if not killing it altogether.

• Members and allied organizations are kept informed and motivated by a series of legislative bulletins prepared by staff lobbyists.

• Because business groups have often found that issues that they thought had been won in the legislature were later lost at the regulatory level, the Michigan chamber has been making increased use of litigation to accomplish its aims. It has also challenged in court the constitutionality of certain laws. It has successfully initiated or intervened in cases involving employee terminations, replacement of strikers, and overcharges to employers for workers compensation. It also mounted an ultimately unsuccessful challenge all the way to the U.S. Supreme Court against a Michigan law that prohibits corporations from making independent election expenditures in support of favored candidates.

• Michigan permits popular referenda in which the voters can have the final say on particular legislative issues. The chamber has actively worked on several campaigns, including two in 1989 that would have increased sales taxes to provide more money for public education. Arguing that educational funds should be increased by reordering public priorities, not by new taxes, the chamber and its allies defeated both measures.

Political Programs. Issues are ultimately settled at the ballot box by the voters' choice of legislators and other elected officials. The Michigan chamber has an extensive program to influence the outcomes of those elections through candidate endorsements, political action committees, and political participation programs.

The organization's candidate endorsements appear to carry unusual weight. A 1986 public opinion survey by *The Detroit News* found that endorsements by the Michigan State Chamber of Commerce were more likely to influence voters' decisions favorably than those of any other interest group or of major newspapers.

The state chamber's PAC currently raises about $175,000 from Michigan business people over the two-year election cycle. Unlike many other PACs, which spread their contributions over a large number of contests, the chamber's PAC has focused on a small number of races that it deemed especially critical and in which it could have a significant impact. Its success record in these campaigns has been over 90 percent. A separate PAC funds state chamber involvement in referendum campaigns.

Local chamber PACs have been stimulated by the state chamber, which coordinates their activities through the Chamber PAC Network. In addition to direct candidate support, the network has made in-kind contributions to candidates, providing them with personal computers and political software.

The chamber or its PAC also sponsors voter opinion polls on key legislative and ballot question campaigns, trains campaign managers of the endorsed candidates, and stimulates business people to become involved in precinct-level politics. The chamber also trains managers of allied PACs and commissions public opinion polls on political matters.

Publications and Meetings. In addition to its bulletins and incidental legislative communications, the Michigan chamber publishes a monthly magazine, *Michigan Forward*. It contains articles on economic and communications topics but, as with everything else in which the Michigan State Chamber of Commerce is involved, the emphasis is on public policy issues. The magazine carries advertising.

The Michigan chamber has no annual meeting as such. Instead it sponsors regional briefings around the state on legislative, political, and other subjects of member interest.

Affiliates. Most of the chamber's economic activities are carried out by its for-profit subsidiary, Michigan State Chamber Services, Inc. The subsidiary manages a variety of taxable, revenue-generating functions for the parent, absorbing or funding program costs in such areas as educational seminars, publications, data processing, and telemarketing. The corporation has an annual operating budget in excess of $800,000. In 1989, a total of sixty-six educational sessions on twenty-three seminar topics were held for chamber members, mostly on labor, tax, environmental, and product liability topics.

Economic service publications are issued, by the parent or the subsidiary, on subjects of concern to Michigan employers. These mainly explain pertinent state and federal regulatory requirements but some deal with matters like the use of alcohol and drugs in the workplace. The chamber also sponsors economic service programs, such as one offered by a commercial consulting firm to reduce unemployment taxes paid by individual employers.

Another subsidiary, the Michigan State Chamber Foundation, a "c-3" organization, conducts a series of educational seminars, called "Leadership Michigan," for future state leaders from all segments of society. The program covers such state issues as criminal justice, education, health care and costs, economic development, and similar topics. Participants must be approved by a selection committee and are often sponsored by individual companies that pay their tuition costs. The foundation is also involved in promoting the privatization of many services of local governments. The foundation's annual expenses, funded through contributions, are about $200,000.

The chamber seeks independent funding for a number of projects and services. These include the construction of its office building and conference center in Lansing, policy studies, litigation, and a combined public relations/advertising program to promote economic education.

The Michigan State Chamber of Commerce is an example of a creatively managed umbrella association that knows what its members want and works energetically to perform for them.

STATE TRADE ASSOCIATIONS

The characteristics of state associations derive from the size of the local industry they represent, the scope and severity of government relations needs, and the mix of member demands between public affairs programs and economic functions. A way of illustrating this point is to compare two associations in the same industry.

Profiled below are two state associations comprised of food and grocery retailers. The New York State Food Merchants Association is one of the oldest and largest state associations in the country; it operates in a state with a very activist governmental philosophy. The Utah Retail Grocers Association represents food retailers in a much smaller state with a very different governmental attitude; its members call on their association for quite another range of services.

An understanding of the structure of grocery retailing is a useful introduction to these two profiles. The industry's configuration has had a major effect on the development of the state and local food retailing associations found in virtually every state. (A few food associations are multi-state.)

The industry was characterized until the 1930s by independent retailers who frequently had only one or two stores, which were neighborhood-oriented and always rather small. Even the few chains that existed were comprised of small stores. These independents were, and still are, serviced by wholesalers who provide most of their grocery products. The two kinds of businesses, retailers and wholesalers, have close but complicated interrelationships. Independents are typically served by only a single primary wholesaler who frequently also provides its retail customers with a range of other services. These generally include advertising and merchandising, but sometimes extend to accounting and store design.

Although some independents are organizationally autonomous from their wholesalers, many of the strongest are affiliated with them in one of two kinds of relationships: cooperatives or voluntaries. A cooperative is a structure in which the wholesaler is owned by its member-retailers. A voluntary organization is a franchise-like arrangement in which the retailers are in effect licensed by the wholesaler, although there is no common ownership. (Wholesalers do occasionally hold a minority financial stake in the stores). From the consumer's point of view, the stores under both arrangements act like corporate chains, usually doing business under a common store name. The stores, however, are really independently owned and operated.

A revolutionary development occurred in the mid-1930s with the invention of the supermarket, a large store with a wider array of goods typically sold at lower prices than small independents could provide. Supermarkets grew rapidly, often owned by great corporate chains against which the independents had considerable difficulty competing. Those that survived often became independent supermarkets themselves.

Independents developed a strong antipathy toward the chains and for a time even sought to have them outlawed. As a result, most state associations, historically comprised of independents, would not admit chains to membership. Some still do not, to this day. Nationally, the chains formed their own trade associations, separate from that representing independents.

A number of state and local associations do not admit wholesalers to their membership either, although that number seems to be declining.

Also widely excluded have been the convenience stores, another food-retailing innovation that arose in the 1940s and 1950s.

In many states, therefore, state and local food associations have consisted only of independents; in others, only independents and wholesalers may join. The chains and convenience stores have generally taken care of their own problems, through a national association, or through a state non-food general retail association.

Profile: New York State Food Merchants Association

Trade associations are typically the prime vehicle by which most companies in the retail food industry handle their state government-relations needs. Even in a state the size of New York, which has many large food distributors, only a few very large firms have government relations personnel on staff. Government relations is therefore the most important service that the New York State Food Merchants Association (NYSFMA) provides its members.

NYSFMA, one of the oldest state associations in the country, was founded in 1900.[6] For many years, it was the largest state association in the food industry and is still one of the biggest, although its size has stabilized while its counterparts in some other states have continued to grow. It also has perhaps the most diverse membership in an industry frequently marked by intense rivalries.

Food retailing is a vast industry. Sales are closely related to population. New York State's food industry does about $25 billion in annual sales, second only to California's. There are about 20,000 food stores in the state.

NYSFMA is exceptional in that it has been the only large state association to which all the major elements in food retailing belong: supermarket chains, wholesalers, cooperatives, voluntaries, independent retailers, convenience stores, and even *bodegas* (small Hispanic food stores). This has given it a strength in the food industry and in the state capital, Albany, that many other state associations can only envy.

The association's membership stretches from Long Island through New York City and west to Buffalo. Its largest concentration of members is in metropolitan New York, followed by the Buffalo-Rochester area. There are eighteen wholesaler members and over 550 retailer members. Most of these retailers are single-store operators, but some of the chains have several hundred stores each.

NYSFMA's primary mission is to represent food retailers in state and local legislative matters. However, the association also provides extensive non-legislative services to grocery manufacturers and other suppliers, as well as to the retailers and wholesalers who are its primary members.

Finance. NYSFMA has several unusual characteristics that set it apart from the vast majority of other trade associations. First, membership dues provide an uncommonly small share of its $2.5 million budget—about 5 percent. Dues, assessed according to sales volume, range from a low of $100 to a maximum of $5,000 per year. Comprehensive dues increases have been massively resisted by most members whose threats to resign have usually been sufficient to bring an end to the subject. Occasional dues increases have occurred in the upper brackets, but the dues ceiling still offers a genuine bargain to the larger retailers and wholesalers who dominate the association.

Second, because dues are so small, the association's budget—and particularly its extensive government relations services—must be financed by income that the IRS considers "unrelated."[7] For that reason, NYSFMA lost its tax exemption many years ago and is therefore a tax-paying entity.

Third, the association has developed a distinctive trade relations program for manufacturers that provides over three-fourths of NYSFMA's income. It is not unusual among either food retailing or other kinds of associations to tap suppliers as a source of income, but few are as dependent on supplier revenues as NYSFMA. Many years ago, the top executive of a large national food manufacturer was asked why companies like his were so willing to donate as generously as most do to retailers' associations and the charitable causes that food retailers often sponsor. He laughed uproariously: "The supplier always pays to get the business, my boy; the supplier always pays."

NYSFMA relies heavily on that willingness, carrying supplier funding to an exceptional length. About 170 suppliers of products, equipment, and services participate in its trade relations program. These suppliers pay annual fees of $5,900 to $8,300 for services that include exhibit space at the association's convention trade show and a certain number of advertisements in NYSFMA's monthly tabloid newspaper, *Food Merchants Advocate*.

It is the intangibles, however, that make participation in the trade relations program attractive to these companies, particularly a series of social opportunities in which they can visit with the top executives of their retail customers. Since sales executives seldom have a chance to meet with anyone higher than store managers and buyers, especially in the metro New York market (the nation's largest), most suppliers consider this a valuable service for which they are willing to pay handsomely.

These companies include not only grocery manufacturers, but also suppliers of equipment and services, including the advertising media. Many of them are mid-sized firms, but a number are among the best-known corporate names in America: Coca-Cola, Campbell Soup, General Mills, Philip Morris, Procter & Gamble, IBM, Kodak, TV Guide, and The New York Times, to name only a few.

Together with other manufacturer advertising, this program provides about 80 percent of NYSFMA's income. Despite the extent of this support, however, these companies have no membership privileges. Many other trade associations do permit some formal involvement by suppliers in return for their financial support. About two-thirds of trade associations (and half of state associations) have some kind of associate membership category for suppliers, often assessing dues on a lower scale than for the primary members.[8] NYSFMA, however, has declined on several occasions to admit suppliers to membership or to give them representation on its board of directors. At the same time, it charges them fees considerably higher than even its largest retail members pay in dues. Most of these companies instead belong to a captive association, the Food Industry Executives Council, which NYSFMA administers. It meets from time to time with top association staff and voluntary leaders to discuss trade relations problems.

In addition to membership dues and its trade relations and other advertising revenue, NYSFMA derives income from both a group insurance program for members and a program that processes the manufacturers' cents-off coupons that food stores redeem from consumers.

Structure. The association's official policy body is its board of directors, a group that fluctuates in size between thirty-five and forty members. Most of the chains and large wholesalers are regularly represented on the board, but a large minority are independent retailers of varying sizes. Although members of the board serve three-year terms, there is no practical bar to indefinite re-election: Almost a third of the directors first joined the board over ten years ago, and a few have been on the board about twice that long.

Most of the governing power lies with the twelve-member executive committee, comprised of the officers plus a few directors appointed by the chairman of the board. The chairman and vice chairmen serve one-year terms and generally are not re-elected. The treasurer is customarily re-elected several times to provide a continuity of financial expertise. The association's general counsel has served as NYSFMA's secretary for many years.

NYSFMA utilizes the usual structure of standing committees and ad hoc task forces. Some of these are administrative, like the finance committee. Program committees, particularly the convention committee, are considered quite important and sometimes prestigious; chairmanship of the convention committee has generally been a steppingstone to election as a vice chairman, putting the individual on the ladder to reach the top elected position eventually.

By far, the most important committee deals with government relations. It evaluates issues based on staff reports and recommends positions on these issues to the executive committee and full board. With rare exceptions, the committee's views are accepted fairly automatically as the association's position.

Staff. Headquartered for many years in New York City's northern suburbs, the association moved its principal office to Albany in 1987. Because metro New York is where the majority of its members and suppliers are located, it maintains a downstate office in New York City that houses half its staff of twenty-four. Located in Albany are the president, James T. Rogers, a director of government relations, a manager of political programs, and most member service and administrative support personnel. Staff members who manage the trade relations program, the convention and other meetings, and the publications office are based in the downstate office. Also in the downstate office is a manager of public and consumer affairs who handles local government relations in New York City and three large suburban counties.

Government Relations. NYSFMA considers government relations its most important function. New York, the nation's second largest state, has an activist government that prides itself on legislative and regulatory initiatives, particularly in the fields of environmental and consumer protection. New York City and some of its suburban areas have an equally activist political philosophy. In consequence, highly visible industries like food retailing are frequently the reluctant recipients of many legislative initiatives at both state and local levels.

NYSFMA therefore lobbies actively on a variety of food packaging and labeling proposals, health and nutrition issues, the regulation of food store sanitation and alcoholic beverage sales, sales tax enforcement, and a broad range of other issues, from employee drug testing to retail store wheelchair accessibility. The association has a high success record on these issues.

NYSFMA's most significant issue continues to be the state's beverage container deposit law, enacted in 1982 after a ten-year battle waged against it by the association and beverage industry suppliers. Shortly after its adoption, NYSFMA succeeded in winning legislative approval for a higher handling fee (paid by beverage suppliers) to compensate retailers partially for the costs of processing returned containers. Ever since, the association has given high priority to a further legislated increase in the handling fee, so far unsuccessfully. Its competitors on this issue are the state beer distribution and soft drink bottling associations and their members, many of whom, ironically, are major participants in the NYSFMA trade relations program.

The association engages in extensive direct lobbying in Albany on these issues, using two full-time lobbyists, plus NYSFMA's president and a retained lobbying firm. Lobbying local governments in metro New York is the responsibility of still another staff member. The association also utilizes aggressive grass-roots lobbying through a system of regional teams of retailers developed in the mid-1980s.

NYSFMA's access to the elected officials who decide the fate of these issues is enhanced by the activities of the Food Industry Political Action Committee (FI-PAC), a captive organization administered by NYSFMA and funded by retailers' corporate political contributions, which are legal in New York State for state and local elections. The PAC collects about $125,000 each year from retailers and wholesalers. Over the course of the two-year election cycle, therefore, FI-PAC contributes over $250,000 to political committees and candidates, making it one of the larger PACs operating in New York State. FI-PAC's recipients include a substantial percentage of incumbent legislators (the vast majority of whom are routinely re-elected), a few non-incumbent candidates, and the legislative campaign committees of both parties. Contributions have also been made to candidates for governor and for key local offices in New York City, Buffalo, and some suburbs.

Meetings and Publications. In addition to its legislative and political functions, NYSFMA organizes two major annual meetings—its convention and trade show, which is one of the largest food industry gatherings in the country, and a mid-year educational conference for independents. It also holds occasional educational seminars on special subjects.

Several publications are issued monthly. The *Food Merchants Advocate,* its tabloid newspaper, circulates to about 25,000 retailers, wholesalers, and supplier executives. (The *Advocate,* over a century old, predates NYSFMA's own establishment.) A members-only newsletter, *FoodScan,* covers government relations developments statewide. Another publication, *Metroline,* reports on local issues in New York City and Long Island for downstate members. NYSFMA has also issued special publications on such topics as the bottle law, sales tax enforcement, and store sanitation issues.

Relations with Other Organizations. NYSFMA has long maintained a close but informal relationship with the Food Marketing Institute (FMI), one of the two national associations representing food retailers. NYSFMA's current C.E.O. is a former FMI staff member. The association has provided grass-roots assistance to FMI in New York State on federal issues, and they cooperate on various other programs and projects. NYSFMA's relations with the National Grocers Association (NGA), an organization considerably smaller than FMI that primarily represents independents, are less close. Many state food associations are NGA members (FMI does not accept memberships from other associations), but NYSFMA is not among them.

Local grocers' associations have existed within the state in the past, but NYSFMA absorbed them many years ago. An exception is a small organization in New York City that works almost exclusively on regulatory issues. A small association of convenience store operators, some of whose members also belong to NYSFMA, was formed in the mid-1980s.

In sum, NYSFMA's programs and activities are skewed by its unusual financial characteristics and the unwillingness of its members to finance more than a fraction of the costs of the government relations and other services from which they benefit considerably. It is thus an extreme example of a problem besetting an increasing number of national and state associations. Given an adequate level of dues support, NYSFMA could probably provide the services that its members want with a staff a quarter to a third smaller than it now has. Taken as a whole, however, NYSFMA mounts a program of services, especially in government relations, that many national associations might envy, and that is far more comprehensive than that of most other state associations in any industry.

Profile: Utah Retail Grocers Association

Utah is a small state that is experiencing the rapid growth characteristic of the Mountain states. Politically and socially conservative, the state rarely exhibits the governmental activism found elsewhere. Nevertheless, the Utah food industry does confront a certain amount of government regulation. The onset of these food issues led to the creation of the Utah Retail Grocers Association (URGA).[9]

Owners of small, independent meat and grocery stores began meeting in Utah around the turn of the century. An informal association operated during the first two decades of this century, although URGA was not formally established until 1924. Originally called the Utah Retail Merchants Association, the name was changed to the present one ten years later when it was decided to limit membership to independent grocers, including neither food chains nor non-food retailers. Both the excluded groups later created their own organization, using URGA's original name.

In Utah as elsewhere, an early issue was keeping the chains out of the state. This failed, of course, for antitrust reasons. Ironically, however, several of the independents began to grow and eventually became chains themselves. Those in this category remained in URGA, and in time the older chains joined as well.

Structure. Primary or regular membership now is open to all food retailers, including chains. Wholesalers and suppliers are associate members who may not vote or serve on the board, but they receive other membership benefits.

There are about 335 regular members representing some 560 stores, plus 152 associate members. Twelve of the retail members are from outside Utah and joined to take advantage of the member rates for URGA's extensive program of economic services. These services are available to non-members but at higher rates.

The association's board is small. Of the fifteen members, most are large independent retailers, but chains and convenience stores are also represented. An executive committee, with the usual functions, consists of the officers. Directors are limited to four two-year terms and are automatically ousted if they fail to attend at least half the board meetings in a twelve-month period.

Staff and Budget. URGA's ten-member staff is headed by its president, James V. Olsen. Other major positions include the coupon service manager, the president of the credit union, assistants for communications and program, and administrative and support personnel.

Although URGA's cash flow is over $7 million annually, primarily because of the stream of coupon funds, the actual budget for the association is a bit over $400,000. Dues provide about 15 percent of the association revenues, of which about a fourth comes from associate members. The organization has a long-term goal to increase dues income to 25 percent of total revenue.

Profits from the coupon program contribute almost 45 percent of URGA's revenues. Fees earned primarily by the operation of the credit union and from services provided to the convenience store association bring in about 10 percent. Another 9 percent derives from rentals of space in URGA's office building in Salt Lake City, and an additional 7 percent comes from its convention and trade show. Interest income and royalties from a computer program sold to other credit unions bring in just under 9 percent. The magazine breaks even or operates at a small loss.

Salaries and employee benefits consume about 60 percent of expenses. The remainder goes for general and administrative costs. Because so much of its revenue falls in categories that the IRS deems "unrelated," URGA pays taxes on its net income.

In the past, the association sought to minimize taxes by coming as close to a break-even position as possible each year. It manages its finances differently now, accepting the payment of taxes as the price for building reserves. URGA's reserve goal is the equivalent of one to two years' income.

Government Relations. URGA was established to provide representation for grocers with the state government, and this continues to be an important function: A survey of the association's membership found that legislative lobbying ranked as the highest association priority, with regulatory liaison ranking nearly as high. Still, the government relations agenda for URGA is not huge. Unlike the legislatures of the large states that, like Congress, are in session virtually full-time, the Utah legislature meets for only short annual sessions. URGA's president is therefore able to handle all aspects of government relations personally while still continuing to run the association.

Legislative problems in recent years have included a variety of advertising issues, alcoholic beverage regulation, product safety, environmental subjects, and labor relations matters. The association has a winning record on most of its issues. URGA has a small political action committee that contributed about $7,500 to state and local candidates in 1988, 90 percent of whom won.

Economic Functions. The bulk of URGA's activities are economic services. The largest of these is its coupon redemption program. Retailers receive a handling fee from grocery manufacturers for each cents-off product coupon they redeem from consumers, the fee increasing with volume. Most state food associations have coupon-clearing programs through which they aggregate and process the coupons from many independent retailers, retaining a percentage as a commission. They thereby gain a higher fee for their members and income for themselves.

URGA's coupon redemption program is considered a valuable service by its members, many of whom (including some out-of-state retailers) have joined just to take advantage of it. The association derives a substantial amount of revenue from coupon commission income, even after paying participants a year-end volume rebate.

URGA has organized a credit union for its members and recently opened a branch office. Other economic activities include group health, life, and casualty insurance programs, as well as other services for retailers. The processing of insurance claims is handled internally by URGA staff, after an unsuccessful experiment in outside processing.

Meetings and Publications. URGA holds a trade show for supplier exhibits in connection with its annual convention. In the past, it also ran an annual consumer food show but subsequently dropped it. Regional legislative conferences and social events for retailers, wholesalers, and suppliers supplement the meeting schedule.

The organization publishes a bi-monthly magazine, the *Intermountain Retailer,* that contains legislative and association news, as well as advertising. A four-page monthly newsletter, the *Alert Bulletin,* keeps members posted on government-relations developments and association activities.

Relations with Other Associations. URGA's relations with NGA have been closer over the years than with FMI, primarily because of NGA's historic representation of independents. Utah retailers have been national leaders of NGA. URGA does, nonetheless, cooperate with FMI in particular areas because of the institute's dominant position in the industry nationally.

Like NYSFMA, URGA absorbed regional grocer associations many years ago. Convenience store operators have their own state association, managed by the URGA staff.

Although it is a small association, URGA's strong program of economic services led it to consider becoming a regional association several years ago, spreading its activities to four neighboring states. Although it chose not to do so, the extent of the services it furnishes to retailers make it increasingly attractive to food distributors outside Utah. Many regard it as the strongest food industry association in its part of the country.

With the increasing activity of state governments and the resulting demand from companies for improved government relations programs, state associations will be far less the junior partners and country cousins of their national kin than they have been historically. As a group, they may never equal national and international associations in size. They will, however, increasingly rival them in importance as power shifts from Washington to the state capitals.

NOTES

1. See, for example: Carl E. Van Horn, ed., *The State of the States* (Washington: CQ Press, 1989).

2. Aspects of business-government relations at the state level are discussed in a collection of essays compiled and published by the Public Affairs Council: *Leveraging State Government Relations: How to Win in Today's Most Critical Public Policy Arenas* (Washington: 1990). (Parts of this chapter appear, in somewhat different form, in an article by the author in that collection.)

3. *State and Regional Associations of the United States* (Washington: Columbia Books, 1990). The same publisher issues *National Trade and Professional Associations of the U. S.*

4. Compensation data: American Society of Association Executives (ASAE), *Association Executive Compensation Study,* 6th ed. (Washington: 1988). For all other data except average dues: ASAE, *Policies and Procedures in Association Management* (Washington: 1987). Average dues calculated from data in *Policies and Procedures.*

5. Michigan State Chamber of Commerce, *Legislative Priorities, 1989–1990* (Lansing, MI: 1989). Information on the Michigan Chamber from publications, reports, and documents it supplied, and from communications with staff and other knowledgeable individuals.

6. Information from publications, reports, and documents supplied by the New York State Food Merchants Association; communications with staff members and other knowledgeable individuals; and the author's personal knowledge of the association.

7. See chapter 9 for an explanation of the tax treatment of associations.

8. ASAE, *Policies and Procedures.*

9. Information from publications, reports, and documents supplied by the Utah Retail Grocers Association, and communications with its staff.

Part V

MEETING THE NEEDS OF THE '90s—AND BEYOND

13

The Alchemy of Vision: Associations and the Future

In all bodies, those who will lead, must also, in a considerable degree, follow. They must conform their propositions to the taste, talent and disposition of those whom they wish to conduct.

Edmund Burke

The task of the leader is to get his people from where they are to where they have not been. Leaders must invoke an alchemy of great vision.

Henry Kissinger

In previous chapters, we have discussed the development and resources of U. S. business associations and the value to their members of utilizing them for maximum effectiveness. As we move into a new decade and, soon enough, a new millennium, it is appropriate to consider both what association members are likely to demand of their organizations in the future and how associations are likely to respond and change.

It is an oft-stated truism that associations exist to serve their members' wants and needs. Perceived needs are wants—but there are also needs that people do not readily recognize as such. Taking the members where they *wish* to go is one dimension of association leadership. Another dimension, however, is identifying where the organization *should* go and persuading its members to move in that direction—a migration that may involve unfamiliar and therefore perhaps frightening territory.

Associations have a fine record of identifying and satisfying members' current wants. On the other hand, while association executives have devoted much rhetoric to planning for the future, in practice business associations have not excelled in forecasting long-term trends and charting new directions for their organizations. There are too many immediate brush-fires and too few firemen to spend much time worrying about fire prevention. Yet, as Peter Drucker and others have frequently pointed out, good planning is the essence of strong management.

Effective association participation requires that members demand of their staff and elected leadership management of the same caliber that the shareholders of individual businesses insist on in their own executives. Surely that includes planning for the future. But to understand the future requires a clear view of the present.

WHAT MEMBERS THINK OF THEIR ASSOCIATIONS

A starting question is how members currently regard their associations. Useful data on this subject were presented in two surveys of association members conducted by the Gallup Organization for the Foundation of the American Society of Association Executives.[1] Although these surveys are now several years old, there is no reason to believe that the attitudes they reflect have changed significantly over time.

Corporate Attitudes

On balance, corporate executives are complimentary if not effusive about their trade associations. A quarter think that their companies gain greatly from their associations, half feel the benefit is moderate, and a fourth say the advantages are small or non-existent. Most think that their associations improved their performance in the previous ten years. On the other hand, 43 percent of corporate members believe that at least some association programs are of little value to them.

Here is a summary of some other principal study findings:

- Over 80 percent said that their companies are at least somewhat active in trade associations. Large companies are more active than mid-sized firms.
- The most common reason given by those not active is a belief that there is either no need for participation or no benefit from it. The second most frequent reason is the claim that the company does not have enough staff people to participate.
- Four out of five said that an executive of the company had been an elected officer or at least served on an association committee within the previous three years.
- Three-quarters said their principal association provided at least a fair amount of guidance and leadership for the members; one-fifth said that there was a great deal of guidance, but another fifth reported very little.
- A modest majority believed that their firms would be handicapped if trade as-

sociations were prohibited, but a third saw very little disadvantage if this were to occur.

- Over half, 55 percent, thought that their trade association would become more important to their company in the future.

- Trade association executives were well-regarded by the members. A rating of good or excellent for association management performance was given by three-quarters of the corporate executives interviewed. Those in medium-sized firms were more complimentary of association managers than were executives with major companies.

- Nearly three out of five corporate executives said that government relations is the most important function that associations provide. No other function was named by more than 20 percent. Fifty percent rated their associations as very effective in carrying out the government-relations function, and another 40 percent rated them as somewhat effective.

- Other functions seen as being of some importance included trade relations ("providing a forum to meet vendors or competitors to discuss mutual problems and make potential client contacts"), information on new industry developments, public relations, and forecasting future problems. Of lesser significance were standards development, continuing education, and research and development.

- Only the information function received a very high rating for effectiveness. Reasonably good grades were given for problem forecasting, standards development, and trade relations. Research and development was largely rated as ineffective.

- Executives of mid-sized companies generally ranked their associations higher on these various activities than did those of major corporations.

- Public relations and government relations ranked highest among *unmet* industry needs.

- Over four out of five executives thought that their companies received adequate consideration for their point of view from their trade associations.

- On particular public policy matters, two-thirds said that their trade groups should work in coalition with other associations on common issues, but three-fifths felt that their associations should not take positions on larger economic, labor, and social policy issues that go beyond the industry's direct interests.

- Almost a third of companies (even more of the largest businesses) have taken actions apart from their trade associations, because they did not think that the associations would be effective; the success of these independent efforts was rated rather highly.

In sum, corporate executives think rather well of their trade associations, particularly in the area of government relations. Because of its great importance, however, this is also an area where further effort is desired.

Views of Professional Associations

The second study surveyed the attitudes of those belonging to individual membership organizations. The needs and satisfactions of this group of association members are quite different from those in the corporate group.

The most important reason that professionals give for joining associations is to gain information from the organization's publications. Opportunities to develop personal contacts and to continue their education are the next most important reasons.

Satisfaction with their associations is much higher among individual members than among company executives. Over 85 percent of professional society members said that they are at least fairly satisfied, and a majority are very satisfied. A large majority believe that they get good value for their dues. Almost three-quarters rate the executives of their associations good or excellent, and only 2 percent think that their performance is declining. Association executives are also given high marks for responsiveness.

Here are other significant survey findings:

- Publications, opportunities to meet other professionals, education, and professional standards development were the functions in which individual membership groups were seen as most effective.
- A mixed judgment was given as to the effectiveness of such activities as future problems forecasting, government relations, research, and public relations.
- Public relations and member education were the top priorities for further association effort. Government relations is not particularly an area where individual members want more from their professional associations. Three-fifths said that their organizations now lobby, and four-fifths thought they do so effectively. Like the trade association members, a majority of those belonging to individual membership groups did not want their organizations to take positions on public policy questions beyond the direct concerns of the association.
- A majority of the members of professional groups said they are not very active in their associations, have never served on a committee, or even attended a meeting within the past year. However, three-quarters of those belonging to a national organization also belong to a related local association and are evenly divided as to which is more valuable.
- Three-fifths thought that there is some duplication of effort among professional associations.
- Three out of four members saw a greater need for professional associations in the future, particularly to deal with the growing complexity or technology in their fields. Only a small group saw a need for expanded government relations.

There were some variations in these attitudes, depending on the size and nature of the association to which the individual belonged, but the patterns of response held fairly constant across the total group surveyed.

In summary, the members of professional associations want information, education, and contact opportunities from their organizations. They generally feel that their needs in these areas are being met.

In contrast, trade association members are a bit less satisfied with their organizations, possibly because trade associations are likely to be less homogeneous than professional societies. The most significant distinction, however, is the widely differing weight given to the government relations function—top priority for trade associations but of relatively minor importance for professional groups.

These differences in emphasis can be at least partially explained by dissimilarities in the groups sampled. The members of trade associations are business enterprises. Only a portion of individual membership groups, however, represent professions in or allied with business. Moreover, those interviewed in the professional society survey represented a cross-section of individual members. The trade association survey, in contrast, interviewed the corporate executive "most knowledgeable" about the company's association memberships, a group much more likely to be sophisticated about associations and their functions.

One suspects that if association executives themselves had been surveyed, the stress on the need for increased involvement on public policy issues would have been even greater. No one else recognizes more clearly the pervasive and growing impact of the public sector on industries and professions of all kinds than do professional association managers.

These distinctions illustrate the differences between what the rank-and-file wants (or thinks it wants) and what more knowledgeable participants understand is required. Leadership involves helping the former to comprehend what the latter readily grasp as critical to the constituency that the organization represents. In any organization, the rank-and-file tend toward a preoccupation with the demands of the present. Guiding them into the future is the task of leaders, leaders with that quality that Kissinger calls the alchemy of vision.

CONFRONTING THE FUTURE

Association members themselves recognize this need. In both surveys, members identified as important their association's capacity to forecast future problems. In neither study were associations given terribly high marks for their performance of this function. It is in this area, more than in any other, that associations face their greatest challenges. Preoccupied with the flood of current problems, managers too frequently fail to identify the tide that drives the flood or to know when the tide has turned or altered its intensity.

Nothing illustrates how unpredictable the tides can be than the events in Eastern Europe in 1989. In the space of five brief months, popular uprisings overthrew established regimes in half a dozen countries, as the rest of the world watched agape and unprepared. If they point up nothing else, the international events of 1989 demonstrate the acceleration of public events and the speed with which the future is rushing on us.

Associations unprepared for sudden shifts in the tides of events are vulnerable to the consequences. Not long ago, one of the most powerful trade associations in Washington lost its credibility almost overnight as the federal government was forced to rescue at great public cost, major savings-and-loan institutions. Their association had sworn, almost to the end, that the industry was healthy and in no need of additional government regulation. The arrogance of its association surely contributed to the severity of the public response when the savings-and-loan industry's economic problems were finally understood.

It can be argued that business associations must be single-minded about their members' needs in times of crisis—so they must. That is not leadership, however. Leadership involves identifying potential hazards, both externally and within the industry (or profession or community), and taking *advance* measures to deal with the underlying causes and problems, as well as to minimize the membership impact.

Certainly, strengthening the association's political and legislative weaponry is an area to which business groups must devote steadily increasing emphasis, a point repeatedly made throughout this book and elsewhere. However, the association that fails to look beyond current issues, that blinds itself to long-term situations that could eventually lead the membership into peril or disaster, is in no significant sense serving its members' real needs. Such an organization may possess strength and yet be wholly lacking in leadership.

The challenge for associations in the 1990s and beyond is to develop the capability to see beyond current problems and issues and to strengthen their ability to forecast future needs, internally and externally. This will require a new kind of credibility with the membership, the credibility necessary to communicate bad news in order to facilitate the voluntary changes needed to forestall public challenge. This is no small task when dealing with a class of corporate members that often look no further than the next quarterly statement and that dislike hearing bad news, especially if it comes from those whom at least some regard as agents and servants, certainly not visionaries.

To confront the future, business associations will have to convince their members of their ability to manage the cause and course of events while still dealing successfully with the current symptoms—a juggling act of no small proportions. This involves challenges to associations themselves, to their members and leaders, and to their professional managers.

Challenges for Associations

The New Environment for Business. There really is no such thing as "American industry" anymore. There may not remain much that can be described as a purely American economy. The challenges that domestic businesses have faced from Japan are likely to pale in the face of competitive pressures from Europe, as Germany unites and as economic unification of the European Community proceeds and as the EEC eventually begins to integrate the national economies of Scandinavia, Austria, Switzerland, and the countries of Eastern Europe. Mikhail Gorbachev's "common European home" will be focused on Brussels long before it centers on Moscow.

As manufacturing continues to become a specialty of developing countries (including those in Eastern Europe), as financial markets merge worldwide, and as the United States becomes an economy based on intellectual, communications, and information services, American business executives are challenging their associations to adapt to the globalization of business.

At the same time, associations must also confront changes in the business climate at national and sub-national level. Amid growing state and local activism, there are also signs that the age of deregulation at the federal level is passing and that Washington will once again impose new controls and costs on business. What is new about this regulatory environment is the extent to which it seeks to make a business a surrogate for government itself. Mandatory personnel benefits are increasingly being proposed, as are sets of "principles" regulating corporate behavior in areas ranging from investment abroad to environmental protection. Business is also making demands on government, sometimes conflicting ones, such as calls to rebuild the nation's decaying transportation infrastructure while urging curbs on government spending and budget deficits.

Thus, U.S. business associations are confronted with the need simultaneously to expand their horizons, both internationally and at the state and local levels, and to cope with new sets of expectations in Washington. This is an extraordinary combination of challenges unlike any that associations have had to contend with in the past. These multi-dimensional demands from their members will require significant alterations in association operations and structure.

· **First,** associations must substantially improve the process of public policy development and implementation. William Ouchi has pointed out[2] how Japanese industry associations and coalitions negotiate unified policy positions among themselves and then jointly press, with considerable success, for their adoption by government. This change would not be easy to achieve in the United States, as he urges, where associations tend to seek the lowest common denominator of policy positions internally and to compete with each other externally.

At least as difficult would be increased business community cooperation with non-business interest groups, as Ouchi recommends—groups that are already major influences on many issues and frequently on the other side from business interests. Some movement in this direction is urgently required, however, if business associations are to be effective in shaping long-term public economic policies.

Whether or not changes of this magnitude actually take place, business organizations need to devote much additional effort to reduce overlapping and competitive situations with other associations—if not through politically difficult mergers (although some have occurred), then at least through greater coordination of positions, strategy, and effort. Increased cooperation through issue coalitions holds out the promise of some progress in this direction.

Coalitions can, however, present competitive problems for associations. As more and more legislatively active companies manage to coordinate their lobbying through coalitions, some come to question the need for associations. Why pay money to support a permanent alliance when less will finance an effective temporary one? Why support ponderous staff bureaucracies that, like some huge supertanker, can be turned in new directions only with great effort when the need is for agile organizations that can turn on a dime?

There are valid answers to those questions, including the importance of staff expertise, continuity, and the value of association information and economic services. That the question is even being asked by member-companies is another signal to associations that cost-effectiveness is constantly being watched. Business executives today frequently are looking for quick competitive edges and cost reductions, even small ones.

• **Second,** modifications in association structure may therefore be required to meet changing needs. In a number of large associations, segments of the membership may have special requirements that the association itself may not be able to meet. An approach being tried in several industries is the establishment of temporary, semi-independent organizations that have at least a ''dotted-line'' relationship with the industry association and that deal with critical but relatively short-term problems affecting only a portion of the member-companies. An example is the Council for Solid Waste Solutions within the plastics industry.

• **Third,** business associations need to refocus their approach to government relations to seek the expansion of markets, domestically and globally. Legislative priorities should be shifted away from the search for special interest protection and toward the vigorous elimination of federal and state barriers to market entry and competitiveness, as well as the even greater impediments found in other countries. This is as much a challenge to state associations as to national ones.

· **Fourth,** U.S. associations need to speed up the development of working relationships with their counterparts in other countries in order to coordinate policies. Global consultative bodies have been established in industries dominated by multinational corporations, because counterpart associations in different countries share so many of the same members. This pattern needs to be broadened even where this is not particularly the case if the common needs of the industry are to be served worldwide.

· **Fifth,** business associations need to reflect the radical changes that have recently taken place in the American corporation as a direct result of increased worldwide competition. The corporation as an institution has grown leaner and far more cost-conscious. While retrenching on dues and indirect outlays, companies simultaneously are demanding both greater service and greater internal efficiency from their associations. It will be very difficult for association executives to resist the internal restructuring that members of their boards of directors have had to make in their own companies. Doing more with less will require considerable ingenuity.

· **Sixth,** associations must recognize the changing patterns of corporate ownership. Many domestic companies now owned by investors from other countries complain of discrimination against them in U.S. business circles, sometimes at the hands of executives of corporations that have experienced similar bias abroad. This behavior is short-sighted and self-defeating in an age of interrelated global commerce. An association based in Washington or Chicago should fairly represent all the members of its constituent industry or profession if those members wish to be treated equally in the business associations of Tokyo and Brussels.

Even among purely domestic companies, associations need to recognize and adapt to important changes. A corporation now privately owned does not do business in the same way that it did when its shares were publicly traded. Moreover, changes affecting associations will undoubtedly occur as large institutional investors (such as pension and mutual funds) take a more active role in corporate management and policy-setting.

Strategic Positioning. Business associations should engage in strategic planning not only for their own long-term operations, but also for the industries, communities, and professions whose interests they champion. This may sound like the same thing but it is not. A trade association may represent the members of a particular industry, but it is itself in a quite different line of work. After all, the association management business has its own discrete interests that are separate and distinct from those of the appliance manufacturers, magazine publishers, or accountants who are its clientele.

The strategic planning processes described in chapter 6 related to the needs of the association as an entity. A parallel process needs to be carried out for the industry or profession as a whole if the collective membership is to be correctly positioned to cope and thrive in the domestic and international economic and public policy environments. The steps in the process are similar. It is the objectives and purposes that differ.

This is an area in which business associations can make a critical leadership contribution. An example lies in the area of research and development—a function of associations that has not received high grades. Increases in industry productivity and competitiveness are beginning to receive greater public attention. Government blessings are being given to such industry-wide programs as Sematech, the semi-conductor industry's R&D consortium. Many other industries could benefit greatly from similar productivity-enhancement approaches. Their associations should take the lead in stimulating their members and public policy-makers to consider appropriate innovative mechanisms.

Applying the Tools of the Information Revolution. Association communications remain heavily print- and meeting-oriented. As a group, business associations lag far behind many of their members in utilizing the new electronic media. Why should members have to wait until the Postal Service works its will on association newsletters and other publications before they can learn of vital developments? The telephone is hardly practical on a daily basis, even for small associations; it is impossible for large ones.

High-speed fax messaging, electronic mail, and local-area networks are all media widely employed by individual companies to communicate among different locations, both domestically and overseas. Computerized fax is now also an emerging technology. The prime obstacle to adopting these communications tools is cost. The alternative, however, is the "danger for any particular association . . . if its members embrace the new technologies at a more rapid rate than their association."[3]

The employment of these new communications media is particularly applicable in government relations. Electronic bulletin boards enable associations to provide immediate information on legislative developments to their members. Electronic mail and fax can greatly speed up advocacy messages to policy-makers.

The impact on grass-roots lobbying alone could be enormous. Imagine a legislative committee meeting at which lawmakers are considering a proposal of importance to a particular group. A quick telephone call from a lobbyist monitoring the proceedings and a fax or e-mail message to members could bring a barrage of grass-roots communications to the legislators while they are still in the committee room debating the issue! There are many other applications on which the new technologies can be employed:

- Videotex can enable members to select among various association data bases, economic services, and publications, instantly bringing materials, texts, and information onto their desk terminals.
- Teleconferencing, never likely to be a complete substitute for face-to-face contacts, nonetheless can be a cost-effective supplement to them, as it can for the personal contacts with members that association executives consider essential.
- Experiments with computer conferencing indicate great potential value, especially for educational programs. The concept also applies to many association meetings requiring a certain amount of interactive participation.

The increasing prevalence of in-office personal computers and work stations readily facilitates the adoption of such computerized and electronic services. Even the traveling business person, equipped with a laptop computer and a portable modem, could access them easily. Fees and subscriptions can alleviate the costs to associations of providing such services.

These technologies are likely to affect business associations in ways that go beyond communications and internal management. For example, instant communication implies the ability for instant board or committee decisions. This may produce faster decisions, not necessarily better ones. Such problems are solvable. The hazard to associations that do not choose to keep up with the technology curve is that they may forfeit a major competitive edge to other organizations serving the same members.

Communicating with the Public. Almost every survey, focus group, or informal discussion of association strengths and weaknesses reveals the frustration of members with the inability of their organizations to mount effective public relations campaigns. Since the problem is hardly the lack of staff communications skills, it becomes one of association costs, priorities, and determination.

One of the major reasons that individual interest groups lose on their government relations issues is the lack of public understanding and support. Of course, there are many situations in which business associations make a conscious and correct decision not to "go public" on their issues, but there are at least as many when this potentially invaluable dimension of support is simply ignored.

Business-related issues are frequently complex. A public relations campaign will fall on sterile ground if the public has not been prepared by long-term advertising, information, and education to improve popular understanding of the situation of the particular industry or profession. It is especially critical to inform citizens and consumers of the stake that they share as individuals in both the outcome of the issue and the welfare of the interest group that the association represents.

The relevance of such efforts to success in government relations objectives is so obvious that it is hard to understand the low priority that public relations continues to receive in most business association programs and budgets.

Revenue Development. As business associations seek out more and more sources of non-dues revenue, decreasing reliance on membership dues may be the wave of the future. That does not make it a healthy development. As dues diminish in importance for associations, so will the individual member's sense of identification with the organization. Likewise, the executives of an association that acquires the bulk of its revenue elsewhere inevitably must develop a sense of distance from their members and their welfare.

If associations encourage their members to undertake rigorous and tough-minded evaluations of the organization's cost-effectiveness and to participate enthusiastically in the process, they may well find less resistance to dues increases. The healthiest association is one fully supported by its members who are repeatedly made aware of the true economic and political value of the organization and of the importance of paying their own way.

One possible approach to dues increases worth experimental consideration would involve a substantial upgrade of the concept of basic dues-funded services. Why should there not be a single annual dues payment that includes all print and electronic subscriptions, convention and educational registration fees, even tickets to association-sponsored dinners and social events? Marketed correctly, such a strategy could justify a large dues increase that might well net the organization considerable additional revenue.

Challenges to Members

Careful attention to conversations among association members is likely to disclose an interesting and almost universal turn of phrase: "The association sent me. . . . A meeting the association organized. . . . The association is lobbying. . . ." Almost invariably, the word "association" is used to mean "the staff."

The association is the membership, *not* the staff. The phrasing is revealing in what it says about members' attitudes toward "ownership" of the organization. There is an analogy with the way most people refer to government; the government may belong to its citizens but few individuals think of it as anything but a distant institution.

For business associations, this is not a healthy point of view. It goes a long way to explain members' resistance to dues increases and their reluctance to devote much effort to association affairs. In a sense, the marketing thrust that many associations are adopting and their growing sense of themselves as entrepreneurial institutions play directly into this "Catch-22" situation. If members perceive the associations that they belong to as only another set of organizations supplying them with services for a fee, they will neither identify with them nor feel any responsibility for their welfare.

The injection of marketing techniques is constructive, but the view of the member-as-client is very different from that of the member-as-owner. The greater the proportion of non-dues revenue, the more likely the association is to become excessively staff-driven. The participative association and the entrepreneurial one are inconsistent concepts.

This is a major reason that business associations should strongly encourage rigorous cost-benefit examinations by their members. The process itself increases membership participation and that inevitably heightens the awareness of the investment the corporation or individual has at stake.

Ultimately, though, it is the members that must accept responsibility for the quality of their participation. Active participation, not mere passive membership, is required to produce the kind of support for corporate objectives that current needs and future challenges require. Companies owe it to their shareholders to assure that they are getting their money's worth from their associations and to take appropriate measures to maximize the value they receive. Unless the association's performance is so inadequate that leaving it is the only practical course, maximizing value will require greater levels of active participation to assure that the member's needs and objectives are fully met. In most situations, alternative means of obtaining services of the same kind and quality offered by associations will be far more costly.

In many cases, optimizing value may well require pressing the association to minimize overlapping programs and wasteful competition with other organizations. This means at least coordinating activities through coalitions to advance common government relations goals.

In their own self-interest, members have an obligation to support the organization's government relations functions fully, especially those involving participation in grass-roots lobbying activities. These programs enable corporate or individual members to advance their own self-interests through collective effort as fully functioning partners in association-wide lobbying campaigns, while retaining the ability to act independently when necessary.

The Challenge to Association Leaders

Kinsey Green, a former association executive, has identified seven critical roles that professional leaders of associations must play to move their organizations successfully into the future:[4]

Visionary

Mentor

Global thinker

Futurist

Program planner and decision-maker

Servant and role model

Coalition builder

These qualities embody a word frequently heard in association circles—leadership—but the most important of these characteristics, and perhaps the rarest, is the quality of vision.

The present is only a moment in time. Preoccupation with today's problems is really management of the past. The ability to plan, to manage the future, is what leadership is all about.

Leadership involves more than taking association members where they want to go. The leader also guides his people where they *need* to go. That implies having a sense of the future as it is *likely* to be and equipping the membership to cope with that future. It also implies envisioning the future as it *could* be and mobilizing the members to alter the march of events in order to attain that future.

It is not sufficient that association executives and elected leaders accept only the "disposition of those whom they wish to conduct," in Burke's phrase.

The alchemy of great vision is what will be required of the leaders of business associations if they are to pilot their organizations through the uncertainties of an onrushing future.

Their members should demand nothing less.

NOTES

1. Gallup Organization, *The Corporate View: How Business Executives Rate Their Trade Associations* (Washington: Foundation of the American Society of Association Executives, 1982); Gallup Organization, *The Verdict: Professionals Evaluate Their Individual Membership Societies* (Washington: Foundation of the American Society of Association Executives, 1983). Other interesting data are found in an even older study of trade and professional association members and non-members: Foundation of the American Society of Association Executives,

The Decision to Join: Insights Based on a Survey of Association Members and Non-Members (Washington: ASAE, 1981).

2. William G. Ouchi, *The M-Form Society* (Reading, MA: Addison-Wesley, 1984).

3. *Foundation of the Amercian Society of Association Executives, Association Communications in the 1990s.* (Washington: ASAE, 1987). This is a useful examination of how associations expect to utilize the new technologies in their operations and membership communications.

4. Kinsey B. Green, "Future Roles of Association Executives," chapter 4 in: Foundation of the ASAE, *Future Perspectives.* (Washington: ASAE, 1985).

Appendix: How Good Associations Get Started

New associations are constantly being formed under a wide variety of circumstances: A new industry or profession may arise and require representation. A segment of an existing organization may decide that its distinctive needs can be better served if it splits off and becomes autonomous. A new technical or specialized challenge to a group of businesses may emerge in the external environment that existing associations lack the capability to handle. The business enterprises in a particular locale may come to believe that they need a community business association where none has existed before.

While each of these groups may have the motivation to found a new organization, starting one from scratch is neither easy nor cheap. It is therefore a good idea to examine carefully if the group's needs can be met satisfactorily by an existing body. All things considered, meeting those needs within existing structures and processes is generally less burdensome than creating new ones. When the justification is great enough to warrant the effort, however, those planning to found the new organization should proceed carefully and systematically through a number of essential stages.

Starting a new association is both harder and easier than it used to be. It is more difficult now because of various legal considerations and because the proliferation of associations makes it harder to justify the need for still another. On the other hand, there is much more experience and advice available today to smooth the way for would-be founding fathers.

A wise course for the founders of new associations to follow is to seek help and advice at a very early stage from both a consultant experienced in association management and an attorney knowledgeable in the various federal and state laws affecting associations.

The material that follows is intended less as a how-to-do-it guide than as an outline of important concerns that merit consideration. Some of these recommendations, particularly those relating to legal and financial matters, are essential. Others are in the area of good management practices that have evolved through the experiences of many associations. References are made to appropriate chapters earlier in this book for additional information on particular topics.

Governance and Legalities

Associations are legal entities, many aspects of which are closely regulated by both federal and state law. That is why new associations appoint and involve legal counsel at a very early stage. The attorney advises and assists the founding group on such matters as incorporation, choice of a name and acronym, structure and governance of the organization, preparation of bylaws, purchase of liability insurance, and sundry other legal necessities. The lawyer's advice will also be essential on such ongoing legal matters as the organization's tax classification, antitrust compliance, and lobbying regulations (see chapter 9).

The organization's governance and internal structure are as much a policy matter for the founders as a legal concern. Decisions will be needed as to the size, composition, and election of the board of directors, the offices to be filled, the policy-making process, and the committee structure (see chapter 7).

Strategic Planning

A sound strategic plan is important to lay a strong foundation for the nascent association. This includes a situation analysis, market analysis, and organizational strategy, comprised of the following elements:

- A clear and specific description of the group or interest that the new association is intended to serve.
- A statement of the precise needs that the new association is being designed to fill. A survey or other study to determine the unmet requirements of the new group's constituency—and why and how they need to be satisfied—will provide essential data for this statement.
- A clear description of the potential membership. Specific membership prospects should be listed if possible; at the very least, the membership description should specify the process by which potential members can be subsequently identified.

- A competitive analysis, including substantiation of the inability of specific existing organizations (or consulting and commercial firms in some cases) to satisfy the needs that the new group intends to fill. This helps to answer the inevitable question that every potential new member asks: "Why do we need another association?"
- A description of the services that the new organization will provide to meet the stated needs, plus a statement strategically positioning the new group relative to existing ones and the services that they offer.
- A formulation of a mission statement, general objectives, and specific goals to be attained in the first year.

In addition, an analysis is needed of first-year staffing needs and office requirements, and a preliminary budget and financial plan prepared. Staff job descriptions and a detailed program budget will follow (see chapter 6).

Funding for the preliminary budget is often a problem. Founding members may advance dues or lend the new association its seed money. Banks are sometimes willing to lend start-up funds, but probably only if the loan is guaranteed by credit-worthy companies or individuals.

An executive director (by whatever title) is usually hired at an early stage to undertake as much of the organizational, planning, and development work as possible, with additional staff put in place as required and as funds permit (see chapter 8).

Program Planning

The services that the new association is being formed to provide need to be delineated. Chapters 4 and 5 furnish a basis for program and service planning, depending on the needs and purposes of the new group.

It is best to start early but also to start small. An early beginning to the delivery of services is important to show new and potential members that the organization is off to a strong start. A small beginning is necessary to proceed carefully and avoid crippling mistakes.

Once a staff and early programs are in place, membership solicitation can begin in earnest. A marketing plan should be developed, focusing on peer contacts, briefing meetings, direct mail, telemarketing, sales calls, or whatever solicitation media are most appropriate for the new organization and the market it wishes to serve.

Communications and Meetings

Communications with the membership are an early and high-priority necessity for any beginning association. A regularly scheduled publication provides content appropriate to the association and its members' needs. It offers visibility for the new group. Content will dictate format, but a newsletter is the easiest and least expensive publication approach.

Many new associations undertake advertising programs as a revenue source if the publication format permits and if justified by the market.

When finances permit the installation of an office computer, software for desktop publishing is frequently an early priority today. This allows the new group to produce a high-quality illustrated publication at a cost that is typically lower than one produced commercially.[1] Costs of a computerized system are shared with its other capabilities, including word processing, financial and membership records, meeting management, and perhaps direct member communications among other functions (see chapters 4 and 13).

Young associations usually organize early informal meetings to introduce and promote the association among its constituency and to recruit members. In addition, a program of formal association meetings is commonly launched as soon as practicable. At a minimum, this includes an annual conference or convention. Later on, consideration can be given to the value of educational seminars, mid-year conferences, and other specialized events.

These meetings offer opportunities for member education, informative speakers, the delivery or at least discussion of other association services, and, perhaps most importantly, peer contacts for the members. Social programs are an important element. Good meetings provide the membership with tangible demonstrations of the group's vitality and a forum in which to promote the new organization and build enthusiasm for it.

Registration fees should be set low enough to encourage attendance and high enough at least to break even. If the market permits, meetings can become an important revenue source, especially if a trade show or exposition can be profitably organized.[2]

Not all new associations thrive. The ones that do are generally those that are the products of sound situation analyses and planning. These processes are not exercises in bureaucratic paperwork. They are essential to demonstrate that the case for the new association has been thought through with great care and that the founders truly know what they are doing.

Examples of the opposite situation abound. New associations sometimes founder because either the need or the group's ability to satisfy it better than competitive groups was not analyzed carefully enough. Others have gotten into trouble, despite a meticulous situation analysis, because of inadequate financial or program planning.

The new associations that survive and prosper are the ones with clear visions of who their clientele is, what its needs are, how the association plans to satisfy those needs, and how governance, programs, finances, and staff will be organized on a multi-year basis.

NOTES

1. A good introduction to association publications is contained in: Debra J. Stratton, "Publications," chapter 17 in American Society of Association Executives (ASAE), *Principles of Association Management: A Professional's Handbook.* (Washington: 1988).

2. See: Wayne H. Gross, "Conventions and Meetings" and "Exhibits," chapters 14 and 15 in ASAE, *Principles of Association Management.*

Resources and Selected Bibliography

A wide range of publications on the management of trade and professional associations is available from the American Society of Association Executives and, to a lesser extent, the U. S. Chamber of Commerce. The Chamber is the prime source of materials on state and local chamber management. Voluntary leaders and other interested citizens will find a number of these quite helpful although most are intended for professional association managers. Current catalogs of these publications can be obtained from:

American Society of Association
  Executives
1575 Eye Street, NW
Washington, DC 20005

U. S. Chamber of Commerce
1615 H Street, NW
Washington, DC 20062

BIBLIOGRAPHY

Local organizations of association executives exist in many states and cities; some of these also publish relevant materials. The local group in the District of Columbia has recently published a comprehensive bibliography of works on association management:

Carey, Stephen W., ed., *A Bibliography of Association Management Literature.*
    Washington: Washington Association Research Foundation, 1990.

Customized bibliographic search and information are available from the same source:

Washington Association Research Foundation
Greater Washington Society of Association Executives
1426 21st Street, NW, Suite 200
Washington, DC 20036

BOOKS

American Society of Association Executives. *ASAE Coalition Directory.* 4th ed. Washington: 1989.

——. *Association Activities.* Washington: 1985.

——. *Association Executive Compensation Study.* 6th ed. Washington: 1988.

——. *Association International Activity.* Washington: 1988.

——. *Association Operating Ratio Report.* 8th ed. Washington: 1989.

——. *Policies and Procedures in Association Management.* Washington: 1987.

——. *Principles of Association Management.* Washington: 1988.

——. *Selecting among Association Management Options.* Washington: 1987.

Astraldi, Romolo. *The Organization of the Chambers of Commerce in the World.* Florence, Italy: L. Macri, 1950.

Bradley, Joseph F. *The Role of Trade Associations and Professional Business Societies in America.* University Park, PA: Pennsylvania State University Press, 1965.

Chamber of Commerce of the United States (Office of Chamber of Commerce Relations). *1988 Survey of State Organizations.* Washington: 1988.

——. *1989 Survey of Local Chambers of Commerce.* Washington: 1989.

Congressional Quarterly. *The Washington Lobby.* Washington: CQ Press, 1989.

Eddy, Arthur J. *The New Competition.* Chicago: A. C. McClurg & Co., 1912.

Foundation of the American Society of Association Executives. *Association Communications in the 1990s.* Washington: 1987.

——. *The Decision to Join: Insights Based on a Survey of Association Members and Non-Members.* Washington: 1981.

——. *Future Perspectives.* Washington: 1985.

Galambos, Louis. *Competition and Cooperation: The Emergence of a National Trade Association.* Baltimore: Johns Hopkins University Press, 1966.

The Gallup Organization. *The Corporate View: How Business Executives Rate Their Trade Associations.* Washington: Foundation of the American Society of Association Executives, 1982.

——. *The Verdict: Professionals Evaluate Their Individual Membership Societies.* Washington: Foundation of the American Society of Association Executives, 1983.

Lynn Hellebust. *State Legislative Sourcebook.* Topeka, KS: Government Research Service, annual editions.

Hudson Institute. *The Value of Associations to American Society.* Washington: Foundation of the American Society of Association Executives, 1990.

Jacobs, Jerald A. *Association Law Handbook,* 2nd ed. Washington: Bureau of National Affairs, 1986.

Lamb, George P., and Carrington Shields. *Trade Association Law and Practice.* Boston: Little, Brown, 1971.

Mack, Charles S. *Lobbying and Government Relations: A Guide for Executives.* Westport, CT: Quorum Books, 1989.

Mitchell, Walter, Jr. *How to Use Your Trade Association.* New York: Prentice-Hall, 1951.

National Industrial Conference Board. *Trade Associations: Their Economic Significance and Legal Status.* New York: 1925.

Ouchi, William G. *The M-Form Society.* Reading, MA: Addison-Wesley, 1984.

Public Affairs Council. *Leveraging State Government Relations; How to Win in Today's Most Critical Public Policy Arenas.* Washington: 1990.

Statham, Robert R., and Richard W. Buek. *Associations and the Tax Laws.* Washington: U. S. Chamber of Commerce, 1978.

U. S. Department of Commerce. *Trade Association Activities.* Washington: Government Printing Office, various editions, the most recent published 1947.

Van Horn, Carl E., ed. *The State of the States.* Washington: CQ Press, 1989.

Webster, George D. and Frederick J. Krebs, *Associations and Lobbying Regulation: A Guide for Non-Profit Organizations.* Washington: Chamber of Commerce of the United States, 1985.

Yamazaki, Hiroaki, and Matao Miyamoto, eds. (International Conference on Business History) *Trade Associations in Business History: Proceedings of the Fuji Conference.* Tokyo: University of Tokyo Press, 1988. (Of particular interest is the paper by Louis Galambos, "The American Trade Association Movement Revisited.")

ESSAYS

Hayward, Jack. "Employer Associations and the State in France and Britain." In Steven J. Warnecke and Ezra N. Suleiman, eds. *Industrial Policies in Western Europe.* New York: Praeger, 1975.

Houghton, Peter D., and Christian Kunz, "Contrasts Between European and American Associations." In *ASAE 4th Annual Management Conference Proceedings.* Washington: American Society of Association Executives, 1986.

Naylor, Emmett Hay. "History of Trade Association Activities." In: U. S. Department of Commerce, *Trade Association Activities.* Washington: Government Printing Office, 1923, pp. 303–304.

DIRECTORIES

Encyclopedia of Associations, 4 vols. Detroit: Gale Research, annually.

Foundation for Public Affairs, *Public Interest Profiles.* Washington; CQ Press, 1989.

National Trade and Professional Associations of the United States. Washington; Columbia Books, annually.

State and Regional Associations of the United States. Washington: Columbia Books, annually.

Index

About the Author

CHARLES S. MACK is a management consultant, writer and public speaker on government relations and trade and business associations. He was previously President and CEO of the New York State Food Merchants Association, Director of Public Government Affairs for CPC International Inc., and a staff executive with the U.S. Chamber of Commerce. His previous book, *Lobbying and Government Relations: A Guide for Executives,* was published by Quorum in 1989.